D0508059

HOW TO USE THIS BOOK

The arrow symbol ◊ indicates that words marked in this way can have another meaning, either in the same topic or in a completely different area. You will find a list of these words at the end of the book, entitled HOMONYMS, together with the page numbers on which the word appears with its different meanings.

Grammatical information

All plurals are included in the text with the exception of nouns which are not usually pluralized in German or in English and feminine nouns ending in -in (which regularly become -innen in the plural). Where the plural form of a noun is the same as its singular, this is shown by a dash (–).

Nouns derived from adjectives take the form:

der Reisende*, -n	traveller
die Reisende*, -n	traveller

This indicates that the noun ending depends on the article being used. Thus:

masculine singular	der Reisende
	ein Reisender
masculine plural	die Reisenden
	Reisende
feminine singular	die Reisende
	eine Reisende
feminine plural	die Reisenden
	Reisende

Phrases and idioms

Expressing yourself in a foreign language involves much more than memorizing large quantities of individual words. Another advantage of your **Collins Pocket 10,000 German Words** is that it includes sections of appropriate phrases and idioms within each topic. These enable you to use and understand the types of genuine German expressions you are likely to need in everyday situations.

Parts of speech section

Supplementary wordlists in the second section of the book group words according to the following parts of speech – adjectives, adverbs, nouns, prepositions, conjunctions and verbs. You will be able to use the words listed here with most or even all of the subject topics.

English index

The English index gives page references for all the ESSENTIAL and IMPORTANT English nouns listed under the individual topics.

HOW TO USE THIS BOOK

We are delighted you have decided to buy **Collins Pocket 10,000 German Words**, which forms part of our range of German Study Pockets. Based on the extremely popular Collins Gem 5000 German Words, this new text offers you a considerably extended guide to modern everyday German vocabulary.

You can benefit from using the graded wordlists if you are revising for school exams, as the topics covered are those included in the syllabuses of a cross-section of international examination boards. However, if you are an ~~adult~~ user wishing to brush up and update your German vocabulary, you ~~would find~~ the book's content equally valuable.

USING YOUR COLLINS POCKET 10,000 GERMAN WORDS

To help you find words and expressions as easily as possible, the information is presented by topic, and the material in each topic is set out in a consistent manner for quick reference. After a key to the abbreviations used in the text, followed by a list of contents, the main part of the book contains over 60 topics of carefully selected vocabulary. The areas covered by the topic wordlists range from Animals to the Weather and from Business and Commerce to Youth Hostelling.

Vocabulary lists

Vocabulary within each topic is divided into the relevant nouns for that topic, in alphabetical order. Vocabulary within the noun sections is graded to help you concentrate on material that suits your particular needs or interests. For example, ESSENTIAL vocabulary includes the basic words that are considered necessary for you to talk or write about a specific subject. IMPORTANT items expand on these and help to improve the level at which you will be able to express yourself in German. Finally, USEFUL material increases your understanding of German by widening the range of words whose meaning you will recognize.

Colour highlighting

The new attractive typography combined with the innovative use of colour makes consultation easier than ever before.

Use of symbols

Two symbols are used in the topics sections. The book symbol ⌂, which you will see in the ESSENTIAL and IMPORTANT categories, indicates words which, at basic exam level, you should be able to recognize and translate into English without necessarily being able to use yourself in German. However, at a more advanced level, you should have an active knowledge of all of these words, meaning that you are able to use them when you write or speak German.

First published in this edition 1994

© HarperCollins Publishers 1994

ISBN 0 00 470157-7

editors
Megan Thomson, Horst Kopleck

editorial staff
Susan Dunsmore

editorial management
Vivian Marr

series editor
Lorna Sinclair-Knight

Based on 5000 German Words © 1979,
compiled by Barbara I. Christie MA (Hons)

A catalogue record for this book
is available from the British Library

Typeset by Tradespools Ltd, Frome, Somerset

Printed in Great Britain by
HarperCollins Manufacturing, Glasgow

COLLINS
10,000
GERMAN
WORDS

HarperCollins*Publishers*

German index

Finally, there is a German index which gives the page references for all the ESSENTIAL and IMPORTANT German nouns.

We hope you will enjoy using your **Collins Pocket 10,000 German Words**. Its practical, everyday vocabulary will help you to understand and to express yourself effectively in written and spoken German.

ABBREVIATIONS			
acc	accusative	jdm	jemandem
adj	adjective	jdn	jemanden
adv	adverb	m	masculine
conj	conjunction	n	noun
dat	dative	nt	neuter
etw	etwas	pl	plural
f	feminine	prep	preposition
gen	genitive	sb	somebody
jd	jemand	sth	something

CONTENTS

CONTENTS

ESSENTIAL WORDS (m)

der Abflug, ¨-e 📖	takeoff; departure
der Ausgang, ¨-e	exit, way out
der Ausstieg, -e 📖	exit
der Dienst, -e	service
der Eingang, ¨-e	entrance
der Fahrausweis, -e 📖	ticket
der Fahrgast, ¨-e 📖	passenger
der Fahrkartenschalter, –	ticket office
der Fahrplan, ¨-e	timetable
der Fahrschein, -e	ticket
der Flug, ¨-e	flight
der Fluggast, ¨-e	airline passenger
der Flughafen, ¨-	airport
der Flugplatz, ¨-e	airfield; airport
der Flugpreis, -e	(air) fare
der Gepäckträger, – ◇	porter
der Hubschrauber, –	helicopter
der Jumbo-Jet, -s	jumbo jet
der Koffer, –	case, suitcase
der Kofferkuli, -s	luggage trolley
der Kontrollturm, ¨-e	control tower
der Nichtraucher, –	non-smoker (*person*)
der Notausgang, ¨-e 📖	emergency exit
der Paß, ¨-sse ◇	passport
der Passagier, -e	passenger
der Pilot, -en	pilot
der Raucher, –	smoker (*person*)
der Reisende*, -n	traveller
der Reisepaß, ¨-sse	passport
der Sicherheitsgurt, -e 📖	seat belt
der Start, -s	takeoff
der Steward, -s	steward
der Terminal, -s ◇	(air) terminal
der Tourist, -en	tourist
der Urlaub, -e	holiday(s)
der Urlauber, –	holiday-maker
der Zoll	customs; duty
der Zollbeamte*, -n	customs officer
der Zuschlag, ¨-e	extra charge

IMPORTANT WORDS (m)

der	**Abstieg**	descent
der	**Absturz, ̈e**	plane crash
der	**Anhänger, –** ◇	label, tag
der	**Aufkleber, –**	sticker, label
der	**Fallschirm, -e**	parachute
der	**Flügel, –** ◇	wing
der	**Fluglotse, -n**	air traffic controller
der	**Geschäftsmann, (-leute)**	businessman

USEFUL WORDS (m)

der	**Direktflug, ̈e**	direct flight
der	**Flugkapitän, -e**	captain
der	**Flugsteig, -e**	(departure) gate
der	**Luftpirat, -en**	hijacker
der	**Pendeldienst, -e**	shuttle (service)

einen Zuschlag zahlen *to pay a supplement*
zuschlagpflichtig *subject to an extra charge*
verspätet *delayed, late*
landen *to land*
wir haben eine Flughöhe von ... *we are flying at a height of ...*
ich packe *I pack*
ich packe aus *I unpack*
ein Hin- und Rückflug nach Köln *a return to Cologne*
gültig *valid*
erhältlich *available*
nichts zu verzollen *nothing to declare*
zollfrei *duty-free*
haben Sie etwas zu verzollen? *do you have anything to declare?*
eine Flugkarte or **ein Ticket lösen** *to buy a (plane) ticket*
durch den Zoll gehen *to go through customs*
"schnallen Sie sich bitte an, bitte anschnallen" *"please fasten your seat belts"*
einen Rückflug buchen/bestätigen *to book/confirm a return flight*

ESSENTIAL WORDS (f)	

die **Ankunft**, ¨-e 📖	arrival
die **Auskunft**, ¨-e ◇	information desk
die **Ausreise**, -n	departure (*from country*)
die **Bordkarte**, -n	boarding card
die **einfache Fahrkarte**, -n -n	single ticket
die **Fahrkarte**, -n	ticket
die **Ferien** (*pl*)	holiday(s)
die **Flugkarte**, -n	(plane) ticket
die **Gepäckaufbewahrung** 📖	left-luggage office
die **Geschwindigkeit**, -en	speed
die **Landung**, -en	landing
die **Luft**	air
die **Maschine**, -n ◇ 📖	plane
die **Nummer**, -n	number
die **Reisende***, -n	traveller
die **Reservierung**, -en	booking, reservation
die **Richtung**, -en	direction
die **Rückfahrkarte**, -n	return (ticket)
die **Startbahn**, -en	runway
die **Stewardeß**, -ssen	air hostess
die **Tasche**, -n ◇	bag
die **Toilette**, -n	toilet
die **Touristin**	tourist
die **Uhr**, -en ◇	clock
die **Urlauberin**	holiday-maker
die **Verbindung**, -en	connection
die **Verspätung**, -en	delay
die **Zollbeamtin**	customs officer
die **Zollkontrolle**	customs control *or* check

IMPORTANT WORDS (f)	

die **Besatzung**, -en	crew
die **Fluggesellschaft**, -en	airline
die **Höhe** ◇	height, altitude
die **Landebahn**, -en	runway; landing strip
die **Rollbahn**, -en	runway
die **Rolltreppe**, -n	escalator
die **Schallmauer**	sound barrier
die **Zwischenlandung**, -en	stopover

die	**Abflughalle, -n**	departure lounge
die	**Einreisekarte, -n**	landing card
die	**Flugzeugentführung, -en**	hijacking
die	**Gepäckausgabe**	baggage reclaim
die	**Luftpiratin**	hijacker
die	**Notlandung, -en**	emergency landing
die	**Turbulenz, -en**	turbulence

das	**Fliegen**	flying
das	**Flugzeug, -e**	plane, aeroplane
das	**Fundbüro, -s**	lost property office
das	**Gepäck**	luggage
das	**Passagierflugzeug, -e**	airliner
das	**Reisebüro, -s**	travel agent's
das	**Reiseziel, -e**	destination
das	**Schließfach, ¨er**	left-luggage locker
das	**Taxi, -s**	taxi
das	**Ticket, -s**	(plane) ticket
das	**zollfreie Geschäft, -n -e**	duty-free shop

das	**Armaturenbrett, -er** ◇	instrument panel
das	**Bodenpersonal**	ground staff
das	**Düsenflugzeug, -e**	jet plane
das	**Übergewicht**	excess luggage

luftkrank *airsick*
fliegen *to fly*
beim Start *during the takeoff*
an Bord *on board*
starten *to take off*
erreichen *to catch*
verpassen *to miss*

ANIMALS

ESSENTIAL WORDS (m)

der Affe, -n 🕮	monkey
der Bär, -en	bear
der Bock, ¨e	buck, ram
der Elefant, -en	elephant
der Fisch, -e	fish
der Hals, ¨e	neck; throat
der Hamster, –	hamster
der Huf, -e	hoof
der Hund, -e	dog
der Löwe, -n 🕮	lion
der Schwanz, ¨e	tail
der Tiergarten, ¨	zoo, zoological park
der Tiger, –	tiger
der Wolf, ¨e	wolf
der Zoo, -s	zoo

IMPORTANT WORDS (m)

der Beutel, –	pouch (*of kangaroo*)
der Bulle, -n	bull
der Eisbär, -en	polar bear
der Esel, – ◇	donkey
der Frosch, ¨e	frog
der Fuchs, ¨e	fox
der Hase, -n	hare
der Hirsch, -e	stag
der Höcker, –	hump (*of camel*)
der Igel, –	hedgehog
der Kater, –	tomcat
der Maulwurf, ¨e	mole
der Ochse, -n	ox
der Panzer, – ◇	shell (*of tortoise*)
der Pelz, -e	fur
der Seehund, -e	seal
der Stachel, -n ◇	spine (*of hedgehog*)
der Stier, -e	bull
der Stoßzahn, ¨e	tusk
der Streifen, –	stripe (*of zebra*)
der Wal(fisch), -e	whale
der Ziegenbock, ¨e	billy goat

USEFUL WORDS (m)

der	Bau, -e ✧	den; burrow
der	Biber, –	beaver
der	Biß, -sse	bite
der	Blutegel, –	leech
der	Büffel, –	buffalo
der	Dackel, –	dachshund
der	Delphin, -e	dolphin
der	Elch, -e	elk, moose
der	Euter, –	udder
der	Fallensteller, –	trapper
der	Galopp	gallop
der	Gepard, -e	cheetah
der	Geruchssinn	sense of smell
der	Giftzahn, ¨e	fang (of snake)
der	Gorilla, -s	gorilla
der	Hengst, -e	stallion
der	Iltis, -se	polecat
der	Jaguar, -e	jaguar
der	junge Hund, -n -e	puppy
der	Käfig, -e	cage
der	Kaninchenstall, ¨e	rabbit hutch
der	Leopard, -e	leopard
der	Löwenbändiger, –	liontamer
der	Marder, –	marten
der	Maulkorb, ¨e	muzzle
der	Maulwurfshügel, –	molehill
der	Mungo, -s	mongoose
der	Nerz, -e	mink
der	Orang-Utan, -s	orang-utan
der	Otter, – ✧	otter
der	Panda, -s	panda
der	Panther, –	panther
der	Pavian, -e	baboon
der	Pit-Bull-Terrier, –	pit bull-terrier
der	Pottwal, -e	sperm whale
der	Pudel, –	poodle
der	Rüssel, –	snout (of pig); trunk (of elephant)
der	Sattel, ¨	saddle
der	Schafbock, ¨e	ram
der	Schäferhund, -e	alsatian (dog)

ANIMALS — 3

der	**Schakal**, -e	jackal
der	**Schimpanse**, -n	chimpanzee
der	**Schnurrbart**	whiskers
der	**See-Elefant**, -en	elephant seal
der	**Seelöwe**, -n	sea lion
der	**Spaniel**, -s	spaniel
der	**Stammbaum**, ¨-e ◇	pedigree
der	**Steigbügel**, –	stirrup
der	**Stierkampf**, ¨-e	bullfight
der	**Stierkämpfer**, –	bullfighter
der	**Tierschutzverein**, -e	RSPCA
der	**Tümmler**, –	porpoise
der	**Vollblüter**, –	thoroughbred (*horse*)
der	**Wallach**, -e	gelding
der	**Waschbär**, -en	raccoon
der	**Windhund**, -e	greyhound
der	**Winterschlaf**	hibernation
die	**Zügel** (*pl*)	reins
der	**Zwinger**, –	kennel

wild *wild*
zahm *tame*
wir haben keine Haustiere *we don't have any pets*
jagen *to hunt; to shoot*
ein Tier freilassen *to set an animal free*
ich habe Angst vor Hunden *I'm afraid of dogs*
laufen *to run*
hüpfen *to hop*
springen *to jump*
kriechen *to slither; to crawl*
schlafen *to sleep*
trinken *to drink*
fressen *to eat*
gehorsam *obedient*

die	**Giraffe**, -n	giraffe
die	**Hundehütte**, -n	kennel
die	**Katze**, -n	cat
die	**Kuh**, ¨-e	cow
die	**Löwin** ▭	lioness
die	**Maus**, ¨-e	mouse
die	**Ratte**, -n	rat
die	**Schlange**, -n ◇ ▭	snake
die	**Tierhandlung**, -en	pet shop
die	**Tigerin**	tigress

die	**Falle**, -n	trap
die	**Fledermaus**, ¨-e	bat
die	**Kralle**, -n ▭	claw; talon
die	**Kröte**, -n	toad
die	**Mähne**, -n	mane
die	**Pfote**, -n	paw (*small*)
die	**Pranke**, -n	paw (*large*)
die	**Ringelnatter**, -n	grass snake
die	**Robbe**, -n	seal
die	**Schildkröte**, -n	tortoise
die	**Schnauze**, -n	snout, muzzle
die	**Tatze**, -n	paw
die	**Ziege**, -n	goat; nanny goat

die	**Amphibien** (*pl*)	amphibians
die	**Beute**	prey
die	**Blindschleiche**, -n	slow-worm
die	**Dressur**	training
die	**Echse**, -n	(large) lizard
die	**Eidechse**, -n	lizard
die	**Färse**, -n	heifer
die	**Feldmaus**, ¨-e	fieldmouse
die	**Giftschlange**, -n	venomous snake
die	**Haselmaus**, ¨-e	dormouse
die	**Höhle**, -n ◇	den

USEFUL WORDS (f) (cont)

die **Hundeausstellung**, -en	dog show
die **Hündin**	bitch
die **Hyäne**, -n	hyena
die **Kaulquappe**, -n	tadpole
die **Klapperschlange**, -n	rattlesnake
die **Kobra**, -s	cobra
die **Leine**, -n	lead, leash
die **Meute**, -n	pack (*of hounds*)
die **Natter**, -n	viper, adder
die **Nüstern** (*pl*)	nostrils (*of horse*)
die **Otter**, -n ◇	viper, adder
die **Rasse**, -n ◇	breed
die **Sau**, ⁻e	sow
die **Schnecke**, -n	snail; slug
die **Viper**, -n	viper
die **Wasserschildkröte**, -n	turtle
die **Wasserstelle**, -n	watering place
die **Wildkatze**, -n	wildcat
die **Wölfin**	she-wolf
die **Zitze**, -n	teat

bellen *to bark*
miauen *to miaow*
beißen *to bite*
schnurren *to purr*
knurren *to growl*
kratzen *to scratch*
füttern *to feed*
die Katze streicheln *to stroke the cat*
ein Löwe ist aus dem Zoo entlaufen *a lion has escaped from the zoo*
in eine Falle gehen *to be caught in a trap*
der Hund wedelt mit dem Schwanz *the dog wags its tail*
"Vorsicht! Bissiger Hund" *"beware of the dog"*
zu Pferd *on horseback*
reiten gehen *to go riding*
auf die Fuchsjagd gehen *to go fox-hunting*

ESSENTIAL WORDS (nt)

das **Bein**, -e	leg
das **Haar**, -e	hair
das **Haustier**, -e	pet
das **Horn**, -̈er	horn
die **Jungen** (*pl*)	young
das **Kamel**, -e	camel
das **Känguruh**, -s	kangaroo
das **Kaninchen**, –	rabbit
das **Krokodil**, -e	crocodile
das **Ohr**, -en	ear
das **Pferd**, -e	horse
das **Pony**, -s ⬦	pony
das **Rhinozeros**, -se	rhinoceros
das **Schaf**, -e	sheep
das **Schwein**, -e	pig
das **Tier**, -e	animal
das **Zebra**, -s	zebra

IMPORTANT WORDS (nt)

das **Eichhörnchen**, –	squirrel
das **Fell**, -e ▭	coat, fur
das **Geweih**, -e	antlers (*pl*)
das **Hufeisen**, –	horseshoe
das **Junge**, -n ⬦	cub, offspring
das **Kalb**, -̈er	calf
das **Kätzchen**, –	kitten
das **Maul**, -̈er	mouth
das **Maultier**, -e	mule
das **Meerschweinchen**, –	guinea pig
das **Merkmal**, -e	characteristic
das **Nashorn**, -̈er	rhinoceros
das **Nilpferd**, -e	hippopotamus
das **Reh**, -e	roe deer

*ein **Tier zähmen*** to tame an animal
ausgestopfte Tiere stuffed animals
*an der **Leine führen*** to keep on a lead

USEFUL WORDS (nt)

das	**Brüllen**	bellowing; roaring
das	**Dromedar, -e**	dromedary
das	**Einhorn, -e**	unicorn
das	**Elefantenbaby, -s**	baby elephant
das	**Fohlen, –**	foal
das	**Frettchen, –**	ferret
das	**Futter** ◇	food
das	**Gebell**	barking
das	**Geschirr, -e** ◇	harness
das	**Gift, -e**	venom, poison
das	**Grunzen**	grunt(ing)
das	**Hundefutter**	dog food
das	**Jaulen**	yelping; howling
das	**Katzenfutter**	cat food
das	**Kläffen**	yap(ping)
das	**Knurren**	growl(ing)
das	**Lamm, ̈-er**	lamb
das	**Lebewesen, –**	creature
das	**Mammut, -s**	mammoth
das	**Männchen, –**	male
das	**Miauen**	miaowing
das	**Muhen**	lowing, mooing
das	**Murmeltier, -e**	marmot
das	**Mutterschaf, -e**	ewe
das	**Nagetier, -e**	rodent
das	**Rehkitz, -e**	fawn (*deer*)
das	**Ren(tier), -e**	reindeer
das	**Reptil, -ien**	reptile
das	**Säugetier, -e**	mammal
das	**Schnauben**	snort
das	**Stachelschwein, -e**	porcupine
das	**Tier, -e**	animal
das	**Tierheim, -e**	animal home
das	**Vieh**	cattle
das	**Walroß, -sse**	walrus
das	**Weibchen, –**	female
das	**Wiehern**	neighing
das	**Wiesel, –**	weasel
das	**Wildpferd, -e**	wild horse
das	**Wildschwein, -e**	(wild) boar

ESSENTIAL WORDS (m)

der **Architekt, -en**	architect
der **Fotoapparat, -e**	camera
der **Fotograf, -en**	photographer
der **Künstler, –**	artist
der **Maler, –** 📖	painter
der **Zeichner, –**	draughtsman

IMPORTANT WORDS (m)

der **Bildhauer, –**	sculptor
der **Landschaftsmaler, –**	landscape painter
der **Pinsel, –**	(paint)brush
der **Rahmen, –**	frame
der **Sammler, –**	collector
der **Schnappschuß, ¨sse**	snapshot

USEFUL WORDS (m)

der **Abzug, ¨e** ◊	print (*photo*)
der **Druck, -e** ◊	print (*picture*)
der **Fries, -e**	frieze
der **Grafiker, –**	graphic artist
der **Mäzen, -e**	patron
der **Porträtmaler, –**	portrait painter
der **Restaurator, –**	restorer
der **Steinmetz, -en**	stonemason
der **Stich, -e** ◊	engraving
der **Wandteppich, -e**	tapestry

verschwommen *blurred*
Hobbymaler/Hobbyfotograf sein *to have painting/photography as a hobby*

ART AND ARCHITECTURE — 2

die **Architektin**	architect
die **Architektur**	architecture
die **Fotografin**	photographer
die **Kamera, -s**	camera
die **Kunst, ⁻e**	art
die **Künstlerin**	artist
die **Malerin** ▭	painter
die **Zeichnerin**	draughtswoman
die **Zeichnung, -en** ▭	drawing

IMPORTANT WORDS (f)

die **Ausstellung, -en**	exhibition
die **Bildhauerin**	sculptor
die **Galerie, -n**	gallery
die **Grafik, -en**	graphic; print
die **Landschaftsmalerin**	landscape painter
die **Sammlerin**	collector
die **Sammlung, -en**	collection
die **schönen Künste** (*pl*)	fine arts

USEFUL WORDS (f)

die **Collage, -n**	collage
die **Dunkelkammer, -n**	darkroom
die **Fälschung, -en**	fake (*painting etc*)
die **Grafikerin**	graphic artist
die **Großaufnahme, -n**	close-up
die **Holzschnitzerei, -en**	wood carving
die **Illustration, -en**	illustration
die **Lithographie, -n**	litho(graphy)
die **Nahaufnahme, -n**	close-up
die **Porträtmalerin**	portrait painter
die **Radierung, -en**	etching
die **Reproduktion, -en**	reproduction
die **Restauratorin**	restorer
die **Skizze, -n**	sketch
die **Skulptur, -en**	sculpture
die **Staffelei, -en**	easel
die **Wandmalerei, -en**	mural (*painting*)

das **Bild**, -er 📖	picture; painting
das **Foto**, -s	photo(graph)
das **Gebäude**, –	building; edifice
das **Gemälde**, – 📖	painting, picture
das **Kunstwerk**, -e	work of art
das **Museum**, (Museen)	museum
das **Werk**, -e ◇	work

das **Aquarell**, -e	watercolour
das **Denkmal**, ̈er	monument
das **Objektiv**, -e	lens
das **Porträt**, -s	portrait
das **Selbstporträt**, -s	self-portrait
das **Stilleben**, –	still life
das **Teleobjektiv**, -e	telephoto lens

das **Blitzlicht**	flash(light)
das **Dia**, -s	slide, transparency
das **Fresko**, (-ken)	fresco
das **Gewölbe**, –	vault
das **Negativ**, -e	negative
das **Ölgemälde**, –	oil painting
das **Pastell**, -e	pastel
das **Relief**, -s	relief
das **Weitwinkelobjektiv**, -e	wide-angle lens

BIKES AND MOTORBIKES

der **Gang**, ¨-e ◇ — gear
der **Gepäckträger**, – ◇ — luggage carrier
der **Motorradfahrer**, – — motorcyclist
der **Rad(fahr)weg**, -e — cycle track *or* path
der **Radfahrer**, – — cyclist
der **Radsport** — cycling
der **Reifen**, – — tyre
der **Sattel**, ¨- — saddle, seat

IMPORTANT WORDS (m)

der **Dynamo**, -s — dynamo
der **Helm**, -e — helmet
der **Korb**, ¨-e ◇ — pannier; basket
der **Rückstrahler**, – — reflector
der **Schmutzfänger**, – — mud flap

USEFUL WORDS (m)

der **Beifahrer**, – — pillion passenger
der **Mopedfahrer**, – — moped rider
der **Scheinwerfer**, – — headlight
der **Schlauch**, ¨-e — (inner) tube
der **Soziussitz**, -e — pillion (*seat*)
der **Ständer**, – — stand

bergab *downhill*
bergauf *uphill*
klingeln *to ring one's bell*
aufsteigen *to get on*
absteigen *to get off*
einen Platten haben *to have a flat tyre*
bremsen *to brake*
reparieren *to repair*
schalten *to change gear*
er kam mit dem Rad *he came on his bike, he came by bike*
geplatzt *burst*
mit dem Rad in die Stadt fahren *to cycle into town*

BIKES

ESSENTIAL WORDS (f)

die	**Bahn,** -en ◇	road, way; (cycle) lane
die	**Bremse,** -n ◇	brake
die	**Ecke,** -n	corner
die	**Fahrradlampe,** -n	cycle lamp
die	**Gefahr,** -en ▭	danger, risk
die	**Geschwindigkeit,** -en	speed
die	**Hauptstraße,** -n	main road
die	**Kette,** -n ◇	chain
die	**Klingel,** -n	bell
die	**Lampe,** -n	lamp
die	**Nebenstraße,** -n	side street; minor road
die	**Pumpe,** -n	pump
die	**Radfahrerin**	cyclist
die	**Reifenpanne,** -n	puncture
die	**Reparatur,** -en	repair; repairing

IMPORTANT WORDS (f)

die	**Lenkstange,** -n	handlebars
die	**Querstange,** -n	crossbar
die	**Satteltasche,** -n	saddlebag; pannier
die	**Speiche,** -n	spoke
die	**Steigung,** -en	gradient
die	**Straßenverkehrsordnung**	Highway Code

USEFUL WORDS (f)

die	**Beifahrerin**	pillion passenger
die	**Gangschaltung**	gears
die	**Hosenklammern** (*pl*)	bicycle clips
die	**Radtour,** -en	bike ride; cycle tour

"Radfahren verboten" *"cycling prohibited"*
Radsport betreiben *to go in for cycling*
mit dem (Fahr)rad fahren *to cycle*
kaputt *broken*
rostig *rusty*

BIKES AND MOTORBIKES — 3

das	**Fahrrad,** ⁻er	bicycle
das	**Hinterrad,** ⁻er	back wheel
das	**Motorrad,** ⁻er	motorbike, motorcycle
das	**Pedal,** -e	pedal
das	**Rad,** ⁻er ◇	wheel; bike
das	**Radfahren**	cycling
das	**Vorderrad,** ⁻er	front wheel

das	**Flickzeug,** -e	puncture repair kit
das	**Katzenauge,** -n	rear light; reflector; cat's eye
das	**Schutzblech,** -e	mudguard

das	**Dreirad,** ⁻er	tricycle
das	**Moped,** -s	moped
das	**Schloß,** ⁻sser ◇	lock
das	**Tandem,** -s	tandem

Leucht- *fluorescent*
glänzend *shiny*
die Reifen aufpumpen *to blow up the tyres*
das Loch flicken *to mend the puncture*

BIRDS AND INSECTS

ESSENTIAL WORDS (m)

der **Flamingo**, -s	flamingo
der **Hahn**, ̈-e ◇	cock, rooster
der **Himmel** ◇	sky
der **Käfig**, -e	cage
der **Kanarienvogel**, ̈-	canary
der **Kuckuck**, -e	cuckoo
der **Moskito**, -s	mosquito
der **Pinguin**, -e	penguin
der **Schwan**, ̈-e	swan
der **Schwanz**, ̈-e	tail
der **Storch**, ̈-e	stork
der **Truthahn**, ̈-e	turkey
der **Vogel**, ̈-	bird
der **Wellensittich**, -e	budgie, budgerigar

IMPORTANT WORDS (m)

der **Adler**, –	eagle
der **Falke**, -n	falcon
der **Fasan**, -e(n)	pheasant
der **Fink**, -en	finch
der **Floh**, ̈-e	flea
der **Flügel**, – ◇	wing
der **Geier**, –	vulture
der **Habicht**, -e	hawk
der **Käfer**, –	beetle
der **Papagei**, -en	parrot
der **Pfau**, -en	peacock
der **Puter**, –	turkey(-cock)
der **Rabe**, -n	raven
der **Schmetterling**, -e	butterfly
der **Schnabel**, ̈- ▢	beak, bill
der **Sittich**, -e	parakeet
der **Spatz**, -en	sparrow
der **Specht**, -e	woodpecker
der **Sperling**, -e	sparrow
der **Star**, -e ◇	starling
der **Stich**, -e ◇	sting
der **Strauß**, -e ◇	ostrich
der **Zaunkönig**, -e	wren

BIRDS

25

BIRDS AND INSECTS — 2

der	Ameisenhaufen, –	anthill
der	Bienenkorb, ¨e	beehive
der	Buchfink, -en	chaffinch
der	Dompfaff, -e	bullfinch
der	Eichelhäher, –	jay
der	Eisvogel, ¨	kingfisher
der	Gesang	singing
der	Honig	honey
der	Leuchtkäfer, –	firefly
der	Marienkäfer, –	ladybird
der	Nachtfalter, –	moth
der	Ohrwurm, ¨er	earwig
der	Raubvogel, ¨	bird of prey
der	Reiher, –	heron
der	Schwarm, ¨e	swarm
der	Sperber, –	sparrowhawk
der	Stachel, -n ◊	sting
der	Taubenschlag, ¨e	dovecot(e)
der	Tausendfüßler, –	centipede
der	Uhu, -s	owl
der	Wandervogel, ¨	migratory bird
der	Watvogel, ¨	wader

Lärm machen to make a noise
in der Luft fliegen to fly in the air
zwitschern to twitter
pfeifen to whistle
stechen to sting
die Biene/die Wespe sticht the bee/the wasp stings
nisten to nest
abfliegen to fly away
singen to sing
ein Nest bauen to build a nest
fliegen to fly
Eier legen to lay eggs

ESSENTIAL WORDS (f)

die	**Biene,** -n	bee
die	**Ente,** -n	duck
die	**Feder,** -n ◇	feather
die	**Fliege,** -n ◇ ▥	fly
die	**Gans,** ⸚e	goose
die	**Henne,** -n	hen
die	**Luft**	air
die	**Nachtigall,** -en	nightingale
die	**Wespe,** -n	wasp

IMPORTANT WORDS (f)

die	**Ameise,** -n	ant
die	**Amsel,** -n	blackbird
die	**Blaumeise,** -n	bluetit
die	**Dohle,** -n	jackdaw
die	**Drossel,** -n	thrush
die	**Elster,** -n	magpie
die	**Eule,** -n	owl
die	**Gespenstheuschrecke,** -n	stick insect
die	**Grille,** -n	cricket
die	**Heuschrecke,** -n	grasshopper
die	**Hornisse,** -n	hornet
die	**Krähe,** -n	crow
die	**Laus,** ⸚e	louse
die	**Lerche,** -n	lark
die	**Libelle,** -n	dragonfly
die	**Meise,** -n	tit(mouse)
die	**Motte,** -n	moth
die	**Möwe,** -n	seagull
die	**Mücke,** -n	midge
die	**Pute,** -n	turkey-hen
die	**Raupe,** -n	caterpillar
die	**Saatkrähe,** -n	rook
die	**Schmeißfliege,** -n	bluebottle
die	**Schwalbe,** -n	swallow
die	**Seidenraupe,** -n	silkworm
die	**Spinne,** -n ▥	spider
die	**Taube,** -n ◇	dove; pigeon
die	**Wanze,** -n	bug

USEFUL WORDS (f)

die	**Bienenkönigin**	queen bee
die	**Blattlaus, ¨-e**	aphid, greenfly
die	**Bremse, -n** ◇	horsefly, gadfly
die	**Brieftaube, -n**	homing pigeon
die	**Honigbiene, -n**	honey-bee
die	**Hummel, -n**	bumble-bee
die	**Krallen** (*pl*)	claws; talons
die	**Küchenschabe, -n**	cockroach
die	**Nisse, -n**	nit
die	**Schnake, -n**	daddy-longlegs
die	**Stange, -n**	perch
die	**Stubenfliege, -n**	housefly
die	**Termite, -n**	termite, white ant
die	**Wachtel, -n**	quail
die	**Zecke, -n**	tick

ESSENTIAL WORDS (nt)

das	**Huhn, ¨-er**	hen; fowl
das	**Insekt, -en**	insect
das	**Nest, -er**	nest
das	**Rotkehlchen, –**	robin (redbreast)
das	**Vogelbauer**	birdcage

USEFUL WORDS (nt)

das	**Ei, -er**	egg
das	**Gackern**	squawking (*of hens*)
das	**Gefieder**	feathers
das	**Glühwürmchen, –**	glow-worm
das	**Gurren**	coo(ing)
das	**Küken, –**	chick
das	**Quaken**	quack
das	**Rebhuhn, ¨-er**	partridge
das	**Spinnennetz, -e**	spider's web; cobweb
das	**Summen**	buzzing; buzz
das	**Ungeziefer**	vermin
das	**Vogelhaus, ¨-er**	aviary
das	**Zirpen**	chirping (*of crickets*)
das	**Zwitschern**	chirping (*of birds*)

ESSENTIAL WORDS (m)

der **Bankrott**, -e	bankruptcy
der **Export**, -e	export
der **Geschäftsmann**, (-leute)	businessman
der **Handel** ◊ ▭	trade, trading
der **Händler**, –	dealer
der **Hersteller**, –	manufacturer, maker
der **Import**, -e	import
der **Industrielle***, -n	industrialist
der **Kaufmann**, (-leute) ◊	merchant; businessman
der **Markt**, ⁻e	market
der **Preisanstieg**, -e	rise in prices
der **Schuldner**, –	debtor
der **Verbraucher**, – ▭	consumer
der **Vertrag**, ⁻e ▭	contract
die **Zinsen** (pl)	interest
der **Zinssatz**, ⁻e	interest rate

IMPORTANT WORDS (m)

der **Aktionär**, -e	shareholder
der **Bestand**, ⁻e	stock
der **Buchhalter**, – ▭	accountant
der **Exporteur**, -e	exporter
der **Festpreis**, -e	fixed price
der **Gläubiger**, –	creditor
der **Handelsüberschuß**, ⁻sse	trade surplus
der **Import-Export-Handel**	import-export trade
der **Investor**, -en	investor
der **Lieferant**, -en	supplier
der **Makler**, –	broker; estate agent
der **öffentliche Sektor**	public sector
der **Partner**, –	partner
der **private Sektor**	the private sector
die **Rückstände** (pl)	arrears
der **Schuldschein**, -e	IOU, promissory note
der **Teilhaber**, –	associate
der **Versicherte***, -n	insured person
der **Vertreter**, –	agent; sales representative

BUSINESS

USEFUL WORDS (m)

der	**Betrüger,** –	swindler
die	**Bezüge** (*pl*) ✧	fees
der	**Bote, -n**	delivery boy; courier
der	**Ecu, -s**	ECU
der	**Freibetrag,** ⁻e	tax allowance
der	**Freihandel**	free trade
der	**Geldschrank,** ⁻e	safe
der	**Geldverleiher,** –	moneylender
der	**Gewerbeschein, -e**	trading licence
der	**Häusermakler,** –	property developer
der	**Kostenvoranschlag,** ⁻e	estimate, quotation
der	**Kreditnehmer,** –	borrower
der	**Kurier, -e**	courier
der	**Magnat, -e**	tycoon
der	**Milliardär, -e**	billionaire
der	**(Multi)millionär, -e**	(multi)millionaire
der	**Papierkrieg**	paperwork
der	**Pfandleiher,** –	pawnbroker
der	**Pressezar, -e**	press baron
der	**Safe, -s**	safe
der	**Schwindel**	swindle
der	**Sparer,** –	saver
der	**Steuernachlaß**	tax relief
der	**Tauschhandel**	barter
der	**Tür-zu-Tür-Verkauf**	door-to-door selling
der	**Versandhandel**	mail-order selling
der	**Verwalter,** –	administrator

sein Konto überziehen to *overdraw one's account*
ein Geschäft aushandeln to *negotiate a deal*
vergriffen out of stock
auf Geschäftsreise sein to *be on a business trip or away on business*
bankrott gehen to *go bankrupt*
sein Vermögen machen to *make one's fortune*
eine Schuld abbezahlen to *pay off a debt*
rentabel profitable; cost-effective

ESSENTIAL WORDS (f)

die	Aktie, -n	share
die	Anleihe, -n	loan
die	Geschäftsfrau, -en ⌑	businesswoman
die	Geschäftsführung	management
die	Gesellschaft, -en ⋄	partnership; company
die	Industrielle*, -n	industrialist
die	Inflation	inflation
die	Kauffrau, -en	businesswoman
die	Konkurrenz	competition
die	Rechnung, -en ⋄	invoice
die	Schulden (pl) ⌑	debts
die	Schuldnerin	debtor
die	Unkosten (pl)	overheads
die	Verbraucherin ⌑	consumer

IMPORTANT WORDS (f)

die	Aktionärin	shareholder
die	Arbeitskräfte (pl)	manpower, labour
die	Auslagen (pl) ⋄	outlay, expenditure
die	Begleichung	payment; settlement
die	Bestandsaufnahme, -n	inventory; stocktaking
die	Bestellung, -en	order
die	Bilanz, -en	balance sheet, statement of accounts
die	Buchführung	book-keeping, accounting
die	Buchhalterin ⌑	accountant
die	Devisen (pl) ⋄	foreign currency
die	EG	EC
die	Fabrik, -en ⌑	factory
die	Garantie, -n	guarantee; warranty
die	Gebühren (pl)	charges
die	Geschäftsreise, -n	business trip
die	Gläubigerin	creditor
die	Inventur, -en	stocktaking
die	Investition, -en	investment
die	Lieferantin	supplier
die	Lieferung, -en	supply; delivery
die	Nebenkosten (pl)	extras
die	Partnerin	partner

BUSINESS AND COMMERCE — 4

IMPORTANT WORDS (f) (cont)

die	**Public Relations** (*pl*)	public relations (PR)
die	**Quittung, -en**	receipt
die	**Teilhaberin**	associate
die	**Versicherte*, -n**	insured person
die	**Versicherung, -en** 🕮	insurance; insurance company
die	**Vertreterin**	agent; sales representative

USEFUL WORDS (f)

die	**Baisse**	fall; slump
die	**Baugenehmigung, -en**	planning permission
die	**Betrügerin**	swindler
die	**Devise, -n** ◇	slogan
die	**Diebstahlversicherung**	insurance against theft
die	**EFTA**	EFTA
die	**Empfangsbestätigung, -en**	acknowledgement of receipt
die	**Expansion**	expansion
die	**Freihandelszone, -n**	free trade area
die	**Hausse, -n**	boom
die	**Kaufkraft**	purchasing power
die	**Kaution, -en**	deposit
die	**Kreditbedingungen** (*pl*)	credit terms
die	**Kreditnehmerin**	borrower
die	**Kreditwürdigkeit**	creditworthiness
die	**Lebensversicherung, -en**	life assurance
die	**Meinungsumfrage, -n**	opinion poll
die	**Prämie, -n**	premium
die	**Rate, -n**	instalment
die	**Reederei, -en**	shipping company
die	**Steuerbefreiung**	tax exemption
die	**Versteigerung, -en**	auction sale
die	**Verwalterin**	administrator

ESSENTIAL WORDS (nt)

das	**Geschäft, -e** ◇	deal, bargain
die	**Geschäfte** (*pl*)	business
das	**Kapital**	capital

IMPORTANT WORDS (nt)

die	**Bücher** (*pl*)	books
das	**Darlehen, –**	loan
die	**Finanzmittel** (*pl*)	funds
das	**Gelände, –**	premises
das	**Handelsdefizit, -e**	trade deficit
das	**Konto, (-ten)** ▭	account
das	**Lager, ⸚ ◇**	warehouse
das	**Monopol, -e**	monopoly
das	**Resultat, -e**	outcome, result
das	**Werk, -e ◇**	factory, works

USEFUL WORDS (nt)

das	**Gebot, -e**	bid
das	**Steuerparadies, -e**	tax haven
die	**Versanddokumente** (*pl*)	shipping documents

THE CALENDAR

THE SEASONS

der	**Frühling**	spring
der	**Sommer**	summer
der	**Herbst**	autumn
der	**Winter**	winter

im Frühling/Sommer/Herbst/Winter in spring/summer/autumn/ winter
der Frühsommer early summer
der Spätherbst late autumn

THE MONTHS

der	**Januar**	January
der	**Februar**	February
der	**März**	March
der	**April**	April
der	**Mai**	May
der	**Juni**	June
der	**Juli**	July
der	**August**	August
der	**September**	September
der	**Oktober**	October
der	**November**	November
der	**Dezember**	December

im September etc in September etc
der erste April April Fools' Day
der erste Mai May Day

THE DAYS OF THE WEEK

der	**Montag**	Monday
der	**Dienstag**	Tuesday
der	**Mittwoch**	Wednesday
der	**Donnerstag**	Thursday
der	**Freitag**	Friday
der	**Samstag**	Saturday
der	**Sonnabend**	Saturday
der	**Sonntag**	Sunday

CALENDAR

freitags etc *on Fridays* etc
nächsten/letzten Freitag etc *next/last Friday* etc
am Freitag etc *on Friday* etc
am nächsten Freitag etc *the following Friday* etc
der Kalender *calendar*
die Jahreszeit *season*
der Monat *month*
die Wochentage *days of the week*
der Feiertag, -e 💭 *(public) holiday*
der Abend vor Allerheiligen *Hallowe'en*
Advent (m) *Advent*
Allerheiligen (nt) *All Saints' Day*
Allerseelen (nt) *All Souls' Day*
Aschermittwoch (m) *Ash Wednesday*
Dreikönigsfest (nt) *Epiphany, Twelfth Night*
Faschingszeit (f) *the Fasching festival, carnival time*
Fastenzeit (f) *Lent*
Fastnacht (f) *carnival time*
der Geburtstag, -e *birthday*
Heiliger Abend, Heiligabend (m) *Christmas Eve*
Karfreitag (m) *Good Friday*
der Namenstag, -e *saint's day*
Neujahr (nt) *New Year*
Neujahrstag (m) *New Year's Day*
Ostern (nt) *Easter*
Ostersonntag (m) *Easter Sunday*
Palmsonntag (m) *Palm Sunday*
Passahfest (nt) *(Feast of the) Passover*
Pfingsten (nt) *Whitsun*
Pfingstmontag (m) *Whit Monday*
der Rosenmontag *Monday preceding Ash Wednesday*
Silvester (nt) *New Year's Eve, Hogmanay*
Valentinstag (m) *St Valentine's Day*
Weihnachten (nt) *Christmas*
Weihnachtsabend (m) *Christmas Eve*
Weihnachtstag (m) *Christmas Day*
zweiter Weihnachtstag (m) *Boxing Day*
den wievielten haben wir heute? *what is today's date?*

CAMPING

ESSENTIAL WORDS (m)

der	**Camper**, –	camper (*person*)
der	**Campingplatz**, ⁻e	camp site
der	**Dosenöffner**, –	tin-opener
der	**Feuerlöscher**, – ▢	fire extinguisher
der	**Liegestuhl**, ⁻e	deck chair
der	**Löffel**, –	spoon
der	**Mülleimer**, –	dustbin
der	**Rucksack**, ⁻e	rucksack, backpack
der	**Schlafsack**, ⁻e	sleeping bag
der	**Teller**, –	plate
der	**Urlaub**, -e	holiday(s)
der	**Waschraum**, ⁻e	washroom
der	**Wohnwagen**, –	caravan
der	**Zuschlag**, ⁻e	extra charge

IMPORTANT WORDS (m)

der	**Aufenthalt**, -e	stay
der	**Campingkocher**, –	camping stove
der	**Klappstuhl**, ⁻e	folding chair
der	**Klapptisch**, -e	folding table
der	**Korkenzieher**, –	corkscrew
der	**Rasierapparat**, -e	razor
der	**Schatten**	shade; shadow
der	**Zeltboden**, ⁻	ground sheet

USEFUL WORDS (m)

der	**Abfall**, ⁻e ◇	rubbish
der	**Anhänger**, – ◇	trailer
der	**Caravan**, -s	caravan
der	**Eimer**, –	bucket, pail
der	**Hering**, -e ◇	(tent) peg
der	**Zeltplatz**, ⁻e	camping ground

ein Zelt aufbauen or **aufschlagen** to pitch a tent
ein Zelt abbauen to take down a tent
"Zelten verboten!" ''no camping''
Camping machen to go camping

ESSENTIAL WORDS (f)

die	**Anmeldung** ◇ ▱	registration
die	**Camperin**	camper (*person*)
die	**Dusche, -n**	shower
die	**Gabel, -n**	fork
die	**Landkarte, -n**	map
die	**Luft**	air
die	**Luftmatratze, -n**	Lilo ®, air bed
die	**Nacht, ¨e**	night
die	**Sache, -n** ◇	thing
die	**Taschenlampe, -n**	torch
die	**Tasse, -n**	cup
die	**Toilette, -n**	toilet
die	**Übernachtung, -en**	overnight stay
die	**Unterkunft, ¨e**	accommodation
die	**Wäsche**	washing
die	**Wäscherei, -en**	laundry (*place*)
die	**Waschmaschine, -n**	washing machine

IMPORTANT WORDS (f)

die	**Büchse, -n** ◇	tin, can; box
die	**Kühltasche, -n**	cool bag
die	**Nachtruhe** ▱	lights out
die	**Ruhe** ◇	peace; rest
die	**Veranstaltung, -en** ▱	organization

ESSENTIAL WORDS (nt)

das	**Camping**	camping
das	**Campinggas**	camping gas
das	**Essen** ◇	food; meal
das	**Fahrzeug, -e** ▱	vehicle
das	**Geschirr** ◇	dishes; pots and pans
das	**Glas, ¨er** ◇	glass
das	**Lagerfeuer, –**	campfire
das	**Messer, –**	knife
das	**Streichholz, ¨er**	match
das	**Taschenmesser, –**	penknife, pocketknife
das	**Wasser**	water
das	**Zelt, -e**	tent

Taschen = Pocket

CAREERS AND EMPLOYMENT

ESSENTIAL WORDS (m)

der	Apotheker, –	(dispensing) chemist, pharmacist
der	Arbeitslohn, ‑e 💬	wages, pay
der	Beruf, -e	profession, occupation
der	Betrieb, -e ◇ 💬	firm, concern
der	Boß, -sse	boss
der	Briefträger, –	postman
der	Feuerwehrmann, ‑er	fireman
der	Filmstar, -s	film star
der	Geschäftsmann, (-leute)	businessman
der	Ingenieur, -e	engineer
der	Job, -s	(spare-time) job
der	Last(kraft)wagenfahrer, –	lorry driver
der	Lehrling, -e	apprentice, trainee
der	LKW-Fahrer, –	lorry driver
der	Lohn, ‑e 💬	wages, pay
der	Maler, –	painter
der	Mechaniker, –	mechanic; engineer
der	Milchmann, ‑er	milkman
der	Pilot, -en	pilot
der	Poet, -en	poet
der	Priester, –	priest
der	Techniker, –	technician

was sind Sie von Beruf? what is your job?, what do you do?
ich bin Elektriker (von Beruf) I am an electrician (by trade)
selbständig self-employed
sparen für to save up for
streiken to strike, be on strike
eine Geschäftsreise machen to be away on business
sein eigenes Geschäft haben to have one's own shop/business
ich möchte Sekretärin werden I'd like to be a secretary
arbeiten to work
arbeitslos werden to be made redundant
Arbeitslosengeld beziehen to be on the dole
seine Stelle verlieren to lose one's job

IMPORTANT WORDS (m)

der **Bauunternehmer**, –	builder, building contractor
der **Bergarbeiter**, –	miner
der **Betriebsleiter**, –	managing director
der **Dichter**, –	poet
der **Fachmann**, (-leute)	specialist, expert
der **Handel** ⟡ ▱	commerce
der **Hausmeister**, – ▱	caretaker
der **Klempner**, –	plumber
der **König**, -e	king
der **Matrose**, -n	sailor
der **Ministerpräsident**, -en	prime minister, premier
der **Mönch**, -e	monk
der **Produzent**, -en ⟡	manufacturer; (film) producer
der **Soldat**, -en	soldier
der **Steinmetz**, -en	stonemason
der **Tischler**, –	joiner, carpenter
der **Verleger**, –	publisher
der **Vertreter**, –	(sales) representative, rep
der **Winzer**, –	wine grower
der **Wirtschaftsprüfer**, –	chartered accountant

USEFUL WORDS (m)

der **Anstreicher**, –	house painter, painter and decorator
der **Arbeitsmarkt**	labour market
der **Arbeitsvertrag**, ¨e	employment contract
der **Bäcker**, –	baker
der **Bankier**, -s	banker
der **Bestattungsunternehmer**, –	undertaker, funeral director
die **Bezüge** (*pl*) ⟡	earnings
der **Bummelstreik**, -s	go-slow
der **Dachdecker**, –	roofer; tiler
der **Drucker**, – ⟡	printer
der **Eisenbahner**, –	railwayman
der **Fleischer**, –	butcher
der **Förster**, –	forest warden
der **Glaser**, –	glazier
der **Handwerker**, –	craftsman

der	**Handwerksberuf**, -e	skilled trade
der	**Installateur**, -e	plumber
der	**Karosseriebauer**, –	coachbuilder
der	**Lehrgang**, ¨e	training course
der	**Leibwächter**, –	bodyguard
der	**Lokomotivführer**, –	train driver
der	**Metallarbeiter**, –	metalworker
der	**Metzger**, –	butcher
der	**Möbelpacker**, –	removal man
der	**Müllmann**, ¨er	dustman
der	**Nachtwächter**, –	night watchman
der	**Page**, -n	pageboy
der	**Rausschmeißer**, –	bouncer
der	**Reeder**, –	shipowner
der	**Sanitäter**, –	ambulance man
der	**Schlosser**, –	locksmith
der	**Schmied**, -e	(black)smith
der	**Schornsteinfeger**, –	(chimney) sweep
der	**Schreiner**, –	cabinetmaker
der	**Schweißer**, –	welder
der	**Seemann**, (-leute)	sailor, seaman
der	**Taucher**, –	diver
der	**Totengräber**, –	gravedigger
der	**Versicherungsvertreter**, –	insurance agent
der	**Zeichner**, –	draughtsman
der	**Zimmermann**, (-leute)	carpenter

entlassen *to dismiss, lay off*
ehrgeizig *ambitious*
arbeitslos sein *to be out of work, be unemployed*
berufstätig sein *to be employed*
bei X arbeiten *to work at X's*
300 Pfund in der Woche verdienen *to earn £300 per week*
mit der Arbeit anfangen *to start work, get down to work*
entlassen werden *to be sacked, get the sack*
langweilig *boring*
sich um eine Stelle bewerben *to apply for a job*

die	**Arbeit, -en** ✧	work; job
die	**Bank, -en** ✧	bank
die	**Berufsberatung**	careers *or* vocational guidance
die	**Bezahlung, -en**	payment
die	**Empfangsdame, -n**	receptionist
die	**Fabrik, -en** ▭	factory
die	**Firma, (-men)**	firm, company
die	**Geschäftsfrau, -en**	businesswoman
die	**Geschäftsreise, -n**	business trip
die	**Gesellschaft, -en** ✧	company
die	**Industrie, -n**	industry
die	**Krankenschwester, -n**	nurse
die	**Lehrzeit, -en**	apprenticeship
die	**Putzfrau, -en**	cleaner, cleaning woman
die	**Schreibkraft, ¨-e**	typist
die	**Stelle, -n** ✧	job, post
die	**Stewardeß, -ssen**	air hostess
die	**Zukunft**	future

die	**Absicht, -en**	intention, aim
die	**Ausbildung**	training, education
die	**Gewerkschaft, -en** ▭	trade union
die	**Königin**	queen
die	**Laufbahn, -en**	career
die	**Lohnerhöhung, -en**	wage *or* pay increase
die	**Nonne, -n**	nun
die	**Platzanweiserin**	usherette
die	**Schneiderin**	dressmaker
die	**Sprechstundenhilfe, -n**	(medical) receptionist
die	**Stenotypistin**	shorthand typist
die	**Verwaltung, -en**	administration

ganztags *full-time*
stundenweise *part-time*
interessant *interesting*
Dienst haben *to be on duty*

die	**Abfindung, -en**	redundancy payment
die	**Anwerbung**	recruiting, recruitment
die	**Arbeitserlaubnis**	work permit
die	**Arbeitslosigkeit**	unemployment
die	**Aushilfe, -n**	temp
die	**Auslagen** (*pl*) ◇	expenses
die	**Baustelle, -n**	building site
die	**Beförderung, -en**	promotion
die	**Berufsaussichten** (*pl*)	job prospects
die	**Berufserfahrung**	(professional) experience
die	**Betriebsferien** (*pl*)	company holidays
die	**Bewerbung, -en**	application
die	**Entlassung**	dismissal; laying-off
die	**Essensmarke, -n**	luncheon voucher
die	**Gehaltserhöhung, -en**	pay rise
die	**Gehaltsskala, (-len)**	salary scale
die	**Geschäftsführung**	management
die	**gleitende Arbeitszeit**	flexitime
die	**Halbtagsbeschäftigung**	part-time job
die	**Haushaltshilfe, -n**	home help
die	**Hierarchie, -n**	hierarchy
die	**Kündigung, -en**	resignation; dismissal
die	**Mittagspause, -n**	lunch break
die	**Schwarzarbeit**	moonlighting
die	**Schwesternhelferin**	auxiliary nurse
die	**Tagesmutter, ̈**	childminder
die	**Tätigkeit, -en** ◇	work; job
die	**Telefonistin**	telephonist
die	**Überstunden** (*pl*)	overtime
die	**Umschulung**	retraining
die	**Verlegerin**	publisher
die	**Versetzung, -en**	transfer

eine Stelle antreten to start a new job
verdienen to earn
jobben to do odd jobs
eine Stelle suchen to look for a job
"Stellenangebote" ''situations vacant''
vorübergehend temporary

ESSENTIAL WORDS (m&f)

der/die **Angestellte***, -n	employee
der/die **Ansager(in)**, – ⌐	announcer
der/die **Arbeiter(in)**, –	worker; labourer
der/die **Arbeitslose***, -n	unemployed person
der/die **Architekt(in)**, -en	architect
der/die **Arzt, ̈-e/Ärztin**	doctor
der/die **Astronaut(in)**, -en	astronaut
der/die **Beamte***, -n/Beamtin	civil servant
der/die **Bibliothekar(in)**, -e	librarian
der/die **Büroangestellte***, -n	office worker, clerk
der/die **Chef(in)**, -s	boss, head
der/die **Elektriker(in)**, –	electrician
der/die **Fotograf(in)**, -en	photographer
der/die **Friseur, -e/Friseuse**, -n	hairdresser
der/die **Gastarbeiter(in)**, –	foreign (guest) worker
der/die **Geschäftsführer(in)**	manager(ess); managing director
der/die **Handlungsreisende***, -n	travelling salesman/-woman
der/die **Journalist(in)**, -en	journalist
der/die **Koch, ̈-e/Köchin**	chef; cook
der/die **Lehrer(in)**, –	(school)teacher
der/die **Politiker(in)**, –	politician
der/die **Polizist(in)**, -en	policeman/-woman
der/die **Präsident(in)**, -en	president
der/die **Premierminister(in)**, –	prime minister, premier
der/die **Reporter(in)**, –	reporter
der/die **Sekretär(in)**, -e ◇	secretary
der/die **Staatsbeamte***, -n/ Staatsbeamtin	civil servant
der/die **Taxifahrer(in)**, –	taxi driver
der/die **Tierarzt, ̈-e/ Tierärztin**	veterinary surgeon, vet
der/die **Verkäufer(in)**, –	salesperson, shop assistant

Frührentner sein *to have taken early retirement*
überarbeitet sein *to be overworked*
als Aushilfe arbeiten *to temp*
Büroarbeit machen *to do office work*
vom Tellerwäscher zum Millionär *from rags to riches*

IMPORTANT WORDS (m&f)

der/die	**Abgeordnete***, -n	M.P., Member of Parliament
der/die	**Autor(in)**, -en	author(ess)
der/die	**Chirurg(in)**, -en	surgeon
der/die	**Dolmetscher(in)**, – ▭	interpreter
der/die	**Forscher(in)**, –	researcher
der/die	**Gewerkschaftler(in)**, –	trade unionist
der/die	**Kameramann**, ¨er/ **Kamerafrau**, -en	cameraman/-woman
der/die	**Künstler(in)**, – ◇	artist
der/die	**Leiter(in)**, – ◇	leader; manager
der/die	**Modeschöpfer(in)**, –	fashion designer
der/die	**Pfarrer(in)**, –	minister, clergyman/-woman
der/die	**Rechtsanwalt**, ¨e/ **Rechtsanwältin**	lawyer, solicitor
der/die	**Schneider(in)**, –	tailor
der/die	**Schriftsteller(in)**, –	writer
der/die	**Vorsitzende***, -n	chair(man/woman)
der/die	**Wissenschaftler(in)**, –	scientist

USEFUL WORDS (m&f)

der/die	**Abenteurer(in)**, –	adventurer/adventuress
der/die	**Anthropologe**, -n/ **Anthropologin**	anthropologist
der/die	**Antiquitätenhändler(in)**, –	antique dealer
der/die	**Archivar(in)**, -e	archivist
der/die	**Assistent(in)**, -en	assistant
der/die	**Augenarzt**, ¨e/ **Augenärztin**	ophthalmologist, eye specialist
der/die	**Auszubildende***, -n	apprentice
der/die	**Betriebsrat**, ¨e/ **Betriebsrätin**	shop steward
der/die	**Biologe**, -n/ **Biologin**	biologist
der/die	**Blumenhändler(in)**, –	florist
der/die	**Buchhalter(in)**, – ▭	accountant
der/die	**Busfahrer(in)**, –	bus driver
der/die	**Direktor(in)**, -en ◇	director
der/die	**Dozent(in)**, -en	lecturer
der/die	**Elektroniker(in)**, –	electronics engineer

USEFUL WORDS (m&f) (cont)

der/die **Entwicklungshelfer(in)**, –	VSO worker
der/die **Gärtner(in)**, –	gardener
der/die **Gastwirt(in)**, -e	innkeeper, hotelier; publican
der/die **Hilfsarbeiter(in)**, –	labourer
der/die **Informatiker(in)**, –	computer scientist
der/die **Innenarchitekt(in)**, -en	interior designer
der/die **Kandidat(in)**, -en	candidate
der/die **Kardiologe**, -n/ **Kardiologin**	cardiologist
der/die **Kassierer(in)**, –	cashier; check-out assistant
der/die **Kellner(in)**, –	waiter/waitress
der/die **Kinderarzt**, ¨e/ **Kinderärztin**	paediatrician
der/die **Kollege**, -n/ **Kollegin**	colleague
der/die **Kosmetiker(in)**, –	beautician
der/die **Laborant(in)**, -en	lab(oratory) technician
der/die **Logopäde**, -n/ **Logopädin**	speech therapist
der/die **Manager(in)**, –	manager/manageress
der/die **Optiker(in)**, –	optician
der/die **Physiker(in)**, –	physicist
der/die **Professor(in)**, -en	professor
der/die **Psychiater(in)**, –	psychiatrist
der/die **Psychologe**, -n/ **Psychologin**	psychologist
der/die **Redakteur(in)**, -e	editor
der/die **Richter(in)**, –	judge
der/die **Romanschriftsteller(in)**, –	novelist
der/die **Saisonarbeiter(in)**, –	seasonal worker
der/die **Schauspieler(in)**, –	actor/actress
der/die **Setzer(in)**, –	typesetter
der/die **Sozialarbeiter(in)**, –	social worker
der/die **Steuerberater(in)**, –	tax consultant
der/die **Streikbrecher(in)**, –	strikebreaker, blackleg
der/die **Streikende***, -n	striker
der/die **Systemanalytiker(in)**, –	systems analyst
der/die **Therapeut(in)**, -en	therapist
der/die **Übersetzer(in)**, –	translator
der/die **Vorgesetzte***, -n	superior
der/die **Zahnarzt**, ¨e/ **Zahnärztin**	dentist

ESSENTIAL WORDS (nt)

das **Büro, -s**	office
das **Einkommen, –**	income
das **Gehalt, -̈er** 🗀	salary
das **Geschäft, -e** ◇	business, trade; shop
das **Handwerk, -e**	trade; craft
das **Interview, -s**	interview
das **Kindermädchen, –**	nanny
das **Leben**	life
das **Mannequin, -s**	model
das **Ministerium, (-ien)**	(government) ministry

USEFUL WORDS (nt)

das **Berufsgeheimnis, -se**	professional secret
das **Dienstalter**	seniority; length of service
das **Dienstmädchen, –**	maid
das **Fotomodell, -e**	model
das **Jahresurlaub**	annual holiday
das **Labor, -e**	laboratory
das **mittlere Management**	middle management
das **Zimmermädchen, –**	chambermaid

mit seiner Arbeit zufrieden sein to get job satisfaction
einstellen to take on, to hire (labour)
kündigen to dismiss; to resign
sich überarbeiten to overwork (o.s.)
krankfeiern to be off "sick"
der/die leitende Angestellte executive
die medizinisch-technische Assistentin medical technician
Schicht arbeiten to work shifts
schnell befördert werden to get quick promotion
sich bewerben (um) to apply (for)
Vollzeit arbeiten to work full-time
Teilzeit arbeiten to work part-time
eine feste Arbeit a permanent or regular job

CEREMONIES AND SPECIAL OCCASIONS

der **Feiertag**, -e ⏢	(public) holiday
der **Gast**, ⸚e	guest
der **Gastgeber**, –	host
der **Geburtstag**, -e ⏢	birthday
der **Tod**, -e	death

IMPORTANT WORDS (m)

der **Fasching**	carnival
der **Festtag**, -e	holiday; red-letter day
der **Feuerwerkskörper**, –	firework
der **Hochzeitstag**, -e	wedding day; wedding anniversary
der **Kalender**, –	calendar
der **Karneval** ⏢	carnival
der **Kuchen**, –	cake
der **Muttertag**	Mother's Day
der **Namenstag**, -e	saint's day
der **Tanz**, ⸚e	dance
der **Trauerfall**, ⸚e	bereavement
der **Trauzeuge**, -n	witness (*at marriage*), best man
der **Verstorbene***, -n	deceased
der **Weihnachtsbaum**, ⸚e	Christmas tree
der **Weihnachtsmann**	Father Christmas

USEFUL WORDS (m)

der **Ball**, ⸚e ◇	dance, ball
der **Festwagen**, –	(*decorated*) float
der **Friedhof**, ⸚e	cemetery, graveyard
der **Heiratsantrag**	(marriage) proposal
der **Jahrmarkt**, ⸚e	fair
der **Kranz**, ⸚e	wreath
der **Lampion**, -s	Chinese lantern
der **Leichenzug**, ⸚e	funeral procession
der **Ruhestand**	retirement
der **Rummelplatz**, ⸚e	fairground
der **Sarg**, ⸚e	coffin
der **Zirkus**, -se	circus

CEREMONIES AND SPECIAL OCCASIONS — 2

die **Einladung**, -en 💬	invitation
die **Feier**, -n	party; celebration
die **Geburt**, -en	birth
die **Hochzeit**, -en 💬	wedding
die **Taufe**, -n	christening, baptism
die **Trauung**, -en	wedding ceremony
die **Verlobung**, -en	engagement

die **Beerdigung**, -en	funeral, burial
die **Flitterwochen** (*pl*)	honeymoon (*time*)
die **Heirat**	marriage
die **Hochzeitsreise**, -n	honeymoon (*trip*)
die **Jahreszeit**, -en	season
die **Nationalhymne**, -n	national anthem
die **Rede**, -n 💬	speech
die **Silvesterfeier**, -n	New Year's Eve party
die **Trauzeugin**	witness (*at marriage*)
die **Verabredung**, -en 💬	date (*with sb*)
die **Verstorbene***, -n	deceased
die **Zeremonie**, -n	ceremony

die **Bescherung**	giving out of Christmas presents
die **Blaskapelle**, -n	brass band
die **Brautjungfer**, -n	bridesmaid
die **Eröffnung**, -en	opening
die **Eröffnungsfeier**, -n	opening ceremony
die **Flagge**, -n	flag
die **Hundertjahrfeier**, -n	centenary celebration
die **Kirche**, -n	church
die **Krönung**	coronation
die **Lichterkette**, -n	fairy lights
die **Messe**, -n ◇	(commercial) fair
die **Weihnachtsbäckerei**	Christmas baking
die **Weihnachtszeit**	the festive season

3 — CEREMONIES AND SPECIAL OCCASIONS

ESSENTIAL WORDS (nt)

das **Fest**, -e	celebration; fête
das **Geschenk**, -e	present, gift

IMPORTANT WORDS (nt)

das **Datum**, (-ten)	date
das **Festival**, -s	festival
das **Standesamt**, ¨-er	registry office
das **Volksfest**, -e	funfair
das **Weihnachtsgeschenk**, -e	Christmas present
das **Weihnachtslied**, -er	(Christmas) carol

USEFUL WORDS (nt)

das **Freudenfeuer**, –	bonfire
das **Grab**, ¨-er	grave; tomb
das **Konfetti**	confetti
das **Lametta**	tinsel
das **Oktoberfest**	Munich beer festival

auf jdn trinken *to drink a toast to sb*
sich (mit jdm) verloben *to get engaged (to sb)*
mein Vater ist vor zwei Jahren gestorben *my father died two years ago*
meine Schwester wurde 1985 geboren *my sister was born in 1985*
die silberne/goldene Hochzeit *silver/golden wedding (anniversary)*
seinen Geburtstag feiern *to celebrate one's birthday*
herzlichen Glückwunsch zum Geburtstag! *happy birthday!*
heiraten *to get married*
sich scheiden lassen *to get divorced*

COLOURS AND SHAPES

beige	beige, fawn
blau	blue
bläulich	bluish
blond	blond
braun	brown
dunkelblau	dark blue
gelb	yellow
gelblich	yellowish
golden	golden
grau	grey
grün	green
grünlich	greenish
hellblau	light blue, pale blue
himmelblau	sky-blue
kastanienbraun	maroon
knallgelb	bright yellow
knallgrün	bright green
knallrot	bright red
königsblau	royal blue
lila	purple
marineblau	navy blue
ockerfarben	ochre
orange	orange
purpurrot	crimson
rehbraun	fawn
rosa	pink
rot	red
rötlich	reddish
scharlachrot	scarlet
schwarz	black
silbern	silver
türkis	turquoise
veilchenblau	violet
violett	violet; purple
weiß	white
zinnoberrot	vermilion

COLOURS

SOME COLOURFUL PHRASES

ein Schwarzer/eine Schwarze *a black man/woman*
das Schwarze Brett *notice board*
ein Weißer/eine Weiße *a white man/woman*
das Weiße Haus *the White House*
schneeweiß *as white as snow*
Schneewittchen *Snow White*
Rotkäppchen *Little Red Riding Hood*
in den roten Zahlen *in the red, in debt*
gelb vor Neid *green with envy*
braun wie eine Haselnuß *as brown as a berry*
braun werden *to go or turn brown*
die Grünen *the Green party, the Greens*
grün und blau *black and blue*
leichenblaß *as white as a sheet*
ein blaues Auge *a black eye*
blau vor Kälte *blue with cold*
eine Fahrt ins Blaue *a mystery tour*
blau steht ihr *blue suits her*
etwas blau anstreichen *to paint something blue*
die Farbe wechseln *to change colour*
uni *self-coloured*
pechschwarz *jet-black*
zweifarbig *two-coloured*
mehrfarbig *multicoloured*

SOME SHAPES

das **Dreieck**, -e	triangle
der **Kreis**, -e ◇	circle
das **Kreuz**, -e ◇	cross
das **Quadrat**, -e	square
das **Rechteck**, -e	rectangle
das **Viereck**, -e	square; rectangle
der **Würfel**, –	cube
der **Zylinder**, – ◇	cylinder

länglich *oblong*
oval *oval*
rautenförmig *diamond-shaped*
rund *round*

COMPUTING

ESSENTIAL WORDS (m)

der	Buchstabe, -n	letter (of alphabet)
der	Computer, –	computer
der	Hacker, –	hacker
der	Heimcomputer, –	home computer
der	Joystick, -s	joystick
der	Monitor, -e	monitor
der	Personalcomputer, –	PC, personal computer
der	Programmierer, –	(computer) programmer
der	Rechner, – ▢	computer; calculator

IMPORTANT WORDS (m)

der	Ausdruck, -e ◇	print-out
der	Bildschirm, -e	monitor, screen
der	Cursor, -s	cursor
der	Drucker, – ◇	printer
der	Laserdrucker, –	laser printer
der	Speicher, – ◇	memory

USEFUL WORDS (m)

der	Chip, -s ◇	chip
der	Informatiker, –	computer scientist
der	Mikrochip, -s	microchip
der	Papiervorschub	form feed
der	Rand, ¨er ◇	margin
der	Seitenwechsel, –	page break
der	Virus, (-ren)	virus
der	Zeilenabstand, ¨e	line spacing
der	Zeilenumbruch	word wrap

tragbar portable
spielen to play
ausdrucken to print out
Informationen abrufen to retrieve information
den Computer programmieren to program the computer
ein Programm schreiben to write a program
sich amüsieren to have fun
Daten eingeben to enter data

ESSENTIAL WORDS (f)

die	**Batterie,** -n	battery
die	**Daten** (*pl*)	data
die	**Funktion,** -en	function
die	**Hardware**	hardware
die	**Informatik**	computer science
die	**Software**	software
die	**Taste,** -n ⟡ ▭	key

IMPORTANT WORDS (f)

die	**Datei,** -en	file
die	**Datenbank,** -en	database
die	**Diskette,** -n	floppy disk
die	**Festplatte,** -n	hard disk
die	**Maus,** ⸚e	mouse
die	**Schnittstelle,** -n	interface
die	**Sicherungskopie,** -n	back-up (copy)
die	**Tastatur,** -en	keyboard

USEFUL WORDS (f)

die	**Ausgabe** ⟡	output
die	**Computerisierung**	computerization
die	**Computersprache,** -n	computer language
die	**EDV-Anlage,** -n	EDP system
die	**Eingabe,** -n	input
die	**Formatierung**	formatting
die	**Hilfefunktion,** -en	help function
die	**Informatikerin**	computer scientist
die	**Leertaste,** -n	space bar
die	**Programmierung**	programming
die	**Rechtschreibprüfung**	spellchecker
die	**Schriftart,** -en	font
die	**Speichereinheit,** -en	storage device
die	**Tabellenkalkulation**	spreadsheet (program)
die	**Wanze,** -n	bug
die	**Ziffer,** -n	digit

den Bildschirm betrachten *to look at the screen*
den Cursor bewegen *to move the cursor*

COMPUTING — 3

das **Kilobyte, -s**	kilobyte
das **Megabyte, -s**	megabyte
das **Menü, -s**	menu
das **Programm, -e** ⟡	program
das **Programmieren**	(computer) programming
das **RAM**	RAM (random access memory)
das **ROM**	ROM (read only memory)

das **Bildschirmgerät, -e**	VDU, visual display unit
das **Computerspiel, -e**	computer game
das **Datensichtgerät, -e**	VDU, visual display unit
das **Diskettenlaufwerk, -e**	disk drive
das **Interface, -s**	interface
das **Modem, -s**	modem
das **Textverarbeitungsgerät, -e**	word processor

das **Bit, -s**	bit
das **Byte, -s**	byte
das **Desktop Publishing (DTP)**	desktop publishing, DTP
das **Dokument, -e**	document
das **Fenster, –**	window
das **Ikon, -e**	icon
das **Softwarepaket, -e**	software package
das **Terminal, -s** ⟡	terminal
das **Zeichen, –** ⟡	character

die Daten speichern *to store the data*
die Daten sichern *to save the data*
editieren *to edit*
ich habe einen Computer zum Geburtstag bekommen *I got a computer for my birthday*
löschen *to delete*
linksbündig/rechtsbündig *left/right justified*
zentrieren *to centre*

COUNTRIES

NB *In German, the definite article is used with masculine and feminine countries and districts and with geographical names preceded by an adjective.*

	Afrika	Africa
	Asien	Asia
	Australien	Australia
	Belgien	Belgium
	Brasilien	Brazil
	Bulgarien	Bulgaria
die	**Bundesrepublik Deutschland (BRD)**	Federal Republic of Germany (FRG)
	China	China
	Dänemark	Denmark
	Deutschland	Germany
	England	England
	Europa	Europe
	Finnland	Finland
	Frankreich	France
	Griechenland	Greece
	Großbritannien	Great Britain
	Holland	Holland
	Indien	India
der	**Irak**	Iraq
der	**Iran**	Iran
	Irland	Ireland
	Italien	Italy
	Japan	Japan
	Kanada	Canada
	Korea	Korea
	Kuwait	Kuwait
der	**Libanon**	Lebanon
	Luxemburg	Luxembourg
	Marokko	Morocco
	Mexiko	Mexico
	Neuseeland	New Zealand
die	**Niederlande** (*pl*)	the Netherlands
	Nordirland	Northern Ireland
	Norwegen	Norway
	Österreich	Austria
	Pakistan	Pakistan
	Polen	Poland

COUNTRIES (cont)

	Portugal	Portugal
	Rumänien	Romania
	Rußland	Russia
	Saudi-Arabien	Saudi Arabia
	Schottland	Scotland
	Schweden	Sweden
die	**Schweiz**	Switzerland
	Skandinavien	Scandinavia
	Slowakien	Slovakia
	Spanien	Spain
	Südafrika	South Africa
	Südamerika	South America
	Tschechien, die tschechische Republik	Czech Republic
die	**Türkei**	Turkey
	Ungarn	Hungary
die	**USA**	USA
das	**Vereinigte Königreich**	the United Kingdom
die	**Vereinigten Staaten**	the United States
	Vietnam	Vietnam
	Wales	Wales

die Staatsangehörigkeit nationality
ein Ausländer, eine Ausländerin a foreigner
ein Fremder, eine Fremde a stranger
ausländisch foreign
fremd strange, foreign
von Übersee from overseas
im Ausland sein to be abroad
ein Land a country
die Hauptstadt capital
die Entwicklungsländer (pl) the developing countries
die Muttersprache native language
ich bin in Deutschland geboren I was born in Germany
nach Deutschland fahren to go to Germany
ins Ausland fahren or *gehen* to go abroad
in die Niederlande/nach Frankreich fahren to go to the Netherlands/to France

NATIONALITIES (m)

ein	**Afrikaner**	an African
ein	**Amerikaner**	an American
ein	**Araber**	an Arab
ein	**Asiat**	an Asian
ein	**Australier**	an Australian
ein	**Belgier**	a Belgian
ein	**Brasilianer**	a Brazilian
ein	**Brite**	a Briton, a British boy *or* man; *(pl)* the British
ein	**Bulgare**	a Bulgar, a Bulgarian
ein	**Chinese**	a Chinese
ein	**Däne**	a Dane, a Danish boy *or* man
ein	**Deutscher**	a German
ein	**Engländer**	an Englishman, an English boy
ein	**Europäer**	a European
ein	**Finne**	a Finn, a Finnish boy *or* man
ein	**Franzose**	a Frenchman, a French boy
ein	**Grieche**	a Greek
ein	**Holländer**	a Dutchman, a Dutch boy
ein	**Inder**	an Indian
ein	**Iraker**	an Iraqi
ein	**Iraner**	an Iranian
ein	**Ire**	an Irishman, an Irish boy
ein	**Italiener**	an Italian
ein	**Japaner**	a Japanese
ein	**Kanadier**	a Canadian
ein	**Kuwaiter**	a Kuwaiti
ein	**Libanese**	a Lebanese
ein	**Luxemburger**	a native of Luxembourg
ein	**Mexikaner**	a Mexican
ein	**Neuseeländer**	a New Zealander
ein	**Norweger**	a Norwegian
ein	**Österreicher**	an Austrian
ein	**Pakistani**	a Pakistani
ein	**Pole**	a Pole, a Polish boy *or* man
ein	**Portugiese**	a Portuguese
ein	**Rumäne**	a Romanian
ein	**Russe**	a Russian
ein	**Schotte**	a Scot, a Scotsman

NATIONALITIES (m) (cont)

ein	**Schwede**	a Swede, a Swedish boy *or* man
ein	**Schweizer**	a Swiss
ein	**Slowake**	a Slovak, a Slovakian boy *or* man
ein	**Spanier**	a Spaniard, a Spanish boy *or* man
ein	**Tscheche**	a Czech
ein	**Türke**	a Turk, a Turkish boy *or* man
ein	**Ungar**	a Hungarian
ein	**Vietnamese**	a Vietnamese
ein	**Waliser**	a Welshman, a Welsh boy

der Gemeinsame Markt *the Common Market*
die Europäische Gemeinschaft (EG) *European Community (EC)*
die Aufenthaltserlaubnis *residence permit*
der Bayer/die Bay(e)rin *Bavarian*
das Deutschlandlied *German national anthem*
die Dritte Welt *Third World*
die ethnische Minderheit *ethnic minority*
die Heimat *home*
das Heimatland *native country*
der/die Indianer(in) *American Indian*
der/die Muttersprachler(in) *native speaker*
die Nationalhymne *national anthem*
der/die Norddeutsche *north German*
der/die Ostdeutsche *East German*
der Sachse/die Sächsin *Saxon*
der/die Staatenlose *stateless person*
der Stamm *tribe*
der/die Süddeutsche *south German*
der/die Westdeutsche *west German*
der/die Zigeuner(in) *gipsy*

NATIONALITIES (f)

eine	**Afrikanerin**	an African
eine	**Amerikanerin**	an American
eine	**Araberin**	an Arabian
eine	**Asiatin**	an Asian
eine	**Australierin**	an Australian
eine	**Belgierin**	a Belgian
eine	**Brasilianerin**	a Brazilian
eine	**Britin**	a Briton, a British girl *or* woman
eine	**Bulgarin**	a Bulgarian
eine	**Chinesin**	a Chinese
eine	**Dänin**	a Dane, a Danish girl *or* woman
eine	**Deutsche**	a German
eine	**Engländerin**	an Englishwoman, an English girl
eine	**Europäerin**	a European
eine	**Finnin**	a Finn, a Finnish girl *or* woman
eine	**Französin**	a Frenchwoman, a French girl
eine	**Griechin**	a Greek
eine	**Holländerin**	a Dutchwoman, a Dutch girl
eine	**Inderin**	an Indian
eine	**Irakerin**	an Iraqi
eine	**Iranerin**	an Iranian
eine	**Irin**	an Irishwoman, an Irish girl
eine	**Italienerin**	an Italian
eine	**Japanerin**	a Japanese
eine	**Kanadierin**	a Canadian
eine	**Kuwaiterin**	a Kuwaiti
eine	**Libanesin**	a Lebanese
eine	**Luxemburgerin**	a native of Luxembourg
eine	**Mexikanerin**	a Mexican
eine	**Neuseeländerin**	a New Zealander
eine	**Norwegerin**	a Norwegian
eine	**Österreicherin**	an Austrian
eine	**Pakistanerin**	a Pakistani
eine	**Polin**	a Pole, a Polish girl *or* woman
eine	**Portugiesin**	a Portuguese

NATIONALITIES (f) (cont)

eine	**Rumänin**	a Romanian
eine	**Russin**	a Russian
eine	**Schottin**	a Scot, a Scotswoman
eine	**Schwedin**	a Swede, a Swedish girl *or* woman
eine	**Schweizerin**	a Swiss
eine	**Slowakin**	a Slovak, a Slovakian girl *or* woman
eine	**Spanierin**	a Spaniard, a Spanish girl *or* woman
eine	**Tschechin**	a Czech
eine	**Türkin**	a Turkish girl *or* woman
eine	**Ungarin**	a Hungarian
eine	**Vietnamesin**	a Vietnamese
eine	**Waliserin**	a Welshwoman, a Welsh girl

die Religion *religion*
christlich *Christian*
evangelisch *Protestant*
katholisch *Catholic*
jüdisch *Jewish*
moslemisch *Muslim, Moslem*

ESSENTIAL WORDS (m)

der **Bach**, ⸚e 🕮	stream, brook
der **Bauer**, -n 🕮	farmer; peasant; (pl) countryfolk
der **Bauernhof**, ⸚e	farm; farmyard
der **Baum**, ⸚e	tree
der **Berg**, -e	mountain; hill
der **Boden**, ⸚ ◊	ground, soil, earth
der **Fluß**, ⸚sse	river
der **Forst**, -e 🕮	forest
der **Frieden** 🕮	peace
der **Gasthof**, ⸚e	inn, hotel
der **Gipfel**, – 🕮	(mountain) top
der **Grund** ◊	ground
der **Gummistiefel**, –	wellington (boot)
der **Hügel**, –	hill
der **Lärm**	noise
der **Markt**, ⸚e	market
der **See**, -n ◊	lake
der **Spazierstock**, ⸚e	walking stick
der **Stein**, -e ◊	stone; rock
der **Stiefel**, –	boot
der **Stock**, ⸚e ◊	cane, stick
der **Strom**, ⸚e ◊	river
der **Tourist**, -en	tourist
der **Turm**, ⸚e	tower; (church) steeple
der **Wald**, ⸚er	wood, forest
der **Wasserfall**, ⸚e	waterfall
der **Weg**, -e ◊	path; way; road

USEFUL WORDS (m)

der **Aussichtspunkt**, -e	viewpoint
der **Dorfplatz**, ⸚e	village square
der **Gebirgler**, –	mountain-dweller
der **Jagdschein**, -e	hunting permit
der **Stacheldraht**	barbed wire
der **Wilderer**, –	poacher
der **Wildhüter**, –	gamekeeper
der **Winzer**, –	wine grower
der **Zaun**, ⸚e	fence

COUNTRY

IN THE COUNTRY — 2

der	**Abhang, ∵e**	slope
der	**Acker, ∵**	field
der	**Bewohner, –**	inhabitant
der	**Dorfbewohner, –**	villager
der	**Erdboden, ∵**	ground
der	**Jäger, –**	hunter
der	**Landwirt, -e**	farmer
der	**Pfad, -e**	path
der	**Schlamm**	mud
der	**Sumpf, ∵e**	marsh, swamp
der	**Teich, -e**	pond
der	**Wegweiser, –**	signpost
der	**Weiher, –**	pond, lake
der	**Weinberg, -e**	vineyard

überqueren *to cross*
bummeln *to wander, stroll*
jagen *to hunt; to shoot*
kultivieren, anbauen *to cultivate, grow*
fließen *to flow*
in der Ferne *in the distance*
sich auf den Weg machen *to set out, set off*
in einer Jugendherberge übernachten *to spend the night in a youth hostel*
steil *steep*
ein Picknick machen *to go for a picnic*
auf dem Bauernhof *on the farm*
auf dem Lande wohnen *to live in the country*
aufs Land gehen *to go into the country*
im Freien *in the open air*
hügelig *hilly*
flach *flat*
fruchtbar *fertile*

ESSENTIAL WORDS (f)

die **Bäu(e)rin** 📖	lady farmer; farmer's wife; peasant
die **Bauersfrau, -en**	farmer's wife
die **Blume, -n**	flower
die **Brücke, -n** ◇	bridge
die **Burg, -en**	castle
die **Erde** ◇	earth, soil
die **Gegend, -en**	district, area
die **Heide, -n** ◇	heath; heather
die **Höhle, -n** ◇	cave; hole
die **Jugendherberge, -n**	youth hostel
die **Kirche, -n**	church
die **Landschaft, -en**	landscape; scenery
die **Landstraße, -n**	country road
die **Landwirtschaft**	agriculture, farming
die **Luft**	air
die **Straße, -n** ◇	road
die **Talsperre, -n** 📖	dam
die **Touristin**	tourist
die **Wiese, -n**	meadow

IMPORTANT WORDS (f)

die **Baumkrone, -n**	treetop
die **Dorfbewohnerin**	villager
die **Ebene, -n**	plain
die **Ernte, -n**	harvest, crop
die **Falle, -n**	trap
die **Gemeinde, -n**	community
die **Hecke, -n**	hedge
die **Jagd, -en**	hunt; hunting
die **Mühle, -n**	mill
die **Quelle, -n**	spring; source
die **Spitze, -n** ◇	tip; peak; point
die **Windmühle, -n**	windmill

USEFUL WORDS (f)

die **Alm, -en**	alpine pasture
die **Berghütte, -n**	mountain hut
die **Bergspitze, -n**	mountain top
die **Dornen** (*pl*)	thorns
die **Dornenhecke, -n**	thorny hedge
die **Gebirglerin**	mountain-dweller
die **Lichtung, -en**	clearing
die **Mündung, -en**	estuary
die **Scheune, -n**	barn
die **Schlucht, -en**	gorge, ravine
die **Winzerin**	wine grower

ländlich *rural*
sich verlaufen *to get lost, lose one's way*
der Weg zum Dorf *the way to the village*
ruhig *peaceful*
schlammig *muddy*
die Einheimischen *the local people, the locals*
die Ernte einbringen *to bring in the harvest*

das Bauernhaus, ⸚er	farmhouse
das Dorf, ⸚er	village
das Feld, -er	field
das Fernglas, ⸚er	(pair of) binoculars
das Flachland, ⸚er	lowlands
das Gasthaus, ⸚er	inn, hotel
das Gebiet, -e ▭	area
das Gebirge, – ▭	mountains, mountain range
das Heideland	heath
das Heu	hay
das Korn	corn, grain
das Land, ⸚er ◇	land; country
das Picknick, -s	picnic
das Schloß, ⸚sser ◇	castle
das Tal, ⸚er ▭	valley
das Tor, -e ◇	gate
das Ufer ◇ ▭	(river) bank; shore (*of lake*)
das Wirtshaus, ⸚er	inn

das Geräusch, -e	sound, noise
das Getreide	grain, cereal crop
das Grundstück, -e ▭	estate; plot of land
das Heidekraut	heather
das Loch, ⸚er ▭	hole

das Dickicht, -e	thicket
das Gestrüpp	scrub(land)
das Marschland	marsh(land), fen
das Moor, -e	moor
das Wildern	poaching

DESCRIBING PEOPLE

ESSENTIAL WORDS (m)

der **Bart**, ¨-e	beard
der **Charakter**	character
der **Gang**, ¨-e ◇ ▭	walk, gait
der **Herr**, -en	gentleman
der **Junge**, -n ◇	boy
der **Mangel**, ¨ ◇	defect, fault
der **Mann**, ¨-er ◇	man
der **Mensch**, -en	human being; man; person
der **Personalausweis**, -e	identity card
der **Schnurrbart**, ¨-e	moustache
der **Zorn**	anger

IMPORTANT WORDS (m)

der **Ausdruck**, ¨-e ◇	expression
der **Faulenzer**, –	lazybones
der **Gesichtszug**, ¨-e	(facial) feature
der **Körperbau**	build
der **Leberfleck**, -e	mole
der **Pickel**, - ◇ ▭	spot, pimple
der **Pony**, -s ◇	fringe
der **Riese**, -n	giant
der **Schönheitsfleck**, -e	beauty spot
der **Schweiß**	sweat, perspiration
der **Taugenichts**, -e	good-for-nothing
der **Teint**, -s	complexion
der **Zug**, ¨-e ◇	feature

gut/schlecht gelaunt *in a good/bad mood*
auf jdn böse sein *to be angry with sb*
(nicht) in der Laune or **in der Stimmung für etw sein** (not) *to be in the mood for sth*
die Gewohnheit haben, etw zu tun *to have a habit of doing sth*
ärgern *to annoy*
lächeln *to smile*
lachen *to laugh*
vor Freude lachen/weinen *to laugh/cry with joy*
eine gute Figur haben *to have a nice figure*
von schlanker Gestalt sein *to be of slender build*

USEFUL WORDS (m)

der **Akzent**, -e	accent
der **Albino**, -s	albino
die **Alten** (pl)	the elderly
der **Backenbart**, ⁝e	sideburns
der **Backenknochen**, –	cheekbone
der **Bauch**, ⁝e ◇	paunch, potbelly
der **Brustumfang**	chest/bust measurement
der **Chauvinist**, -en	chauvinist
der **Doppelgänger**, –	double
der **Dummkopf**, ⁝e	fool; idiot
der **Einfaltspinsel**, –	simpleton
der **Esel**, – ◇	ass
der **Faulpelz**, -e	idler, loafer
der **Geist** ◇	wit
der **(gesunde) Menschenverstand**	common sense
der **Haaransatz**	hairline
der **Haarschnitt**, -e	haircut
der **Hippie**, -s	hippie
der **Humor**	(sense of) humour
der **Idiot**, -en	idiot
der **Junggeselle**, -n	bachelor
der **Kerl**, -e	lad, fellow
der **Klatsch**	gossip
der **Krauskopf**, ⁝e	curly-head
der **Kriecher**, –	crawler, boot-licker
der **Lebensstil**, -e	lifestyle
der **Menschenfeind**, -e	misanthropist
der **Pedant**, -en	pedant
der **Pferdeschwanz**, ⁝e	ponytail
der **Phantast**, -en	dreamer
der **Rotschopf**, ⁝e	redhead
der **Rüpel**, –	boor
der **Scheitel**, –	parting (*of hair*)
der **Schurke**, -n	villain, scoundrel
der **Schwachkopf**, ⁝e	moron
der **Skinhead**, -s	skinhead
der **Sonderling**, -e	eccentric
der **Spätentwickler**, –	late developer
der **Spitzname**, -n	nickname

USEFUL WORDS (m) (cont)

der **Trottel**, –	clot, dummy
der **Typ**, -en ◊	chap, bloke, guy
der **Vamp**, -s	vamp
der **Verstand**	reason; mind
der **Wildfang**, ¨e	tomboy
der **Wirrkopf**, ¨e	muddle-head
der **Zopf**, ¨e	plait
der **Zwerg**, -e	dwarf

albern silly
alt old
altmodisch old-fashioned
angenehm pleasant
ängstlich nervous; worried
attraktiv attractive
auffallend striking
aufrichtig ingenuous
bärtig bearded
blaß pale
blind blind
borniert narrow-minded
böse angry; evil
bucklig hunch-backed
chauvinistisch chauvinistic
clever clever, cunning
cool cool, laid-back
dick fat
dickköpfig stubborn
dumm stupid
dünn thin
egoistisch selfish
ehrgeizig ambitious
ehrlich honest
eifersüchtig (auf + acc**)** jealous (of)
eingebildet conceited
einsam lonely
enttäuscht disappointed
ernst serious
exzentrisch eccentric

ESSENTIAL WORDS (f)

die **Ähnlichkeit**, -en ▢	similarity
die **Bewegung**, -en ▢	movement, motion
die **Brille**, -n	(pair of) glasses
die **Dame**, -n ◇	lady
die **Figur**, -en ◇	figure
die **Frau**, -en ◇	woman
die **Freude**	joy; delight
die **Gesichtsfarbe**, -n	complexion
die **Geste**, -n	gesture
die **Größe**, -n ◇	height; size
die **Kontaktlinsen** (*pl*)	contact lenses
die **Natur**, -en	nature
die **Neugierigkeit** ▢	curiosity
die **Person**, -en	person
die **Schönheit**	beauty
die **Schüchternheit**	shyness

IMPORTANT WORDS (f)

die **Ängstlichkeit**	nervousness
die **Dauerwelle**, -n	perm
die **Eigenschaft**, -en	quality, attribute
die **Falte**, -n ◇	wrinkle
die **Faulenzerin**	lazybones
die **Frisur**, -en ▢	hairstyle
die **Gestalt**, -en	figure
die **Gewohnheit**, -en	habit
die **Glatze**, -n	bald head
die **Häßlichkeit**	ugliness
die **Laune**, -n	mood, humour, temper
die **Locke**, -n	curl
die **Narbe**, -n	scar
die **Runzel**, -n	wrinkle
die **Schlafmütze**, -n	dope (*person*)
die **Sommersprosse**, -n	freckle
die **Stimmung**, -en ◇	mood, frame of mind
die **Träne**, -n	tear
die **Wut** ▢	fury, rage

USEFUL WORDS (f)

die **Blondine**, -n	blonde
die **Doppelgängerin**	double
die **Erscheinung**, -en	appearance
die **Gewissenhaftigkeit**	assiduousness
die **Güte** ◇	kindness
die **Haltung**	posture
die **Hasenscharte**, -n	harelip
die **Hexe**, -n	witch
die **Kragenweite**, -n	collar size
die **Oberweite**, -n	chest measurement
die **Pedantin**	pedant
die **Perücke**, -n	wig
die **Schuhgröße**, -n	shoe size
die **Schwäche**, -n	weakness; weak spot
die **Selbstsicherheit**	self-assurance
die **Taillenweite**	waist measurement
die **Tätowierung**, -en	tattoo

farbenblind colour-blind
faul lazy, idle
frauenfeindlich misogynous, woman-hating
frech (zu) cheeky (to)
fremdenfeindlich xenophobic
freundlich (zu) friendly (to); kind (to)
froh, fröhlich glad, happy
galant courteous, gentlemanly
gebräunt tanned
geduldig patient
gelassen relaxed; laid-back
gelenkig agile, nimble
gepflegt smart
geschickt skilful, clever
gesellig sociable
glattrasiert clean-shaven
glücklich happy
grausam cruel
groß tall; big
gutmütig good-natured

USEFUL WORDS (m&f)

der/die **Angeber(in)**, –	braggart, poser
der/die **Außenseiter(in)**, –	outsider
der/die **Aussteiger(in)**, –	dropout
der/die **Behinderte***, -n	handicapped *or* disabled person
der/die **Betrüger(in)**, –	cheat
der/die **Blinde***, -n	blind man/woman
der/die **Bucklige***, -n	hunchback
der/die **Eigenbrötler(in)**, –	loner; oddball
der/die **Einarmige***, -n	one-armed man/woman
der/die **Einäugige***, -n	one-eyed man/woman
der/die **Einsiedler(in)**, –	hermit, recluse
der/die **Einzelgänger(in)**, –	loner
der/die **Erwachsene***, -n	grown-up, adult
der/die **Frühaufsteher(in)**, –	early riser
der/die **Heuchler(in)**, –	hypocrite
der/die **Individualist(in)**, -en	individualist
der/die **Langschläfer(in)**, –	late riser

häßlich *ugly*
heimtückisch *insidious; malicious*
hell *fair* (skin)
höflich *polite*
homosexuell *homosexual*
hübsch *pretty*
intelligent *intelligent*
jung *young*
kindisch *childish*
kindlich *childlike*
klein *short, small*
kleinlich *petty*
klug *clever*
komisch *funny*
kräftig *strong*
kurz *short*
kurzsichtig *short-sighted*
lächerlich *ridiculous*
lahm *lame*
lang *long*
lässig *casual, off-hand*

USEFUL WORDS (m&f) (cont)

der/die	**Linkshänder(in)**, –	left-handed person
der/die	**Lügner(in)**, –	liar
der/die	**Opportunist(in)**, -en	opportunist
der/die	**Optimist(in)**, -en	optimist
der/die	**Pessimist(in)**, -en	pessimist
der/die	**Realist(in)**, -en	realist
der/die	**Rechtshänder(in)**, –	right-handed person
der/die	**Rentner(in)**, –	(old age) pensioner
der/die	**Säufer(in)**, –	boozer
der/die	**Schmeichler(in)**, –	flatterer
der/die	**Schnorrer(in)**, –	scrounger
der/die	**Schwarzseher(in)**, –	pessimist
der/die	**Schwindler(in)**, –	swindler
der/die	**Sexist(in)**, -en	sexist
der/die	**Spielverderber(in)**, –	killjoy
der/die	**Streber(in)**, –	pushy person; swot
der/die	**Taube***, -n ♢	deaf man / woman
der/die	**Taubstumme***, -n	deaf-mute
der/die	**Träumer(in)**, –	dreamer
der/die	**Trinker(in)**, –	drunkard

laut noisy
linkshändig left-handed
mager skinny, thin; lean; *mürrisch* sullen
nachdenklich thoughtful
nachlässig careless
nackt bare, naked; *naiv* naive
neidisch (auf +acc*)* envious or jealous (of)
nervös nervous; *nett* neat; nice
neugierig curious, nosy
ordentlich tidy, neat
pickelig spotty; *pingelig* pernickety
prahlerisch boastful
raffiniert cunning; crafty
rechtshändig right-handed
reizend charming
reserviert reserved
rothaarig red-haired
rücksichtslos reckless

ESSENTIAL WORDS (nt)

das	**Alter** ◇ ▭	age
das	**Auge, -n**	eye
das	**Aussehen**	appearance
das	**Gewicht, -e**	weight
das	**Haar, -e**	hair
das	**Mädchen, –**	girl
das	**Wesen**	character, personality

rund *round*
sadistisch *sadistic*
schlagfertig *quick-witted*
schlank *slender, slim*
schlau *smart, clever*
schnurrbärtig *with a moustache*
schön *beautiful*
schüchtern *shy*
schwach *weak*
seltsam *strange*
senil *senile*
sensibel *sensitive*
snobistisch *snobbish*
sorgfältig *careful; painstaking, meticulous*
stämmig *burly, stocky*
stark *strong*
stolz (auf +acc**)** *proud (of)*
streng *hard, harsh; strict*
stumm (vor) *dumb (with)*
stur *obdurate; pig-headed*
sympathisch *nice, likeable*
tapfer *brave*
taub *deaf*
taubstumm *deaf and dumb*
tolpatschig *ungainly, clumsy*
traurig *sad*
unartig *naughty*
ungeschickt *clumsy, awkward*
ungesellig *unsociable*

IMPORTANT WORDS (nt)

das	**Benehmen**	behaviour
das	**Doppelkinn, -e**	double chin
das	**Gebiß, -sse**	false teeth
das	**Gefühl, -e**	feeling
das	**Gewissen**	conscience
das	**Grübchen, –**	dimple
das	**Lebewesen, –**	creature
das	**Selbstvertrauen**	self-confidence

USEFUL WORDS (nt)

das	**Äußere**	outward appearance
das	**besondere Merkmal, -n -e**	distinguishing mark
das	**Geschlecht, -er** ⌑	sex
das	**Haarbüschel, –**	tuft of hair
das	**Individuum, (-duen)**	individual
das	**Lispeln**	lisp
das	**Muttermal, -e**	birthmark
das	**Original, -e**	character (*person*)
das	**Talent, -e**	gift, talent
das	**Verhalten**	behaviour
das	**Zucken**	(nervous) twitch

unverschämt *outrageous; impertinent*
verführerisch *seductive*
vernünftig *sensible*
verrückt *crazy, mad*
verschieden *different*
vorsichtig *careful; cautious*
waghalsig *bold, daring*
weise *wise*
weitsichtig *long-sighted*
winzig *tiny*
zerstreut *scatterbrained; absent-minded*
zornig *angry*
zufrieden (mit) *pleased (with)*
zurückgeblieben *backward*

---

mit nacktem Oberkörper *stripped to the waist*
(ein) Talent haben für *to have a gift for*
Scheuklappen tragen *to wear blinkers, be blinkered*
leicht zugänglich sein *to be approachable*
er stottert *he has a stutter*
er ist im Stimmbruch *his voice is breaking*
Herr/Frau Soundso *Mr/Mrs so-and-so*
mit bloßen Beinen *barelegged*
barfuß, barfüßig *barefoot*
wieviel wiegst du? *what do you weigh?*
zunehmen *to put on weight*
Durchschnitts- *average*
wie heißen Sie? *what is your name?*
ich heiße Wolfgang *my name is Wolfgang*
erkennen *to recognize*
sich benehmen *to behave (oneself)*
wie alt sind Sie? *how old are you?, what age are you?*
ich bin 16 Jahre alt *I am 16 (years old)*
mittleren Alters *middle-aged*
in den Vierzigern/Achtzigern sein *to be in one's forties/eighties*
Kontaktlinsen/eine Brille tragen *to wear contact lenses/ glasses*
gut/schlecht aussehen *to look well/poorly*
er sieht schäbig aus *he is shabby-looking*
er sieht wie sein Vater/wie seine Mutter aus *he looks like his father/ his mother*
er ist seinem Vater/seiner Mutter ähnlich *he resembles his father/ his mother*
müde/zornig/komisch aussehen *to look tired/angry/funny*
ein gutaussehender Mann *a handsome or good-looking man*
grüne/blaue/braune Augen haben *to have green/blue/brown eyes*
eine schöne Frau *a beautiful woman*
die Selbstbeherrschung verlieren *to lose one's composure*
ein dynamischer Typ sein *to be a go-getter*
introvertiert/extrovertiert sein *to be an introvert/extrovert*

SIGNS OF THE ZODIAC	

das	**Tierkreiszeichen**	sign of the zodiac
das	**Horoskop**	horoscope

Widder	Aries
Stier	Taurus
Zwillinge	Gemini
Krebs	Cancer
Löwe	Leo
Jungfrau	Virgo
Waage	Libra
Skorpion	Scorpio
Schütze	Sagittarius
Steinbock	Capricorn
Wassermann	Aquarius
Fische	Pisces

(ein) Stier sein to be Taurus or a Taurean
sie ist Fische, sie ist ein Fisch she is Pisces or a Piscean
lockiges/welliges/glattes Haar curly/wavy/straight hair
er hat blonde/dunkle/schwarze/rote/graue Haare he has blond or fair/ dark/ black/red/grey hair
eine Glatze bekommen to be going bald
ihre neue Frisur steht ihr gut her new hairstyle suits her
sie ist 1 Meter 70 groß she is 1 metre 70 tall
ein Mann von mittlerer Größe a man of medium height

ESSENTIAL WORDS (m)

der	**Austausch**, -e	exchange
der	**Bleistift**, -e	pencil
der	**Buchstabe**, -n	letter (*of alphabet*)
der	**Computer**, –	computer
der	**Erfolg**, -e ▭	success
der	**Fehler**, –	mistake, error; fault
der	**Feiertag**, -e ▭	holiday, day off
der	**Fernseher**, –	television set
der	**Filzstift**, -e	felt-tip (pen)
der	**Kindergarten**, ¨	nursery school
der	**Kugelschreiber**, – ▭	ballpoint (pen), Biro ®
der	**Kuli**, -s	Biro ®, ballpoint (pen)
der	**Kurs**, -e ◇	course
der	**Preis**, -e ◇	prize
der	**Schlafsaal**, (-säle)	dormitory
der	**Schreibtisch**, -e	desk
der	**Schulanfang**	beginning of term
der	**Schülerlotse**, -n ▭	*pupil who helps with school crossing patrol*
der	**Schulhof**, ¨e	playground
der	**Speisesaal**, (-säle)	dining hall; refectory
der	**Spielplatz**, ¨e	playground
der	**Stundenplan**, ¨e	timetable
der	**Test**, -s	test
der	**Unterricht**, -e	instruction; (*pl*) lessons
der	**Versuch**, -e ◇	experiment
der	**Zettel**, –	piece of paper; note; form

studieren to study
lernen to learn
zuhören to listen
aufpassen to pay attention
vergessen to forget
lesen to read
sprechen to speak
schreiben to write
arbeiten to work

IMPORTANT WORDS (m)

die **Anwesenden** (*pl*)	those present
der **Aufsatz**, ̈e ▭	essay, composition
der **Aufsichtsschüler**, –	prefect
der **Bericht**, -e ▭	report
der **Bleistiftspitzer**, –	pencil sharpener
der **Drehbleistift**, -e	propelling pencil
die **Fortschritte** (*pl*)	progress
der **Füller**, –	fountain pen
der **Füllfederhalter**, –	fountain pen
der **Gang**, ̈e ⇦	corridor
der **Gesang**	singing
der **Internatsschüler**, –	boarder
der **Irrtum**, ̈er	error
der **Klecks**, -e	blot, stain
der **Religionsunterricht**	religious education
der **Satz**, ̈e ⇦	sentence
der **Tagesschüler**, –	dayboy
der **Vortrag**, ̈e	talk, lecture

USEFUL WORDS (m)

der **Deutschunterricht**	German class
der **Fernunterricht**	multi-media (correspondence) course
der **Hörsaal**, (-säle)	lecture theatre
der **Kommentar**, -e	commentary
der **Lehrgang**, ̈e	course
der **Lehrstuhl**, ̈e	chair (*university*)
der **Magister**, –	Master (*of arts/science*)
der **Prüfling**, -e	candidate
der **Prüfungsausschuß**, ̈sse	board of examiners
der **Prüfungstermin**, -e	date of examination
der **Radiergummi**, -s	rubber
der **Schulbus**, -se	school bus
der **Schwamm**, ̈e	sponge
der **Sportunterricht**	physical education

ESSENTIAL WORDS (f)

die	**Abschlußprüfung, -en**	final exam
die	**Algebra**	algebra
die	**Antwort, -en**	answer, reply
die	**Arbeit, -en** ⋄	work; test
die	**Arithmetik**	arithmetic
die	**Aufgabe, -n**	exercise, task
die	**Aula, (-len)**	(assembly) hall
die	**Berufsschule, -n** ▭	vocational *or* trade school
die	**Bibliothek, -en**	library
die	**Biologie**	biology
die	**Chemie**	chemistry
die	**Computerlehre**	computer studies
die	**Erdkunde**	geography
die	**Erziehung**	education, schooling
die	**Fach(hoch)schule, -n**	technical college
die	**Ferien** (*pl*)	holidays
die	**Frage, -n**	question
die	**Fremdsprache, -n**	foreign language
die	**Ganztagsschule, -n**	all-day school *or* schooling
die	**Garderobe, -n** ⋄	cloakroom
die	**gemischte Schule**	mixed school, co-ed
die	**Geographie**	geography
die	**Geometrie**	geometry
die	**Gesamtschule, -n**	comprehensive school
die	**Geschichte, -n** ⋄	history; story
die	**Grammatik**	grammar
die	**Grundschule, -n**	primary school
die	**Gruppe, -n**	group
die	**Halbtagsschule, -n** ▭	half-day school
die	**Handarbeit**	handicrafts; needlework
die	**Hauptschule, -n** ▭	secondary school
die	**Hochschule, -n**	college; university
die	**höhere Schule, -n -n**	secondary school
die	**Holzarbeiten** (*pl*)	woodwork
die	**Karte, -n** ⋄	map; card
die	**Klasse, -n** ⋄	class, form
die	**Klassenarbeit, -en** ▭	test
die	**Klassenfahrt, -en** ▭	(class) trip, outing
die	**Kreide**	chalk
die	**Kunst**	art

79

ESSENTIAL WORDS (f) (cont)

die **Lehre**	teaching
die **Leistung, -en** 💬	achievement
die **Lektion, -en**	lesson, unit
die **Mappe, -n**	briefcase; folder
die **Mathematik**	mathematics, maths
die **Methode, -n**	method
die **Mittagspause, -n**	lunch break
die **Musik**	music
die **Nachhilfe** 💬	private coaching or tuition
die **Naturwissenschaft** 💬	natural history
die **neueren Sprachen** (*pl*)	modern languages
die **Note, -n** ◇	mark, grade
die **Oberstufe**	upper school
die **Pause, -n** ◇	break, interval
die **Physik**	physics
die **Prüfung, -en**	exam, examination
die **Realschule, -n** 💬	secondary school
die **Reihe, -n** ◇	row (*of seats etc*)
die **Religion**	religion
die **Schule, -n**	school
die **Schülermitverwaltung (SMV), -en** 💬	school or student council
die **Schultasche, -n**	school bag, satchel
die **Seite, -n** ◇	page
die **Sozialkunde**	modern studies
die **Sprache, -n**	language
die **Strafarbeit, -en**	punishment exercise
die **Stunde, -n** ◇	lesson, period
die **Tafel, -n** ◇	blackboard
die **Technik**	technology
die **Technische Hochschule, -n -n**	polytechnic
die **Tinte**	ink
die **Turnhalle, -n**	gym(nasium)
die **Übersetzung, -en**	translation
die **Übung, -en**	practice; exercise
die **Uni, -s**	uni(versity)
die **Universität, -en**	university
die **Volksschule, -n**	primary school
die **Zeichnung, -en** 💬	drawing (*piece of work*)

IMPORTANT WORDS (f)

die	**Abwesenden** (*pl*)	absentees
die	**Aktentasche, -n**	briefcase
die	**Aufsichtsschülerin**	prefect
die	**Dichtung**	poetry
die	**Handelsschule, -n**	commercial college
die	**Hauswirtschaft**	home economics
die	**Internatsschülerin**	boarder
die	**Kantine, -n**	canteen
die	**Lektüre**	reading
die	**Pädagogische Hochschule, -n -n**	College of Education
die	**Preisverleihung, -en**	prize-giving
die	**Rechtschreibung**	spelling
die	**Regel, -n** ◊	rule
die	**Tagesschülerin**	daygirl
die	**Vorlesung, -en**	lecture

USEFUL WORDS (f)

die	**Blindenschrift**	Braille
die	**Disziplin**	discipline
die	**Einschreibung**	enrolment
die	**Entschuldigung, -en**	letter of excuse
die	**Erwachsenenbildung**	adult education
die	**Fernuniversität, -en**	Open University
die	**Förderklasse, -n**	remedial class
die	**große Pause, -n -n**	(main) break
die	**Hausaufgaben** (*pl*)	homework
die	**Klassenstärke, -n**	class size
die	**Klingel, -n**	bell
die	**Mittelstufe**	middle school
die	**Paukerei**	cramming
die	**Prüfungsunterlagen** (*pl*)	exam papers
die	**Semesterferien** (*pl*)	vacation
die	**Sommerferien** (*pl*)	summer holidays
die	**Strafe, -n** ◊	punishment
die	**Tagesschule, -n**	day school
die	**Unterstufe**	lower school
die	**Vokabeln** (*pl*)	vocabulary
die	**Vorschulerziehung**	pre-school education

ESSENTIAL WORDS (m&f)

der/die	**Direktor(in), -en** ⬦	principal, head(master/mistress) *(secondary)*
der/die	**Freund(in), -e**	friend
der/die	**Hochschüler(in), –**	college/university student
der/die	**Klassenlehrer(in), –**	form teacher
der/die	**Klassensprecher(in), –** 🕮	form prefect
der/die	**Lehrer(in), –**	(school)teacher
der/die	**Mitschüler(in), –**	classmate; schoolmate
der/die	**Prüfer(in), –**	examiner
der/die	**Rektor(in), -en**	headmaster/mistress *(primary)*; rector
der/die	**Schüler(in), –**	schoolboy/girl, pupil, student
der/die	**Schulfreund(in), -e**	schoolfriend
der/die	**Schulkamerad(in), -en**	schoolfriend
der/die	**Student(in), -en**	student

seit wieviel Jahren lernen Sie Deutsch? how many years have you been learning German?
sprichst du Deutsch? do you speak German?
ich gehe in die Schule I'm going to school
mein Lieblingsfach my favourite subject
letztes Jahr habe ich einen Austausch gemacht I did an exchange last year
schulfrei haben to have a day off
fleißig hard-working
klug clever
faul lazy
streng strict
in der Schule at school
die Schule besuchen to attend school
interessant interesting
langweilig boring
hitzefrei haben to have a day off because of very hot weather
versetzt werden to move up (to higher class)

USEFUL WORDS (m&f)

der/die **Abiturient(in), -en**	holder of the Abitur
der/die **Analphabet(in), -en**	illiterate (man/woman)
der/die **Aushilfslehrer(in), –**	supply teacher
der/die **Dekan(in), -e**	dean *(of faculty)*
der/die **Deutschlehrer(in), –**	German teacher
der/die **Dozent(in), -en**	lecturer
der/die **Erstsemester(in), –**	first-year student
der/die **Fachlehrer(in), –**	specialist teacher
der/die **Gasthörer(in), –**	unregistered student, observer
der/die **Gymnasiast(in), -en**	grammar school pupil
der/die **Hochschullehrer(in), –**	college/university lecturer
der/die **Kandidat(in), -en**	candidate
der/die **Klassenbeste*, -n**	best pupil
der/die **Klassenkamerad(in), -en**	classmate
der/die **Praktikant(in), -en**	trainee
der/die **Professor(in), -en**	professor
der/die **Realschüler(in), –**	secondary school pupil
der/die **Schulleiter(in), –**	head(master/mistress)
der/die **Schulrat, ¨e/**	
Schulrätin	schools inspector
der/die **Stipendiat(in), -en**	grant-holder
der/die **Tutor(in), -en**	tutor

intelligent *intelligent*
die Schule verlassen *to leave school*
abschreiben *to copy*
Fortschritte machen *to make progress*
dumm *stupid*
fragen *to ask*
einfach *easy*
eine Frage beantworten *to answer a question*
jdm eine Frage stellen *to ask sb a question*
antworten *to answer, reply*
sitzenbleiben *to repeat a year*
der Französischlehrer the French teacher (teacher of French)
ich möchte Lehrer werden *I'd like to be a teacher*

ESSENTIAL WORDS (nt)

das	**Abitur**	German school-leaving certificate/ exam
das	**Blatt, ̈er** ◇	sheet (*of paper*)
das	**Buch, ̈er**	book
das	**Deutsch**	German
das	**Diplom, -e**	diploma
das	**Englisch**	English
das	**Ergebnis, -se** 🕮	result (*of exam*)
das	**Examen, –**	exam, examination
das	**Fach, ̈er** ◇	subject
das	**Französisch**	French
das	**Gymnasium, (-ien)**	grammar school
das	**Heft, -e**	exercise book, jotter
das	**Italienisch**	Italian
das	**Klassenzimmer, –**	classroom, schoolroom
das	**Labor, -e**	laboratory
das	**Latein**	Latin
das	**Lehrerzimmer, –**	staff room
das	**Lineal, -e**	ruler
das	**Papier, -e**	paper
das	**Pflichtfach, ̈er**	compulsory subject
das	**Rechnen**	arithmetic
das	**Semester, –**	term (*2 per year*)
das	**Spanisch**	Spanish
das	**Sprachlabor, -e**	language lab
das	**technische Zeichnen**	technical drawing
das	**Trimester, –**	term (*3 per year*)
das	**Turnen** ◇	P.E.; gymnastics
das	**Vokabular**	vocabulary
das	**Wahlfach, ̈er**	optional subject
das	**Werken**	handicrafts
das	**Wörterbuch, ̈er** 🕮	dictionary
das	**Zeichnen**	drawing (*subject*)
das	**Zeugnis, -se**	school report

loben to praise
bestrafen to punish

IMPORTANT WORDS (nt)

das	**Benehmen**	behaviour
das	**Diktat, -e**	dictation
das	**Griechisch**	Greek
das	**Internat, -e**	boarding school
das	**Nachsitzen**	detention
das	**Notizbuch, ¨er**	notebook
das	**Pult, -e**	desk
das	**Russisch**	Russian
das	**Studenten(wohn)heim, -e**	students' hall of residence
das	**Tonbandgerät, -e**	tape recorder

lehren, unterrichten to teach
das Abitur machen to sit one's A-levels (approx)
wiederholen to repeat; to revise
den ersten Preis gewinnen to win first prize
eine Prüfung machen to sit an exam
eine Prüfung bestehen/nicht bestehen to pass/fail an exam
durchfallen to fail
schriftlich written
mündlich oral
ich lerne seit 3 Jahren Deutsch I've been learning German for 3 years
schwierig difficult
die Schule schwänzen to skip school
jdn nachsitzen lassen to keep sb in (after school)
nachsitzen müssen to be kept in
hat es schon geklingelt? has the bell gone?
ich hatte (eine) Mattscheibe my mind went blank
von der Schule verwiesen werden to be expelled from the school
ein intelligenter Schüler a bright pupil
ein Jahr wiederholen müssen to have to repeat a year
zurückgeblieben backward

das	**Abc**	ABC
das	**Abendgymnasium, (-ien)**	night school
das	**Arbeitsblatt, ¨-er**	handout
das	**Hauptfach, ¨-er**	main subject
das	**Klassenbuch, ¨-er**	class register
das	**Lexikon, (-ka)**	encyclopaedia; dictionary
das	**Lieblingsfach, ¨-er**	favourite subject
das	**Mikroskop, -e**	microscope
das	**Nebenfach, ¨-er**	subsidiary subject
das	**Praktikum, (-ka)**	training period; training course
das	**Schulessen**	school meals
das	**Schulgeld**	school fees
das	**Sekretariat, -e**	(secretary's) office
das	**Stipendium, (-ien)**	grant
das	**Wahlfach, ¨-er**	optional subject
das	**Wunderkind, -er**	child prodigy

sehr gut *very good*
gut *good*
befriedigend *fair*
ausreichend *satisfactory*
mangelhaft *poor*
ungenügend *unsatisfactory*

ESSENTIAL WORDS (m)

der **Abfall**, ⸚e ◇	waste
der **Baum**, ⸚e	tree
der **Berg**, -e	mountain; hill
der **Einwohner**, –	inhabitant
der **Fisch**, -e	fish
der **Fluß**, ⸚sse	river
der **Forst**, -e ▱	forest
der **Kanal**, ⸚e ◇	canal
der **Mond**	moon
der **Planet**, -en	planet
der **Regen**	rain
der **Saure Regen**	acid rain
der **See**, -n ◇	lake
der **Strand**, ⸚e ◇	shore; beach
der **Strom**, ⸚e ◇	river
der **tropische Regenwald**, -n ⸚er	tropical rainforest
der **Wald**, ⸚er	wood, forest

IMPORTANT WORDS (m)

der **Brennstoff**, -e	fuel
der **Dieselkraftstoff**	diesel oil
die **FCKWs** *(pl)*	CFCs
der **Forscher**, –	researcher
der **Katalysator**, -en	catalytic converter
der **Ökologe**, -n	ecologist
der **Ozean**, -e	ocean
der **Schaden**, ⸚	damage, harm
der **Schadstoff**, -e	harmful substance
der **Treibhauseffekt**	greenhouse effect
der **Treibstoff**, -e	fuel *(for vehicles)*
der **Umweltschutz** ▱	conservation
der **Umweltschützer**, –	conservationist, environmentalist
der **Wissenschaftler**, –	scientist

THE ENVIRONMENT — 2

der	**Atombunker,** –	fallout shelter
der	**Atomreaktor,** -en	nuclear reactor
die	**Bodenschätze** (*pl*)	mineral resources
der	**Bohrturm,** ⸚e	drilling *or* oil rig
der	**Damm,** ⸚e	dam
der	**Eisberg,** -e	iceberg
der	**Energieverbrauch**	energy consumption
der	**Erdrutsch,** -e	landslide
der	**Krater,** –	crater
der	**Müll**	rubbish, refuse
der	**Müllabladeplatz,** ⸚e	rubbish tip *or* dump
der	**radioaktive Niederschlag**	(radioactive) fallout
der	**Smog**	smog

umweltfreundlich *environment-friendly*
biologisch abbaubar *biodegradable*
umweltschädlich *harmful to the environment*
bleifrei *unleaded*
verbleit *leaded* (petrol)
organisch *organic*
grün *green*

ESSENTIAL WORDS (f)

die **Blume**, -n	flower
die **Einwohnerin**	inhabitant
die **Erde** ◇	the earth
die **Fabrik**, -en ▥	factory
die **Flasche**, -n	bottle
die **Frage**, -n	question
die **Gegend**, -en	region, area
die **Grünen** (*pl*)	the Greens
die **Hitze**	heat
die **Insel**, -n	island
die **Katastrophe**, -n	catastrophe
die **Küste**, -n	coast; shore
die **Lösung**, -en	solution
die **Luft**	air
die **Pflanze**, -n	plant
die **See**, -n ◇	sea
die **Temperatur**, -en	temperature
die **Welt**	world
die **Zeit**, -en	time
die **Zeitschrift**, -en	magazine
die **Zeitung**, -en	newspaper
die **Zukunft**	future

IMPORTANT WORDS (f)

die **Bevölkerung**, -en ▥	population
die **Chemikalien** (*pl*)	chemicals
die **globale Erwärmung**	global warming
die **Krise**, -n	crisis
die **Ökologin**	ecologist
die **Ozonschicht**	ozone layer
die **Regierung**, -en ▥	government
die **Sprühdose**, -n	aerosol
die **Steuer**, -n ◇	tax
die **Umwelt**	environment
die **Umweltverschmutzung** ▥	environmental pollution
die **Verschmutzung**	pollution
die **Wüste**, -n ▥	desert

USEFUL WORDS (f)

die **Atomkraft**	nuclear power
die **Ausgrabungen** (pl)	excavations
die **Bestrahlung**	irradiation
die **Bewässerung**	irrigation
die **Dunstglocke**	haze
die **Entgiftung**	decontamination
die **Entseuchung**	decontamination (*from radioactivity*)
die **Erosion**	erosion
die **Fauna**	wildlife, fauna
die **Flora**	flora
die **Lärmbelästigung**	noise pollution
die **Lava**	lava
die **Luftverschmutzung**	air pollution
die **Mülldeponie, -n**	waste disposal site
die **Radioaktivität**	radioactivity
die **Reinigung**	purification
die **Schwerkraft**	gravity
die **Städteplanung**	town planning
die **Verschwendung**	waste
die **Wiederauf-** **bereitungsanlage, -n**	reprocessing plant
die **Wiederverwertung**	recycling, reprocessing
die **Windkraft**	wind power

wiederaufbereiten, recyceln *to recycle*
retten *to save*
verunreinigen *to contaminate*
zerstören *to destroy*
verschmutzen *to pollute*
etw verbieten *to ban sth*
in der Zukunft *in future*
Energie sparen *to save energy*
auslaufende Chemikalien *a leakage of chemicals*
gesundheitsschädlich sein *to be damaging to one's health*
"aus Altpapier hergestellt" *"made from recycled paper"*

ESSENTIAL WORDS (nt)

das **Auto**, -s	car
das **Benzin**	petrol
das **Deodorant**, -s	deodorant
das **Gas**, -e	gas
das **Gebiet**, -e 💬	area
das **Gemüse**, –	vegetable(s)
das **Glas** ◇	glass
das **Holz**	wood
das **Klima**, -s	climate
das **Land**, ¨er ◇	country
das **Meer**, -e	ocean; sea
das **Obst**	fruit
das **Produkt**, -e	product; (*pl*) produce
das **Spülmittel**, –	washing-up liquid
das **Tier**, -e	animal
das **Waschmittel**, –	detergent
das **Waschpulver**, –	washing powder
das **Wasser**	water
das **Wetter**	weather

IMPORTANT WORDS (nt)

die **Abwässer** (*pl*)	sewage
das **Erdbeben**, –	earthquake
das **Ereignis**, -se	event
das **Loch**, ¨er	hole
das **Ozonloch**, ¨er	hole in the ozone layer
das **Weltall**	universe

USEFUL WORDS (nt)

das **Aluminium**	aluminium
das **Atomkraftwerk**, -e	nuclear power station
das **Blei**	lead
das **Insektengift**, -e	insecticide
das **Kohlenmonoxyd**	carbon monoxide
das **Ökosystem**, -e	ecosystem
das **Recycling**	recycling
das **Schädlingsbekämpfungs-** mittel, –	pesticide

THE FAMILY

der	Alte*, -n	old man
der	Babysitter, –	baby-sitter
der	Bekannte*, -n	acquaintance
der	Bruder, ¨	brother
der	Cousin, -s	cousin
der	Ehemann, ¨er	married man; husband
die	Eltern (pl)	parents
der	Enkel, – ▭	grandson; (pl) grandchildren
der	Erwachsene*, -n	grown-up, adult
der	Familienname, -n	surname, family name
der	Freund, -e	friend; boyfriend
der	Großvater, ¨	grandfather
der	Jugendliche*, -n ▭	teenager, young person
der	Junge, -n ◇	boy
der	Mädchenname, -n	maiden name
der	Mann, ¨er ◇	man; husband
der	Mensch, -en	human being, person
der	Nachbar, -n	neighbour
der	Nachname, -n	surname, family name
der	Name, -n	name
der	Neffe, -n ▭	nephew
der	Onkel, –	uncle
der	Opa, -s	grandpa
der	Rentner, – ▭	(old age) pensioner
der	Schwiegersohn, ¨e	son-in-law
der	Schwiegervater, ¨	father-in-law
der	Sohn, ¨e	son
der	Vater, ¨	father
der	Vati, -s ▭	dad, daddy
der	Verlobte*, -n	fiancé
der	Verwandte*, -n	relation, relative
der	Vetter, -n	cousin
der	Vorname, -n	first name, Christian name
der	Witwer, – ▭	widower
der	Zuname, -n	surname
die	Zwillinge (pl)	twins
der	Zwillingsbruder, ¨	twin brother

der	**Bräutigam,** -e	bridegroom
die	**Drillinge** (*pl*)	triplets
der	**Junggeselle,** -n ▢	bachelor
die	**Jungverheirateten** (*pl*)	newly-weds
der	**Pate,** -n	godfather
der	**Rufname,** -n	first name, usual name
der	**Säugling,** -e	baby, infant
der	**Schwager,** ¨	brother-in-law
der	**Spitzname,** -n	nickname
der	**Stiefbruder,** ¨	stepbrother
der	**Stiefvater,** ¨	stepfather
der	**Vorfahr,** -en	ancestor
der	**Vormund,** -e	guardian

der	**Adoptivsohn,** ¨e	adopted son
der	**Alleinerbe,** -n	sole heir
der	**Angehörige*,** -n	relative
die	**Blutsverwandten** (*pl*)	kith and kin
der	**Clan,** -s	clan
der	**Erbe,** -n ◇	heir
der	**Familienkreis**	family (circle)
der	**Familienstand**	marital status
die	**Fünflinge** (*pl*)	quintuplets, quins
der	**Gatte,** -n	husband, spouse
der	**große Bruder,** -n ¨	older brother
der	**Großonkel,** –	great-uncle
der	**Inzest**	incest
der	**kleine Bruder,** -n ¨	younger brother
die	**nächsten Verwandten** (*pl*)	next of kin
der	**Patensohn,** ¨e	godson
der	**Stammbaum,** ¨e ◇	family tree
der	**Stammhalter,** –	son and heir
der	**Stiefsohn,** ¨e	stepson
der	**Taufschein,** -e	baptismal certificate
der	**Totenschein,** -e	death certificate
der	**Urenkel,** –	great-grandson
der	**Urgroßvater,** ¨	great-grandfather
die	**Vierlinge** (*pl*)	quadruplets, quads

ESSENTIAL WORDS (f)

die **Alte***, -n	old woman
die **Bekannte***, -n	acquaintance
die **Cousine**, -n	cousin
die **Dame**, -n ⋄	lady
die **Ehefrau**, -en	married woman; wife
die **Enkelin** ⌑	granddaughter
die **Erwachsene***, -n	grown-up, adult
die **Familie**, -n	family
die **Frau**, -en ⋄	woman; wife
die **Freundin**	friend; girlfriend
die **Großmutter**, ¨	grandmother
die **Hausfrau**, -en	housewife
die **Jugend**	youth (*stage of life*)
die **Jugendliche***, -n ⌑	teenager, young person
die **Kusine**, -n ⌑	cousin
die **Leute** (*pl*)	people
die **Mutter**, ¨ ⋄	mother
die **Mutti**, -s ⌑	mum, mummy
die **Nachbarin**	neighbour
die **Nichte**, -n ⌑	niece
die **Oma**, -s	granny
die **Person**, -en	person
die **Rentnerin** ⌑	(old age) pensioner
die **Schwester**, -n	sister
die **Schwiegermutter**, ¨	mother-in-law
die **Schwiegertochter**, ¨	daughter-in-law
die **Tante**, -n	aunt
die **Tochter**, ¨	daughter
die **Verlobte***, -n	fiancée
die **Verwandte***, -n	relation, relative
die **Witwe**, -n ⌑	widow
die **Zwillingsschwester**, -n	twin sister

heiraten *to get married*
verheiratet *married*
sich verloben *to get engaged*
verlobt *engaged*

IMPORTANT WORDS (f)

die	**alte Jungfer, -n -n**	spinster, old maid
die	**Braut, ⁻e**	bride
die	**Hochzeit, -en** 📖	wedding
die	**Junggesellin**	unmarried woman
die	**Patin**	godmother
die	**Schwägerin**	sister-in-law
die	**Stiefmutter, ⁻**	stepmother
die	**Stiefschwester, -n**	stepsister
die	**Waise, -n**	orphan

geschieden *divorced*
meine Eltern leben getrennt *my parents are separated*
ledig *single*
streiten *to quarrel*
sich vertragen *to get along*
tot *dead*
mein Großvater ist 1990 gestorben *my grandfather died in 1990*
bei uns *at our place* or *house*
die ganze Familie *the whole family*
wie heißt du? *what's your name?*
wie alt bist du? *how old are you?*
männlich *male*
weiblich *female*
wir nennen das Baby Max *we're calling the baby Max*
ich bin 17 Jahre alt *I am 17 (years old)*
ich heiße Karl *my name is Karl*
kennen *to know*
kennenlernen *to get to know*
wir wohnen jetzt in Österreich *we live in Austria now*
unsere Familie stammt aus Polen *our family comes from Poland*
erinnern (an +acc**)** *to remind (of)*
vorstellen *to introduce*
ich bin 1979 geboren *I was born in 1979*
familiäre Bindungen *family ties*
das Sorgerecht über die Kinder haben *to have custody of the children*
der Familienkreis *the family circle*

USEFUL WORDS (f)

die	**Adoptivtochter, ¨**	adopted daughter
die	**Alimente** (*pl*)	maintenance (allowance), alimony
die	**Alleinerbin**	sole heiress
die	**Angehörige*, -n**	dependant
die	**Erbin**	heiress
die	**Erbschaft**	inheritance
die	**Familienähnlichkeit**	family resemblance
die	**Gattin**	wife, spouse
die	**Geburtsurkunde, -n**	birth certificate
die	**Gouvernante, -n**	governess
die	**große Schwester**	older sister
die	**Großfamilie, -n**	extended family
die	**Großtante, -n**	great-aunt
die	**Haushaltshilfe, -n**	mother's help
die	**Heiratsurkunde, -n**	marriage certificate
die	**Kindertagesstätte, -n**	day nursery
die	**kleine Schwester, -n -n**	younger sister
die	**Kleinfamilie, -n**	nuclear family
die	**ledige Mutter, -n ¨**	unmarried mother
die	**Mitgift**	dowry
die	**Patentochter, ¨**	goddaughter
die	**Schwiegereltern** (*pl*)	in-laws
die	**Stieftochter, ¨**	stepdaughter
die	**Tracht Prügel**	spanking
die	**Urenkelin**	great-granddaughter
die	**Urgroßeltern** (*pl*)	great-grandparents
die	**Urgroßmutter, ¨**	great-grandmother
die	**Verwandtschaft**	relations, relatives

in eine Familie einheiraten to marry into a family
mit jdm verwandt sein to be related to sb
mit jdm verschwägert sein to be related by marriage to sb

ESSENTIAL WORDS (nt)

das **Alter** ◇ ▢	age; old age
das **Au-pair, -s**	au pair
das **Baby, -s**	baby
das **Ehepaar, -e** ▢	married couple
das **Einzelkind, -er**	only child
das **Enkelkind, -er**	grandchild
die **Geschwister** (*pl*)	brothers and sisters
das **Kind, -er**	child
das **Kindermädchen, –**	nanny
das **Mädchen, –**	girl
das **Paar, -e** ◇	couple

IMPORTANT WORDS (nt)

das **Greisenalter**	(extreme) old age
das **Kleinkind, -er**	little child
das **Waisenhaus, ̈-er**	orphanage

USEFUL WORDS (nt)

das **Erbe** ◇	inheritance
das **Familienfest, -e**	family party
das **Familiengrab, ̈-er**	family grave
das **Familienmitglied, -er**	member of the family
das **Familienoberhaupt, ̈-er**	head of the family
das **Nesthäkchen, –**	youngest child, baby of the family
das **uneheliche Kind, -n -er**	illegitimate child

älter/jünger als ich *older/younger than me*
sich scheiden lassen *to get divorced*
mütterlicherseits *maternal, on the mother's side*
väterlicherseits *paternal, on the father's side*
ein Kind adoptieren *to adopt a child*

FARMING AND AGRICULTURE

ESSENTIAL WORDS (m)

der **Bach**, ¨e 📖	stream, brook
der **Bauer**, -n 📖	farmer; peasant; countryman
der **Bauernhof**, ¨e	farm; farmyard
der **Boden**, ¨ ◇	ground, earth; floor; loft
der **Bulle**, -n	bull
der **Hahn**, ¨e ◇	cock, rooster
der **Hügel**, –	hill
der **Hund**, -e	dog
der **Landarbeiter**, –	farm labourer
der **Lieferwagen**, –	van
der **Markt**, ¨e	market
der **Ochse**, -n	ox
der **Puter**, –	turkey(-cock)
der **Traktor**, -en	tractor
der **Wald**, ¨er	wood, forest
der **Weizen**	wheat
der **Zaun**, ¨e	fence

IMPORTANT WORDS (m)

der **Acker**, ¨	field
der **Brunnen**, – ◇	well
der **Dünger**, –	dung, manure; fertilizer
der **Eimer**, –	bucket, pail
der **Esel**, – ◇	donkey
der **Graben**, ¨	ditch
der **Hafer**	oats
der **Hase**, -n 📖	hare
der **Haufen**, –	heap, pile
der **Heuboden**, ¨	hayloft
der **Karren**, –	cart
der **Kuhstall**, ¨e	cowshed, byre
der **Landwirt**, -e	farmer
der **Mähdrescher**, –	combine harvester
der **Mais** ◇	maize
der **Pferdestall**, ¨e	stable
der **Pflug**, ¨e	plough
der **Roggen**	rye
der **Schäfer**, –	shepherd
der **Schäferhund**, -e 📖	alsatian (dog)

FARMING

der	**Schlamm**	mud
der	**Schuppen, –**	shed
der	**Stall, ⸚e**	stable; sty; (hen)house
der	**Stapel, –**	pile
der	**Staub**	dust
der	**Stier, -e**	bull
der	**Teich, -e**	pond
der	**Truthahn, ⸚e**	turkey(-cock)
der	**Widder, –**	ram

der	**Ackerbau**	farming
der	**Futtertrog, ⸚e**	feeding trough
der	**Gärtner, –**	gardener
der	**Hopfen**	hop
der	**Hufschmied, -e**	blacksmith, farrier
der	**Kuhhirte, -n**	cowherd
der	**Müller, –**	miller
der	**Pächter, –**	tenant farmer
der	**Raps**	rape(seed)
der	**Schafbock, ⸚e**	ram
der	**Schmied, -e**	blacksmith
der	**Stallbursche, -n**	groom
der	**Torf**	peat
der	**Trog, ⸚e**	trough
der	**Viehzüchter, –**	stockbreeder
der	**Weinbauer, -n**	wine-grower
der	**Ziegenbock, ⸚e**	billy goat
der	**Ziegenhirte, -n**	goatherd

die Ernte einbringen *to bring in the harvest*
Ackerbau und Viehzucht *mixed farming*

ESSENTIAL WORDS (f)

die	Bäu(e)rin ▭	lady farmer; farmer's wife; peasant
die	Bauersfrau, -en	farmer's wife
die	Ente, -n	duck
die	Erde ◇	earth, soil
die	Feldmaus, ¨e	fieldmouse
die	Gans, ¨e	goose
die	Heide, -n ◇ ▭	heath
die	Henne, -n	hen
die	Herde, -n	herd; flock
die	Heugabel, -n	pitchfork
die	Katze, -n	cat
die	Kuh, ¨e	cow
die	Landschaft	countryside; scenery
die	Landwirtschaft	agriculture, farming
die	Milchkanne, -n	milk churn
die	Pute, -n	turkey(-hen)
die	Wiese, -n	meadow

IMPORTANT WORDS (f)

die	Ernte, -n	harvest, crop
die	Erntezeit, -en	harvest (time)
die	Furche, -n	furrow
die	Garbe, -n	sheaf
die	Gerste	barley
die	Kleie	bran
die	Leiter, -n ◇	ladder
die	Schäferin	shepherdess
die	Scheune, -n	barn
die	Vogelscheuche, -n	scarecrow
die	Weide, -n ◇	pasture
die	Windmühle, -n	windmill
die	Ziege, -n	goat; nanny goat

USEFUL WORDS (f)

die	**Fischzucht**	fish farming
die	**Hirse**	millet
die	**Legehenne, -n**	laying hen
die	**Melkmaschine, -n**	milking machine
die	**Milch**	milk
die	**Milchkuh, ¨-e**	milk cow
die	**Molkerei, -en**	dairy
die	**Paarung**	mating
die	**Pächterin**	tenant farmer
die	**Plantage, -n**	plantation
die	**Rinderzucht**	cattle breeding
die	**Schafhürde, -n**	sheepfold
die	**Schafschur**	sheepshearing
die	**Sichel, -n**	sickle
die	**Viehzucht**	cattle breeding
die	**Weinlese**	grape harvest

der Bauer sorgt für die Tiere *the farmer looks after the animals*
die Felder pflügen *to plough the fields*
zur Erntezeit *at harvest-time*
Ferien auf dem Bauernhof *farm holidays*
auf einem Bauernhof wohnen *to live on a farm*
melken *to milk*
mähen *to reap, cut*

ESSENTIAL WORDS (nt)

das	Bauernhaus, ⁇er	farmhouse
das	Dorf, ⁇er	village
das	Feld, -er	field
das	Gebäude, –	building
das	Heu	hay
das	Huhn, ⁇er	hen; (pl) poultry
das	Hühnerhaus, ⁇er	henhouse
das	Kalb, ⁇er	calf
das	Korn	corn, grain
das	Lamm, ⁇er	lamb
das	Land, ⁇er ◇	land; country
das	Pferd, -e	horse
das	Schaf, -e	sheep
das	Schwein, -e	pig
das	Stroh	straw
das	Tier, -e	animal

IMPORTANT WORDS (nt)

das	Gatter, –	gate; railing
das	Geflügel ▭	poultry
das	Geschirr, -e ◇	harness
das	Getreide	grain, cereal crop
das	Küken, –	chick
das	Vieh ▭	cattle; livestock
das	Zugpferd, -e	carthorse

USEFUL WORDS (nt)

das	Ferkel, –	piglet
das	Futter ◇	fodder
das	Gehöft, -e	farm(stead)
das	Gestüt, -e	stud farm
das	Kaninchen, –	rabbit
das	Maultier, -e	mule
das	Perlhuhn, ⁇er	guinea fowl
das	Pflügen	ploughing
das	Rind, -er	cow; (pl) cattle
das	Schlachthaus, ⁇er	slaughterhouse
das	Weideland	pasture

FASHION AND CLOTHES

der	**Anorak, -s**	anorak
der	**Anzug, ⸚e**	suit
der	**Badeanzug, ⸚e**	swimming *or* bathing costume
der	**BH, -s**	bra
der	**Büstenhalter, –**	bra
der	**Gürtel, –**	belt
der	**Handschuh, -e**	glove
der	**Hausschuh, -e**	slipper
der	**Hut, ⸚e** *Hüte*	hat
der	**Kleiderschrank, ⸚e**	wardrobe
der	**Knopf, ⸚e**	button
der	**Mantel, ⸚**	coat, overcoat
der	**Overall, -s**	(set of) overalls
der	**Pulli, -s**	pullover, jumper
der	**Pullover, –**	pullover, jumper
der	**Pyjama, -s**	(pair of) pyjamas
der	**Regenmantel, ⸚**	raincoat
der	**Regenschirm, -e**	umbrella
der	**Rock, ⸚e** *Röcke.*	skirt
der	**Schal, -s**	scarf
der	**Schlafanzug, ⸚e**	(pair of) pyjamas
der	**Schlips, -e**	tie
der	**Schuh, -e**	shoe
der	**Spazierstock, ⸚e**	walking stick
der	**Stiefel, –**	boot
der	**Strumpf, ⸚e**	stocking; (long) sock
der	**Trainingsanzug, ⸚e**	tracksuit
die	**Turnschuhe** (*pl*)	trainers, training shoes
der	**Unterrock, ⸚e**	underskirt, slip

groß big
klein small
das steht Ihnen (gut) *that suits you*
passen *to fit; to suit*
seine Schuhe/seinen Mantel anziehen *to put on one's shoes/coat*
eine Hose/einen Mantel tragen *to wear trousers/a coat*
darf ich dieses Kleid anprobieren? *may I try on this dress?*

FASHION

103

IMPORTANT WORDS (m)

der **Ärmel**, –	sleeve
der **Brustumfang**	chest/bust measurement
der **Gesellschaftsanzug**, ¨-e	evening dress (man's)
der **Hosenanzug**, ¨-e	trouser suit
der **Hosenrock**, ¨-e	culottes
der **Hosenträger**, –	braces (pl)
der **Kragen**, –	collar
die **Lumpen** (pl)	rags
der **Morgenrock**, ¨-e	dressing gown
der **Pfennigabsatz**, ¨-e	stiletto heel
der **Reißverschluß**, ¨-sse	zip
der **Rollkragenpullover**, –	polo-neck sweater
der **Schnürsenkel**, –	shoelace
der **Smoking**, -s ▭	dinner or evening suit

USEFUL WORDS (m)

der **Absatz**, ¨-e	heel
der **Ausschnitt** ◇	neck(line)
der **Bademantel**, ¨-	bathrobe
der **Button**, -s	badge
die **Clogs** (pl)	clogs
der **Druckknopf**, ¨-e	press stud
der **Faltenrock**, ¨-e	pleated skirt
der **Fausthandschuh**, -e	mitt(en)
der **Fleck**, -en	stain, mark
der **Frack**, ¨-e	tails, tailcoat
der **Hemdkragen**, –	shirt collar
die **Hemdsärmel** (pl)	shirt-sleeves
der **Hemdschoß**, ¨-e	shirt tail
der **Holzschuh**, -e	wooden shoe, clog
der **Hosenschlitz**	fly, flies (of trousers)
der **Hüfthalter**, –	girdle
der **Kittel**, –	overall
die **Kniestrümpfe** (pl)	knee-length socks
der **Kopfschmuck**	headdress
die **Manschettenknöpfe** (pl)	cufflinks
der **Maskenball**, ¨-e	fancy-dress party
der **Minibikini**, -s	scanty bikini
der **Minirock**, ¨-e	miniskirt

USEFUL WORDS (m) (cont)

der	**Modeschöpfer**, –	fashion designer
der	**Modezeichner**, –	dress designer
die	**Netzstrümpfe** (pl)	fishnet stockings
der	**Ohrring**, -e	earring
der	**Pantoffel**, -n	slipper
der	**Pelzmantel**, ¨	fur coat
die	**Plateauschuhe** (pl)	platform shoes
der	**Pullunder**, –	slipover, tank top
der	**Pumps**, –	court shoe
der	**Ring**, -e	ring
der	**Riß**, -sse	tear
der	**Saum**, ¨e	hem(line)
der	**Schleier**, –	veil
der	**Schneeschuh**, -e	snow shoe
die	**Skistiefel** (pl)	ski boots
der	**Slip**, -s	briefs
der	**Strumpfgürtel**, –	suspender belt
der	**Strumpfhalter**, –	suspender
der	**Taucheranzug**, ¨e	diving suit
die	**Tennisschuhe** (pl)	tennis shoes
der	**Umhang**, ¨e	cloak
der	**V-Ausschnitt**, -e	V-neck
die	**Wollstrümpfe** (pl)	woollen socks
der	**Zylinder**, – ⇨	top hat

seine Schuhe/seinen Mantel ausziehen to take off one's shoes/coat
einen Hut tragen to wear a hat
den Hut abnehmen to take off one's hat
einen Hut aufsetzen to put on a hat
tragen to wear
bunt (multi)coloured
kariert checked
gestreift striped
in Mode in fashion
"vor Nässe schützen" "keep dry"
chemisch reinigen to dry-clean
passend matching
waschen to wash

ESSENTIAL WORDS (f)

die	**Badehose, -n**	swimming *or* bathing trunks
die	**Bermudashorts** (*pl*)	Bermuda shorts
die	**Bluse, -n**	blouse
die	**Brille, -n**	(pair of) glasses
die	**Fliege, -n** ⟡	bow tie
die	**Freizeitkleidung**	casual clothes
die	**Größe, -n** ⟡	size
die	**Handtasche, -n**	handbag
die	**Herrenkonfektion** ▭	menswear
die	**Hose, -n**	(pair of) trousers
die	**Jacke, -n**	jacket
die	**Jeans, –**	jeans
die	**Kleidung**	clothing
die	**Krawatte, -n**	tie
die	**Lederhose, -n**	(pair of) leather shorts
die	**Mode, -n**	fashion
die	**Modenschau, -en**	fashion show
die	**Mütze, -n**	cap
die	**Sandale, -n**	sandal
die	**Schultertasche, -n**	shoulder bag
die	**Shorts** (*pl*)	shorts
die	**Socke, -n**	sock
die	**Strumpfhose, -n**	(pair of) tights
die	**Tasche, -n** ⟡	pocket; bag
die	**Umkleidekabine, -n**	fitting room
die	**Uniform, -en**	uniform
die	**Unterhose, -n**	(under)pants (*pl*)
die	**Unterwäsche**	underwear

bügeln to iron
das paßt mir nicht that doesn't suit me
modisch fashionable
unmodisch out of fashion
altmodisch old-fashioned
in trendy
ich ziehe mich um I get changed, I change my clothes
sich verkleiden to disguise oneself
von der Stange off the peg

IMPORTANT WORDS (f)

die **Falte, -n** ◇	pleat
die **Hüftweite**	hip measurement
die **Kappe, -n**	cap, hood
die **Kragenweite, -n**	collar size
die **Latzhose, -n**	dungarees
die **Melone, -n** ◇	bowler hat
die **Schuhgröße, -n**	shoe size
die **Schürze, -n**	apron
die **Strickjacke, -n**	cardigan
die **Taille, -n**	waist
die **Taillenweite**	waist measurement
die **Tracht, -en**	costume, dress
die **Weste, -n**	waistcoat
die **Wolljacke, -n**	cardigan

maßgeschneidert *made to measure*
sehr schick *very smart*
ich ziehe mich an *I get dressed, I put on my clothes*
ich ziehe mich aus *I get undressed, I take off my clothes*
etw links herum anhaben *to wear sth inside out*
sich in Schale werfen *to get dressed up*
sich die Haare färben *to dye one's hair*
sich die Haare legen lassen *to have one's hair set*
wasserfest *waterproof*
flicken *to patch*
wieder annähen *to sew back on*
stopfen *to darn*
aufkrempeln *to roll up* (sleeves)
eng *tight*
weit *loose*
gepunktet *spotted*
ein einteiliger/zweiteiliger Badeanzug *a one-piece/two-piece swimsuit*

USEFUL WORDS (f)

die	Änderung, -en ◇	alteration
die	Aufmachung	get-up, rig-out
die	Badekappe, -n	swimming cap
die	Bettjacke, -n	bedjacket
die	Brusttasche, -n	breast pocket
die	Bügelfalte, -n	crease (*in trousers*)
die	chemische Reinigung	dry cleaning
die	Farbe, -n ◇	colour
die	Gamasche, -n	gaiter
die	Haarspange, -n	(hair) slide
die	Halskette, -n	necklace
die	Haube, -n	bonnet, cap
die	Kapuze, -n	hood, cowl
die	Kapuzenmütze, -n	Balaclava
die	Kniehose, -n	knee breeches
die	Kollektion, -en	collection
die	Manschette, -n	cuff
die	Modeschöpferin	fashion designer
die	Modezeichnerin	dress designer
die	Modistin	milliner
die	Paillette, -n	sequin, spangle
die	Pelzjacke, -n	fur jacket
die	Pelzmütze, -n	fur hat
die	Pumphose, -n	baggy breeches
die	Regenhaut, ¨e	plastic raincoat
die	Safarijacke, -n	safari jacket
die	Skihose, -n	ski pants
die	Sohle, -n	sole
die	Turnhose, -n	gym shorts
die	Verkleidung, -en	disguise; fancy dress
die	Wollsachen (*pl*)	woollens

IMPORTANT WORDS (nt)

das	Hochzeitskleid, -er	wedding dress
das	Kopftuch, ¨er ⌑	headscarf, headsquare
das	Zubehör	accessories (*pl*)

ESSENTIAL WORDS (nt)

das	**Abendkleid**, -er	evening dress (*woman's*)
das	**Band**, ¨er ◇	ribbon
das	**Blouson**, -s	bomber jacket
das	**Hemd**, -en	shirt
das	**Jackett**, -s	jacket
das	**Kleid**, -er	dress
die	**Kleider** (*pl*)	clothes, clothing
das	**Kostüm**, -e ◇	costume; fancy dress; (*lady's*) suit
das	**Nachthemd**, -en	nightdress; nightshirt
das	**Sweatshirt**, -s	sweatshirt
das	**Taschentuch**, ¨er	handkerchief
das	**T-Shirt**, -s	T-shirt, tee-shirt
das	**Unterhemd**, -en	vest

USEFUL WORDS (nt)

das	**Cape**, -s	cape
das	**Dekolleté**, -s	low neck(line)
das	**Dirndl(kleid)**, -s (-er)	dirndl
das	**Futter**, – ◇	lining
das	**Halstuch**, ¨er	scarf
das	**Korsett**, -s	corset
das	**Kostümfest**, -e	fancy-dress party
das	**kurzärmelige Hemd**, -en	short-sleeved shirt
das	**Lätzchen**, –	bib (*baby*)
das	**Mannequin**, -s	model
das	**Muster**, – ◇	design, pattern
das	**Negligé**, -s	négligée
das	**Ölzeug**	oilskins
das	**Polohemd**, -en	polo shirt
das	**Revers**, –	lapel
das	**Sakko**, -s	sports jacket
das	**Schulterpolster**, –	shoulder pad
das	**Schultertuch**, ¨er	scarf (*round shoulders*), shawl, wrap
das	**Söckchen**, –	ankle sock
das	**Stirnband**, ¨er	headband
das	**Strumpfband**, ¨er	garter
das	**Umstandskleid**, -er	maternity dress

FEELINGS AND RELATIONSHIPS

ESSENTIAL WORDS (m)

der	**Ärger**	irritation, annoyance
der	**Haß**	hatred
der	**Mut**	courage
der	**Neid**	envy
der	**Schrecken** 🕮	terror, dread

IMPORTANT WORDS (m)

der	**Ekel**	revulsion
der	**Konflikt, -e**	conflict, clash
der	**Schock**	shock
der	**Streit, -e** ⇨	quarrel

USEFUL WORDS (m)

der	**Bekannte*, -n**	acquaintance
der	**Ehebruch**	adultery
der	**Ehekrach, ̈-e**	marital row
der	**Freund, -e**	friend; boyfriend
der	**Gefährte, -n**	companion
der	**Geliebte*, -n**	lover
der	**Groll**	grudge; resentment
der	**Hintergedanke, -n**	ulterior motive
der	**Kosename, -n**	pet name
der	**Krach, ̈-e** ⇨	row, quarrel
der	**Liebhaber, –**	lover
der	**Rivale, -n**	rival
der	**Stolz**	pride
der	**Trost**	comfort

viel von jdm halten *to think highly of sb*
wenig von jdm halten *not to think much of sb*
Todesangst haben *to be scared stiff*
etw bereuen *to regret sth*
jdn mögen *to like sb*
jdn umarmen *to embrace sb*
jdn in den Arm nehmen *to give sb a cuddle*
jdn erschrecken *to give sb a fright*

FEELINGS

ESSENTIAL WORDS (f)

die **Angst**, ⸚e ▭	anxiety; fear
die **Emotion**, -en	emotion
die **Enttäuschung**, -en ▭	disappointment
die **Freude**	joy; delight
die **Furcht**	fear
die **Liebe** ▭	love
die **Sorge**, -n	worry
die **Wut** ▭	fury, rage

IMPORTANT WORDS (f)

die **Abscheu**	disgust
die **Aggression**, -en	aggression
die **Begeisterung**	enthusiasm
die **Beleidigung**, -en	insult
die **Depression**, -en	depression
die **Entrüstung**	indignation
die **Erleichterung**	relief
die **Hilfe**	help
die **Krise**, -n	crisis
die **Meinungsverschieden-** heit, -en	disagreement
die **Nervosität**	nervousness
die **Panik**	panic
die **Rache**	revenge
die **Spannung**, -en	tension
die **Trauer**	sorrow, grief; mourning
die **Ungeduld**	impatience
die **Unruhe**	agitation, disquiet
die **Verwirrung**	disorientation
die **Verwunderung**	wonder
die **Zufriedenheit**	happiness, contentment
die **Zuneigung**	affection

jdn betrügen to be unfaithful to sb
aufgeregt agitated, excited
im siebten Himmel sein to be in seventh heaven
ein reines Gewissen haben to have a clear conscience
aus Sentimentalität for sentimental reasons

USEFUL WORDS (f)

die **Affäre, -n**	affair
die **Auseinandersetzung, -en**	quarrel, argument
die **Bekannte*, -n**	acquaintance
die **Beklommenheit**	trepidation
die **Bitterkeit**	bitterness, rancour
die **Ehekrise, -n**	marital crisis
die **Ekstase**	ecstasy
die **Freundin**	friend; girlfriend
die **Freundschaft**	friendship
die **Gefährtin**	companion
die **Geliebte*, -n**	mistress, lover
die **Kühnheit**	daring
die **Liebelei, -en**	flirtation; affair
die **Liebhaberin**	lover
die **Phantasie**	imagination
die **Rivalin**	rival
die **Rivalität, -en**	rivalry
die **Scheidung, -en**	divorce
die **Selbstachtung**	self-esteem
die **Untreue**	unfaithfulness
die **Vergeltung**	vengeance, revenge
die **Zärtlichkeit**	tenderness, affection

*die **Fassung behalten/verlieren*** *to keep/lose one's cool*
sich über etw freuen *to be delighted about sth*
es ist mir peinlich *I feel embarrassed about it*
böses Blut *ill feeling*
Zwietracht säen *to sow discord*
getrennt leben *to live apart*
verliebt *in love*
ärgern *to annoy; to bother*
begehren *to covet*
irritieren *to irritate*
neidisch *envious*
treu *faithful*
untreu *unfaithful*
verlegen *embarrassed*
besorgt *worried*

ESSENTIAL WORDS (nt)

das **Entsetzen**	horror
das **Erstaunen**	astonishment, amazement
das **Gefühl, -e**	feeling
das **Glück** ◇ ⊡	happiness
das **Mitleid** ⊡	pity; sympathy

IMPORTANT WORDS (nt)

das **Mißverständnis, -se**	misunderstanding
das **Schimpfwort, ¨er**	term of abuse
das **Vorurteil, -e** ⊡	prejudice

USEFUL WORDS (nt)

das **Flirten**	flirting
das **Ressentiment, -s**	(feeling of) resentment

reagieren *to react*
unterdrücken *to suppress*
sich aufregen *to get excited* or *worked up*
(gut/schlecht) miteinander auskommen *to get on (well/badly)*
verraten *to betray*
geschieden *divorced*
(sich) duzen *to use the familiar ''du'' form*
(sich) siezen *to use the formal ''Sie'' form*
sich schämen *to be* or *feel ashamed*
Vorurteile haben *to be prejudiced*

FISH AND SHELLFISH

der **Fisch**, -e	fish
der **Goldfisch**, -e	goldfish
der **Schwanz**, ⸚e	tail

der **Aal**, -e	eel
der **Frosch**, ⸚e	frog
der **Hai(fisch)**, -e	shark
der **Hecht**, -e	pike
der **Hering**, -e ✧	herring
der **Hummer**, –	lobster
der **Kabeljau**, -e	cod
der **Krebs**, -e ✧	crab; crayfish
der **Lachs**, -e	salmon
der **Schellfisch**, -e	haddock
der **Thunfisch**, -e	tuna fish
der **Tintenfisch**, -e	(small) octopus, squid
der **Weißfisch**, -e	whiting
der **Wurm**, ⸚er	worm

der **Angler**, –	angler
der **Barsch**, -e	perch
der **Fischer**, –	fisherman
der **Fischteich**, -e	fishpond
der **Flußkrebs**, -e	crayfish
der **Haken**, – ✧	hook
der **Karpfen**, –	carp
der **Köder**, –	bait
der **Rochen**, –	skate, ray
der **Sägefisch**, -e	sawfish
der **Schwarm**, ⸚e	shoal
der **Schwertfisch**, -e	swordfish
der **Seehecht**, -e	hake

FISH

ESSENTIAL WORDS (f)

die	**Forelle,** -n	trout
die	**Sardine,** -n	sardine

IMPORTANT WORDS (f)

die	**Auster,** -n	oyster
die	**Flosse,** -n	fin
die	**Garnele,** -n	shrimp; prawn
die	**Kaulquappe,** -n	tadpole
die	**Krabbe,** -n	shrimp; prawn
die	**Krake,** -n	octopus
die	**Languste,** -n	crayfish
die	**Muschel,** -n	mussel
die	**Qualle,** -n	jellyfish
die	**Schuppe,** -n	scale
die	**Seezunge,** -n	sole

USEFUL WORDS (f)

die	**Brasse,** -n	bream
die	**Kammuschel,** -n	scallop
die	**Kiemen** (*pl*)	gills
die	**Makrele,** -n	mackerel
die	**Meeräsche,** -n	(grey) mullet
die	**Reuse,** -n	shrimping net
die	**Scholle,** -n	plaice
die	**Sprotte,** -n	sprat
die	**Venusmuschel,** -n	clam

ESSENTIAL WORDS (nt)

das	**Aquarium,** (-ien)	aquarium
das	**Schalentier,** -e	shellfish
das	**Seepferdchen,** –	sea horse
das	**Wasser**	water

"Angeln verboten" *"no fishing"*
im Wasser schwimmen *to swim in the water*

FOOD AND DRINK

der	Alkohol	alcohol
der	Apfelsaft	apple juice
der	Apfelstrudel, –	apple strudel
der	Apfelwein	cider
der	Appetit	appetite
der	Aschenbecher, –	ashtray
der	Aufschnitt	cold meats
der	Becher, – ◊	mug; tumbler
der	Champagner	champagne
die	Chips (pl) ◊	crisps
der	Dessertlöffel, –	dessert spoon
der	Durst	thirst
der	Einkaufswagen, –	shopping trolley
der	Eintopf ▥	stew
der	Eßlöffel, –	tablespoon
der	Essig	vinegar
der	Fisch, -e	fish
der	Geschmack, ¨e	taste
der	Gulasch	goulash
der	Hamburger, –	hamburger
der	Honig	honey
der	Hunger	hunger
der	Imbiß, -sse	snack
der	Joghurt, -s	yoghurt
der	Kaffee	coffee
der	Kakao, -s	cocoa
der	Käse, –	cheese
der	Keks, -e	biscuit
der	Kellner, –	waiter
der	Knödel, –	dumpling
der	Kognak, -s	brandy
der	Korken, –	cork
der	Kuchen, –	cake
der	Löffel, –	spoon
der	Nachtisch, -e	dessert, sweet
der	Pfeffer	pepper
der	Reis	rice
der	Rinderbraten, –	roast beef
der	Saft, ¨e	juice
der	Salat, -e ◊	salad

FOOD

ESSENTIAL WORDS (m) (cont)

der	**Schinken**	ham
der	**Schnaps, ¨e**	schnapps; spirits
der	**Schnellimbiß, -sse** ⊡	snack bar; fast-food outlet
der	**Sekt**	champagne
der	**Senf, -e**	mustard
der	**Sprudel**	fizzy mineral water; fizzy drink
der	**Stammtisch, -e** ⊡	table for the regulars
der	**Strohhalm, -e**	(drinking) straw
der	**Tabak**	tobacco
der	**Tee**	tea
der	**Teelöffel, –**	teaspoon
der	**Teller, –**	plate
der	**Tisch, -e**	table
der	**Toast**	toast
der	**Wein, -e**	wine
der	**Whisky, -s**	whisky
der	**Zucker**	sugar
der	**Zuschlag, ¨e**	extra charge

alkoholfrei *non-alcoholic*
ein weichgekochtes/hartgekochtes Ei *soft-boiled/hard-boiled egg*
ein gekochtes Ei *boiled egg*
Eier mit Speck *ham and eggs*
aus der Flasche trinken *to drink from the bottle*
gedünstet *steamed*
Trinkwasser *drinking water*
vakuumverpackt *vacuum-packed*
mit Beilage *with side-dish/vegetables/ side-salad etc*
eine Schlankheitskur machen *to be on a diet*
er muß Diät leben *he must observe a strict diet*
eine Obstkur machen *to go on a fruit diet*
zum Kochen bringen *to bring to the boil*
wie wär's mit einem Apfelsaft? *do you fancy an apple juice?*
schlucken *to swallow*

FOOD AND DRINK — 3

IMPORTANT WORDS (m)

der **Eiswürfel, –**	ice cube
der **Krug Wasser, ̈e –**	jug of water
der **Pfannkuchen, –**	pancake
der **Rahm**	cream
der **Schinkenspeck**	ham
der **Speck**	bacon
der **Teig**	dough
der **Wackelpeter**	jelly
der **Weinbrand**	brandy
der **Zwieback**	(small) rusk

schmecken to taste (good)
das schmeckt ihm he likes it
könnte ich bitte eine Cola haben? could I have a Coke please?
bestellen to order
rauchen to smoke
danke, ich rauche nicht no thanks, I don't smoke
abtrocknen to dry the dishes
reichen to hand; to pass
bitten um to ask for
essen to eat
bedienen Sie sich! help yourself!
guten Appetit! enjoy your meal!
alkoholisch alcoholic
den Tisch decken/abräumen to lay or set/clear the table
abwaschen, (das Geschirr) spülen to wash up, do the dishes
kühl servieren serve chilled
blutig/medium/durchgebraten rare/medium/well-cooked (steak)
eine Scheibe Wurst a slice of sausage
probieren to taste, try
anstoßen to clink glasses
verdauen to digest
gierig gluttonous, greedy

USEFUL WORDS (m)

der **Aperitif**, -s	aperitif
der **Appetitanreger**, –	appetizer
der **Auflauf**, ¨e	baked pudding
der **Backteig**	batter
der **Berliner**, –	jam doughnut
der **Bierkeller**, –	beer cellar
der **Blätterteig**	puff or flaky pastry
der **Braten**, –	roast
der **Bratfisch**	fried fish
der **Christstollen**, –	Yule log
der **Curry**	curry (spice)
der **Eierlikör**	advocaat
der **Feinschmecker**, –	gourmet
der **Fruchtsaft**, ¨e	fruit juice
der **Gast**, ¨e	customer
der **Gastgeber**, –	host
der **Gastwirt**, -e	restaurateur; publican
der **Gin**	gin
der **Grieß**	semolina
der **Gurkensalat**	cucumber salad
der **Hasenpfeffer**	jugged hare
der **Honigkuchen**	gingerbread
der **Ingwer**	ginger
der **Jahrgang**, ¨e	year; vintage
der **Kabeljau**, -e	cod
der **Kamillentee**	camomile tea
der **Käsekuchen**, –	cheesecake
der **Kaugummi**, -s	chewing gum
der **Kebab**, -s	kebab
der **Kinderteller**, –	children's portion
der **Knoblauch**	garlic
der **Koch**, ¨e	chef; cook
der **Kopfsalat**, -e	lettuce
der **Kräutertee**, -s	herbal tea
der **Krautsalat**	coleslaw
der **Kronkorken**, –	crown cap
der **Kümmel**	caraway, cumin
der **Lebkuchen**	gingerbread
der **Likör**, -e	liqueur
der **Lutscher**, –	lollipop

USEFUL WORDS (m) (cont)

der	**Maiskolben,** –	corn on the cob
der	**Mokka, -s**	mocha coffee
der	**Mürbeteig**	shortcrust pastry
der	**Nachgeschmack**	aftertaste
der	**Ober,** –	waiter
der	**Orangensaft**	orange juice
der	**Oregano**	oregano
der	**Parmesankäse**	parmesan cheese
der	**Pfefferminztee**	peppermint tea
der	**Portwein**	port (*wine*)
der	**Pudding, -s**	blancmange
der	**Pulverkaffee**	instant coffee
der	**Pumpernickel**	pumpernickel
der	**Qualitätswein, -e**	wine of certified quality
der	**Quark**	quark
der	**Rauch**	smoke
der	**Räucherhering, -e**	smoked herring, kipper
der	**Räucherlachs**	smoked salmon
der	**Rollmops, ̈-e**	rollmops
der	**Rosé (wein)**	rosé (wine)
der	**Rotwein**	red wine
der	**Rum**	rum
der	**Sauerbraten**	braised beef (*marinated*)
der	**Schaschlik, -s**	(shish) kebab
der	**Schmalz**	lard
der	**Schnittlauch**	chives
der	**Snack, -s**	snack
der	**Spießbraten,** –	joint roasted on a spit
der	**Stammgast, ̈-e**	regular customer
der	**Tafelwein, -e**	table wine
der	**Teebeutel,** –	tea bag
der	**Thunfisch**	tuna
der	**Trüffel,** –	truffle
der	**Vegetarier,** –	vegetarian
der	**Weißwein**	white wine
der	**Wodka**	vodka
der	**Würfelzucker**	lump sugar
der	**Zahnstocher,** –	toothpick
der	**Zimt**	cinnamon
der	**Zuckerguß**	icing

ESSENTIAL WORDS (f)

die	**Auswahl (an** +*dat*) ◇	choice (of)
die	**Bedienung**	service; service charge
die	**Bestellung, -en**	order
die	**Bockwurst, ⁻e**	type of pork sausage
die	**Bratensoße**	gravy
die	**Bratwurst, ⁻e**	grilled *or* fried sausage
die	**Butter**	butter
die	**Cola, -s**	Coke ®
die	**Currywurst, ⁻e**	curried sausage
die	**Dose, -n** ▭	box; tin, can
die	**Erfrischung, -en** ▭	refreshment
die	**Flasche, -n**	bottle
die	**Frucht, ⁻e**	(piece of) fruit
die	**Gabel, -n**	fork
die	**Getränkekarte, -n** ▭	wine list
die	**Imbißstube, -n**	snack bar
die	**Kaffeekanne, -n**	coffeepot
die	**kalte Platte, -n -n**	cold meal
die	**Kartoffel, -n**	potato
die	**Kellnerin**	waitress
die	**Kneipe, -n**	pub
die	**Leberwurst**	liver sausage
die	**Limonade, -n**	lemonade
die	**Mahlzeit, -en**	meal
die	**Margarine**	margarine
die	**Marmelade, -n**	jam
die	**Mayonnaise**	mayonnaise
die	**Milch**	milk
die	**Nachspeise, -n**	dessert, sweet
die	**Orangenmarmelade**	marmalade
die	**Pizza, -s**	pizza
die	**Pommes frites** (*pl*)	chips, French fries
die	**Portion, -en**	portion, helping
die	**Praline, -n**	chocolate (*individual*)
die	**Rechnung, -en** ◇	bill
die	**Sahne**	cream
die	**Salami**	salami
die	**Salatsoße, -n**	salad dressing
die	**Salzkartoffeln** (*pl*) ▭	boiled potatoes
die	**Schale, -n** ◇	bowl

ESSENTIAL WORDS (f) (cont)

die Scheibe, -n	slice
die Schenke, -n 📖	inn
die Schlagsahne	whipped cream
die Schokolade	chocolate
die Schüssel, -n	bowl, dish
die Soße, -n	sauce
die Speisekarte, -n	menu
die Suppe, -n	soup
die Tageskarte, -n	(set) menu of the day
die Tasse, -n	cup
die Teekanne, -n	teapot
die Theke, -n	bar; counter
die Torte, -n	flan, tart
die Untertasse, -n	saucer
die Vanillesoße	custard
die Vorspeise, -n	hors d'oeuvre, starter
die Wirtschaft, -en ⬦	pub
die Wurst, ¨e	sausage (*large*)
die Zigarette, -n	cigarette
die Zigarre, -n	cigar

IMPORTANT WORDS (f)

die Büchse, -n ⬦	tin, can
die Eisdiele, -n	ice-cream parlour
die Frikadelle, -n	rissole
die Kaffeemaschine, -n	coffee machine
die Konserven (*pl*)	preserved foods
die Niere, -n	kidney
die Pfeife, -n	pipe
die Serviette, -n	napkin, serviette
die Thermosflasche, -n	Thermos ® flask

braten to fry
backen to bake
kochen to cook
vorbereiten to prepare
grillen to grill
würzen to season

USEFUL WORDS (f)

die	**Anchovis**, –	anchovy
die	**Apfeltasche**, -n	apple turnover
die	**Asche**	ash
die	**Austern** (*pl*)	oysters
die	**Beilage**, -n	side dish
die	**Bierdose**, -n	beer can
die	**Bierflasche**, -n	beer bottle
die	**Blutwurst**	black pudding
die	**Bouillon**	broth, stock
die	**Bowle**, -n	punch
die	**Bratkartoffeln** (*pl*)	fried potatoes
die	**Buttercremetorte**, -n	cream cake (*with buttercream*)
die	**Currysoße**	curry sauce
die	**Feinschmeckerin**	gourmet
die	**Filterzigarette**, -n	filter(-tipped) cigarette
die	**Fingerschale**, -n	finger bowl
die	**Fleischpastete**, -n	meat pie
die	**Frittenbude**, -n	chip shop
die	**Frühlingsrolle**, -n	spring roll
die	**Füllung**, -en ◇	stuffing
die	**Gastgeberin**	hostess
die	**Gaststätte**, -n	restaurant; pub
die	**Gastwirtin**	restaurateur; pub landlady
die	**Gefräßigkeit**	greed, gluttony
die	**Gewürzgurke**, -n	gherkin
die	**Götterspeise**	jelly
die	**Gräte**, -n	(fish)bone
die	**Grillparty**, -s	barbecue (*party*)
die	**Haferflocken** (*pl*)	oatflakes, porridge oats
die	**Innereien** (*pl*)	offal; giblets
die	**Käseplatte**, -n	cheeseboard
die	**Knackwurst**, ¨e	sausage
die	**Knoblauchzehe**, -n	clove of garlic
die	**Köchin**	chef; cook
die	**Krabben** (*pl*)	shrimps; prawns
die	**Kruste**	crust; crackling
die	**Lammkeule**, -n	leg of lamb
die	**Leber**	liver
die	**Literflasche**, -n	litre bottle

USEFUL WORDS (f) (cont)

die **Makkaroni** (*pl*) (mit Käsesoße)	macaroni (cheese)
die **Maß**, – ◇	litre (tankard) of beer
die **Mokkatorte**, -n	mocha cake
die **Muskatnuß**	nutmeg
die **Nudeln** (*pl*)	noodles, pasta
die **Obsttorte**, -n	fruit tart
die **Ochsenschwanzsuppe**, -n	oxtail soup
die **Ölsardinen** (*pl*)	sardines
die **Pastete**, -n	pie; paté
die **Petersilie**	parsley
die **Pizzeria**, (-ien)	pizzeria
die **Rindfleischsuppe**	beef broth
die **Runde**, -n ◇	round (*of drinks*)
die **Salatplatte**, -n	selection of salads
die **Sardelle**, -n	anchovy
die **Schweinshaxe**, -n	knuckle of pork
die **Sojabohnen** (*pl*)	soya beans
die **Sojasprossen** (*pl*)	beansprouts
die **Spaghetti** (*pl*)	spaghetti
die **Spätzle** (*pl*)	*type of (home made) pasta*
die **Stärke** ◇	starch
die **Streichholzschachtel**, -n	matchbox
die **Süßigkeiten** (*pl*)	sweets
die **Tagessuppe**, -n	soup of the day
die **Teestube**, -n	tearoom
die **Tiefkühlkost**	(deep-)frozen food
die **Vanille**	vanilla
die **Vegetarierin**	vegetarian
die **Waffel**, -n	waffle; wafer
die **Weinprobe**, -n	wine-tasting session
die **Zigarettenspitze**, -n	cigarette holder
die **Zitronenschale**, -n	lemon peel
die **Zwiebelsuppe**	onion soup
die **Zwischenmahlzeit**, -en	snack (*between meals*)

streichen *to spread*
schneiden *to cut*
einschenken *to pour* (tea etc)
anzünden *to light up*

ESSENTIAL WORDS (nt)

das	**Abendbrot**	evening meal, supper
das	**Abendessen**	evening meal, supper
das	**belegte Brot, -n -e**	open sandwich
das	**Bier, -e**	beer
das	**Bonbon, -s**	sweet, sweetie
das	**Brathähnchen, –**	roast chicken
das	**Brot, -e**	bread; loaf
das	**Brötchen, –**	(bread) roll
das	**Butterbrot, -e**	piece of bread and butter
das	**Café, -s**	café
das	**deutsche Beefsteak, -n -s**	hamburger
das	**Ei, -er**	egg
das	**Eis** ◊	ice cream
das	**Essen** ◊	food; meal
das	**Feuerzeug, -e**	lighter
das	**Fleisch** ◊	meat
das	**Frühstück**	breakfast
das	**Gemüse, –**	vegetable(s)
das	**Gericht, -e** ◊	dish, course
das	**Geschirr** ◊	dishes; crockery; pots and pans
das	**Getränk, -e**	drink
das	**Glas, ¨er** ◊	glass
das	**Hauptgericht, -e**	main course
das	**Kalbfleisch**	veal
das	**Kotelett, -e**	chop
das	**Lammfleisch**	lamb
das	**Menü, -s**	set menu
das	**Messer, –**	knife
das	**Mineralwasser**	mineral water
das	**Mittagessen**	lunch
das	**Mus**	purée
das	**Obst**	fruit
das	**Öl**	oil
das	**Omelett, -s**	omelette
das	**Picknick, -s**	picnic
das	**Pils** ▭	lager
das	**Restaurant, -s**	restaurant
das	**Rezept, -e** ◊	recipe
das	**Rindfleisch**	beef

ESSENTIAL WORDS (nt) (cont)

das	**Rührei, -er**	scrambled egg
das	**Salz**	salt
das	**Sandwich, -s**	sandwich
das	**Schnitzel, –**	(veal) cutlet
das	**Schwarzbrot**	(dark) rye bread
das	**Schweinefleisch**	pork
das	**Spiegelei, -er**	fried egg
das	**Steak, -s**	steak
das	**Tablett, -s**	tray
das	**Trinkgeld, -er**	tip
das	**Wasser**	water
das	**Wiener Schnitzel, – –**	Wiener schnitzel
das	**Wirtshaus, ̈-er**	inn
das	**Würstchen, –**	sausage (*small*)

paniert *in breadcrumbs*
frühstücken *to have breakfast*
hast du schon gegessen? *have you eaten yet?*
ich trinke gern Tee *I like (drinking) tea*
ich esse gern Käse *I like (eating) cheese*
das schmeckt scheußlich! *that tastes dreadful!*
ich mag Käse/Tee nicht, ich mag keinen Käse/Tee *I don't like cheese/tea*
ich esse lieber Brot/trinke lieber Bier *I prefer bread/beer*
ich sterbe vor Hunger! *I'm starving!*
durstig sein, Durst haben *to be thirsty*
hungrig sein, Hunger haben *to be hungry*
schmeckt Ihnen der Wein? *do you like the wine?*
um Feuer bitten *to ask for a light*
"Rauchen verboten" *"no smoking"*
trinken *to drink*
ich versuche, das Rauchen aufzugeben *I'm trying to give up smoking*
Meeresfrüchte (pl) *seafood, shellfish*
was können Sie empfehlen? *what do you recommend?*
ein Essen bei Kerzenschein *a candlelit dinner*
sich vollstopfen mit *to stuff oneself with*

IMPORTANT WORDS (nt)

das	**Geflügel**	poultry
das	**Kartoffelpüree**	mashed potatoes
das	**Mehl, -e** ▭	flour
das	**Rosinenbrötchen, –**	(currant) bun
das	**Streichholz, ¨er**	match
das	**Tischtuch, ¨er**	tablecloth
das	**Trifle, -s**	trifle
das	**Wild**	game (*meat*); venison

bitter bitter
eßbar edible
gebacken roast
gebraten fried
gefüllt stuffed
gekocht cooked; boiled
giftig poisonous
knusprig crisp, crunchy
köstlich delicious
pikant savoury
ranzig rancid
roh raw
saftig juicy
salzig salty
sauer sour
schal stale
scharf pungent; hot
sehnig stringy
süß sweet
würzig spicy
zäh tough

USEFUL WORDS (nt)

das Apfelmus	stewed apples
das Aroma, (-men)	aroma
das Basilikum	basil
das Eis am Stiel	ice lolly
das Eisbein	knuckle of pork
das Faß, ¨sser	barrel, cask
das Faßbier, -e	draught beer
das Festessen, –	feast, banquet
das Filet, -s	fillet
das Filetsteak, -s	fillet steak
das Fischstäbchen, –	fish finger
das Flaschenbier	bottled beer
das Fleischgericht, -e	meat dish
das Gasthaus, ¨er	inn, hotel
das Gehackte	mince
das Gewürz, -e	seasoning
das Graubrot	brown/wholemeal bread
das Jägerschnitzel, –	veal *or* pork with mushrooms
das Knoblauchbrot	garlic bread
das Krustenbrot	crusty bread
das Lakritz	liquorice
das Löffelbiskuit, -s	sponge finger (*biscuit*)
das Lokal, -e	pub; inn
das Lorbeerblatt, ¨er	bayleaf
das Marzipan	marzipan
das Orangeat	candied orange peel
das Paniermehl	breadcrumbs
das Plätzchen, –	biscuit
das Ragout, -s	ragout
das Roggenbrot	rye bread
das Schnellgericht, -e	convenience food
das Stangenbrot, -e	baguette
das Stück, -e ◇	piece
das Tomatenpüree	tomato purée
das Vanilleeis	vanilla ice cream
das Weißbrot	white bread
das Zigeunerschnitzel, –	veal *or* pork with peppers
das Zitronat	candied lemon peel

| ESSENTIAL WORDS (m) |

der **Ausflug**, ⸚e	trip, outing
der **Besuch**, -e	visit; visitor
der **Brieffreund**, -e	penfriend
der **CD-Spieler**, –	CD player
der **Computer**, –	computer
der **Fan**, -s	fan
der **Film**, -e	film
der **Fotoapparat**, -e	camera
der **Freund**, -e	friend; boyfriend
der **Jugendklub**, -s	youth club
der **Karneval** ▭	carnival
der **Kassettenrecorder**, –	cassette recorder
der **Krimi**, -s	thriller, detective story
der **Nachtklub**, -s	night club
der **Pfadfinder**, –	boy scout
der **Plattenspieler**, –	record player
der **Roman**, -e	novel
der **Sänger**, –	singer
der **Schlager**, –	hit (record)
der **Spaziergang**, ⸚e	walk
der **Sport**	sport
der **Tanz**, ⸚e	dance
der **Treffpunkt**, -e ▭	meeting place
der **Verein**, -e	club, association
der **Walkman** ®, -s	personal stereo, Walkman ®
der **Zoo**, -s	zoo

wir treffen uns jeden Freitag *we meet* or *get together every Friday*
hast du Lust, zu meiner Party zu kommen? *do you fancy coming to my party?*
eine Party geben *to have a party*
schreiben *to write*
Radio hören *to listen to the radio*
einen Spaziergang machen *to go for a walk*
umschalten *to turn over, change channels*

die **Comics** (*pl*)	cartoons, comic strips
der **Fortsetzungsroman**, -e	serial
der **Musikautomat**, -en	jukebox
der **Spielautomat**, -en	slot machine
der **Wettbewerb**, -e	competition
der **Zeitvertreib**, -e	pastime

der **Babysitter**, –	baby-sitter
der **Bube**, -n	jack, knave (*cards*)
der **Camcorder**, –	camcorder
der **Drachen**, –	kite
der **Flipper**, –	pinball machine
der **Fotoroman**, -e	(romantic) picture story
der **Fußballplatz**, ⸚e	football pitch
der **Fußballtoto**	football pools
der **Hacker**, –	hacker
der **Klub**, -s	club
der **Knobelbecher**, –	dice cup
der **König**, -e	king (*cards*)
der **Liebesroman**, -e	romantic novel
der **Pauschalurlaub**, -e	package holiday
der **Sammler**, –	collector
der **Sandkasten**, ⸚	sandpit
der **Skat**	skat (*German card game*)
der **Spieler**, –	player; gambler
der **Spielplatz**, ⸚e	playground
der **Spionageroman**, -e	spy novel
der **Trumpf**, ⸚e	trump
der **Urlauber**, –	holiday-maker
der **Vergnügungspark**, -s	amusement park
der **Videorekorder**, –	video recorder
der **Wahrsager**, –	fortune-teller
der **Wanderverein**, -e	rambling club

ESSENTIAL WORDS (f)

die	**Aufnahme, -n** ◇	shot (*photo*); recording
die	**Ausstellung, -en**	exhibition
die	**Besichtigung, -en** ▭	visit
die	**Brieffreundin**	penfriend
die	**Briefmarkensammlung, -en**	stamp collection
die	**CD, -s**	CD
die	**Compact Disc, - -s**	compact disc
die	**Diskothek, -en**	disco
die	**Einladung, -en** ▭	invitation
die	**Eintrittskarte, -n** ▭	(admission) ticket
die	**Ermäßigung, -en**	reduction
die	**Fotografie, -n**	photograph; photography
die	**Freizeit**	free time, spare time
die	**Freizeitbeschäftigung, -en**	hobby, spare-time activity
die	**Freundin**	friend; girlfriend
die	**Führung, -en** ▭	conducted tour
die	**Illustrierte, -n** ▭	magazine
die	**Karten** (*pl*)	(playing) cards
die	**Kassette, -n**	cassette
die	**Langspielplatte, -n**	long-playing record, LP
die	**Maxi-Single, -s**	12-inch single
die	**Messe, -n** ◇ ▭	fair; mass
die	**Musik**	music
die	**Nachrichten** (*pl*) ▭	news
die	**Pfadfinderin**	girl scout
die	**Sängerin**	singer
die	**Schallplatte, -n**	record
die	**Sendung, -en** ▭	programme
die	**Stereoanlage, -n**	stereo (system)
die	**Unterhaltung, -en** ◇	entertainment; talk
die	**Verabredung, -en** ▭	date, appointment
die	**Videokassette, -n**	video (cassette)
die	**Wanderung, -en**	walk, hike
die	**Zeitschrift, -en**	magazine
die	**Zeitung, -en**	newspaper

ich interessiere mich für (+acc) *I am interested in*
aufnehmen *to record*
zeichnen *to draw*

IMPORTANT WORDS (f)

die **Begeisterung**	enthusiasm
die **Familienserie, -n**	soap opera
die **Filmkamera, -s**	cine camera
die **Hitparade**	charts, hit parade
die **Party, -s**	party
die **Seifenoper, -n**	soap opera
die **Stickerei**	embroidery
die **Versammlung, -en**	meeting, gathering

USEFUL WORDS (f)

die **Babysitterin**	baby-sitter
die **Dame, -n** ◇	queen (*cards*)
die **Entspannung**	relaxation
die **Geschichte, -n** ◇	story, tale
die **Kaffeepause, -n**	coffee break
die **Kartenlegerin**	fortune teller (*who reads cards*)
die **Kegelbahn, -en**	bowling lane; bowling alley
die **Mitgliedschaft**	membership
die **Rutschbahn, -en**	slide
die **Sammlerin**	collector
die **Schaukel, -n**	swing
die **Sehenswürdigkeiten** (*pl*)	places of interest
die **Spielerin**	player; gambler
die **Urlauberin**	holiday-maker
die **Videokamera, -s**	video camera
die **Wahrsagerin**	fortune-teller

fernsehen to watch television
lesen to read
Platten hören to play records
fotografieren to take photos (of)
toll! terrific!
ausgezeichnet! excellent!
die Zeit mit etw verbringen to spend one's time doing sth
in meiner Freizeit in my free or spare time

ESSENTIAL WORDS (nt)

das	**Band, -̈er** ◊	recording tape
das	**Dia, -s**	slide, transparency
das	**Fernsehen**	television
das	**Foto, -s**	photo(graph)
das	**Hobby, -s**	hobby
das	**Interesse, -n**	interest
das	**Kartenspiel, -e**	game of cards; pack of cards
das	**Kino, -s**	cinema
das	**Konzert, -e**	concert
das	**Lesen**	reading
das	**Magazin, -e**	magazine
das	**Mitglied, -er**	member
das	**Museum, (-een)**	museum
das	**Nähen**	sewing
das	**Programm, -e** ◊	(TV) programme
das	**Radio, -s**	radio
das	**Schach**	chess
das	**Singen**	singing
das	**Spiel, -e** ◊	game
das	**Stricken**	knitting
das	**Taschenbuch, -̈er** ▭	paperback
das	**Taschengeld**	pocket money
das	**Theater, –**	theatre
das	**Transistorradio, -s**	transistor radio
das	**Videogerät, -e**	video (recorder)
das	**Wandern**	hiking, rambling
das	**Wochenende, -n**	weekend

sammeln to collect
es hat mir wirklich gut gefallen *I really liked it*
am Wochende *at the weekend(s)*
malen to paint
treffen to meet
amüsiere dich gut! *enjoy yourself, have fun!*
beschließen to decide
sich ausruhen to rest
wo sollen wir uns treffen? *where shall we meet?*

das **Album, (-ben)**	album
das **Damespiel**	draughts
das **Feriendorf, ¨-er**	holiday centre
das **Ferienlager, –**	school camp
das **Kreuzworträtsel, –** ⌑	crossword (puzzle)
das **Lied, -er**	song
das **Modell, -e** ◇	model
das **Rollbrett, -er**	skateboard
das **Skateboard, -s**	skateboard

ich hole dich ab *I'll pick you up*
meine Lieblingsbeschäftigung *my favourite hobby*
"mit oder ohne Filter?" *"plain or tipped?"* (of cigarette)
einem Verein beitreten *to join a club*
Patiencen legen *to play patience*
sich ausschlafen *to have a lie-in*
ein Nickerchen machen *to have a snooze or nap*
auf der Straße spielen *to play in the street*
mit Murmeln spielen *to play marbles*
Verstecken spielen *to play hide-and-seek*
einen Drachen fliegen lassen *to fly a kite*
knobeln *to play dice*
um etw knobeln *to toss up for sth*
mit Puppen spielen *to play with dolls*
Bockspringen spielen *to play leapfrog*
Kopf oder Zahl? *heads or tails?*
seilspringen *to skip* (with a rope)
unterhaltsam *entertaining*
durchblättern *to leaf through*
etw durch das Los bestimmen *to decide sth by drawing lots*
"Pik/Kreuz ist Trumpf" *"spades/clubs are trumps"*

USEFUL WORDS (nt)

das	**Angeln**	fishing, angling
das	**As, -se**	ace (*cards*)
das	**Backgammon**	backgammon
das	**Bowling**	(tenpin) bowling
das	**Brettspiel, -e**	board game
das	**Bridge**	bridge
das	**Buch, ¨er**	book
das	**Comic-Heft, -e**	comic
das	**Computerspiel, -e**	computer game
das	**Damebrett, -er**	draughtboard
das	**Darts(spiel)**	darts
das	**Drachenfliegen**	hang-gliding
das	**Geschwätz**	gossip, gossiping
das	**Gesellschaftsspiel, -e**	parlour game
das	**Golf**	golf
das	**Herz ◇**	hearts (*cards*)
das	**Karo**	diamonds (*cards*)
das	**Kartenlegen**	card-reading
das	**Karussell, -s**	merry-go-round
das	**Kegeln**	ninepins, skittles
das	**Knetgummi**	Plasticine ®
das	**Korbflechten**	wickerwork, basketwork
das	**Kreuz ◇**	clubs (*cards*)
das	**Lotto**	lotto
das	**Malbuch, ¨er**	colouring book
das	**Märchen, –**	fairy tale
das	**Minigolf**	crazy *or* miniature golf
das	**Pfand, ¨er**	forfeit
das	**Pferderennen, –**	horse racing; horse race
das	**Pik**	spades (*cards*)
das	**Puzzle, -s**	jigsaw (puzzle)
das	**Roulette**	roulette
das	**Schachbrett, -er**	chessboard
das	**Spielkasino, -s**	casino
das	**Surfen**	surfing
das	**Tanzen**	dancing
das	**Tanzlokal, -e**	dance hall
das	**Töpfern**	pottery
das	**Video, -s**	video
das	**Zoomobjektiv, -e**	zoom (lens)

FRUIT

der **Apfel**, ⸚	apple
der **Apfelbaum**, ⸚e	apple tree
der **Birnbaum**, ⸚e	pear tree
der **Obstbaum**, ⸚e	fruit tree
der **Obstgarten**, ⸚	orchard
der **Pfirsich**, -e	peach
der **Pfirsichbaum**, ⸚e	peach tree
der **Weinstock**, ⸚e	vine

IMPORTANT WORDS (m)

der **Granatapfel**, ⸚	pomegranate
der **Kern**, -e	pip; stone (*in fruit*)
der **Nußbaum**, ⸚e	walnut tree
der **Rhabarber**	rhubarb
der **Walnußbaum**, ⸚e	walnut tree
der **Weinberg**, -e	vineyard

USEFUL WORDS (m)

der **Brombeerstrauch**, ⸚er	blackberry bush
der **Johannisbeerstrauch**, ⸚er	red *or* blackcurrant bush
der **Kirschbaum**, ⸚e	cherry tree
der **Mandelbaum**, ⸚e	almond tree
der **Stein**, -e ⸰	stone

sammeln *to gather*
essen *to eat*
pflücken *to pick*
saftig *juicy*
blaue/grüne Trauben *black/green grapes*
beißen *to bite*
hart *hard*
weich *soft*
unreif *not ripe*
reif *ripe*

ESSENTIAL WORDS (f)

die	**Apfelsine**, -n	orange
die	**Banane**, -n	banana; banana tree
die	**Birne**, -n ◇	pear
die	**Erdbeere**, -n	strawberry
die	**Frucht**, ¨e	(piece of) fruit
die	**Himbeere**, -n	raspberry
die	**Kirsche**, -n	cherry
die	**Melone**, -n ◇	melon
die	**Olive**, -n	olive
die	**Orange**, -n	orange; orange tree
die	**Pflaume**, -n	plum
die	**Schale**, -n ◇	skin; peel; shell
die	**Weintraube**, -n	grape; bunch of grapes
die	**Zitrone**, -n	lemon

USEFUL WORDS (f)

die	**Avocado**, -s	avocado (pear)
die	**Cashewnuß**, ¨sse	cashew nut
die	**Guave**, -n	guava
die	**Honigmelone**, -n	honeydew melon
die	**Klementine**, -n	clementine
die	**Kokospalme**, -n	coconut palm *or* tree
die	**Mandel**, -n ◇	almond
die	**Mango**, -s	mango
die	**Mirabelle**, -n	small yellow plum
die	**Nektarine**, -n	nectarine
die	**Pistazie**, -n	pistachio (nut)
die	**Reneklode**, -n	greengage
die	**Sauerkirsche**, -n	Morello cherry
die	**Wassermelone**, -n	watermelon
die	**Zitrusfrüchte** (*pl*)	citrus fruits

süß *sweet*
sauer *sour, sharp*
bitter *sour; bitter*

---

das	**Kerngehäuse, –**	core
das	**Kompott, -e**	stewed fruit
das	**Obst**	fruit
das	**Stück Obst**	piece of fruit

IMPORTANT WORDS (f)

die	**Ananas, –**	pineapple
die	**Aprikose, -n**	apricot; apricot tree
die	**Backpflaume, -n**	prune
die	**Beere, -n**	berry
die	**Brombeere, -n**	blackberry, bramble
die	**Dattel, -n**	date
die	**Erdnuß, ̈-sse**	peanut, monkeynut
die	**Feige, -n**	fig
die	**Grapefruit, -s**	grapefruit
die	**Haselnuß, ̈-sse**	hazelnut
die	**Heidelbeere, -n**	bilberry
die	**Johannisbeere, -n**	redcurrant
die	**Kastanie, -n**	chestnut; chestnut tree
die	**Kiwi, -s**	kiwi (fruit)
die	**Kokosnuß, ̈-sse**	coconut
die	**Mandarine, -n**	tangerine
die	**Nuß, ̈-sse**	nut
die	**Pampelmuse, -n**	grapefruit
die	**Passionsfrucht, ̈-e**	passion fruit
die	**schwarze Johannisbeere, -n -n**	blackcurrant
die	**Stachelbeere, -n**	gooseberry
die	**Traube, -n**	grape; bunch of grapes
die	**Traubenlese**	grape harvest, vintage
die	**Walnuß, ̈-sse**	walnut
die	**Weinrebe, -n**	vine
die	**Zwetsch(g)e, -n**	plum

ESSENTIAL WORDS (m)

der Elektroherd, -e	electric cooker
der Fernsehapparat, -e	television set
der Gasherd, -e	gas cooker
der Herd, -e ⌑	cooker
der Kassettenrecorder, –	cassette recorder
der Kleiderschrank, ⸚e	wardrobe
der Kühlschrank, ⸚e	fridge, refrigerator
der Nachttisch, -e	bedside table
der Ofen, ⸚	oven
der Plattenspieler, –	record player
der Raum, ⸚e ◇ ⌑	room
der Schrank, ⸚e	cupboard
der Sessel, –	armchair
der Spiegel, –	mirror
der Stecker, –	plug
der Strom ◇	(electric) current
der Stuhl, ⸚e	chair
der Tisch, -e	table
der Videorekorder, –	video recorder
der Walkman ®, -s	personal stereo, Walkman ®
der Wecker, –	alarm clock

(die Möbel) umräumen *to move the furniture around*
ein Zimmer ausräumen *to clear out a room*
sich setzen *to sit down*
sich hinlegen *to lie down*
sich ausruhen *to rest*
es funktioniert nicht *it's not working*
gemütlich *comfortable, cosy*
ausmachen, ausschalten *to turn or switch off*
anmachen, einschalten *to turn or switch on*
staubsaugen *to hoover ®*
elektrisch *electric*
Staub putzen *to dust*
anrufen *to phone, call*
fernsehen *to watch television*
Musik hören *to listen to music*
telefonieren *to telephone*
im Fernsehen *on television*

FURNITURE

IMPORTANT WORDS (m)	

der	Anrufbeantworter, –	telephone answering machine
der	Backofen, ⸚	oven
der	Bücherschrank, ⸚e	bookcase
der	Couchtisch, -e	coffee table
der	Eßtisch, -e	dining table
der	Frisiertisch, -e	dressing table
der	Heizofen, ⸚	heater
der	Kleiderhaken, –	coat hook
der	Lehnsessel, –	armchair
der	Mikrowellenherd, -e	microwave (oven)
der	Möbelwagen, –	furniture van, removal van
der	Nachtspeicherofen, ⸚	(night) storage heater
der	Rahmen, – ⌑	frame
der	Satz ⸖ Tische, ⸚e –	nest of tables
der	Schaukelstuhl, ⸚e	rocking chair
der	Schirmständer, –	umbrella stand
der	Schnellkochtopf, ⸚e	pressure cooker
der	Schreibtisch, -e	(writing) desk
der	Sekretär, -e ⸖	bureau, writing desk
der	Staubsauger, – ⌑	vacuum cleaner, Hoover ®
der	Teewagen, –	trolley
der	Umzug, ⸚e ⸖	removal

USEFUL WORDS (m)	

der	Ausziehtisch, -e	extending table
der	CD-Spieler, –	CD *or* compact disc player
der	Diwan, -e	divan
der	Fön, -e	hair dryer
der	Hocker, –	stool
der	Klappstuhl, ⸚e	folding chair
der	Klapptisch, -e	folding table
der	Kronleuchter, –	chandelier
der	Lampenschirm, -e	lampshade
der	Liegestuhl, ⸚e	deck chair; lounger
der	Radiowecker, –	clock radio
der	Trockenautomat, -en	tumble dryer
der	Ventilator, -en	fan

3 — FURNITURE AND APPLIANCES

die **Kuckucksuhr**, -en	cuckoo clock
die **Lampe**, -n	lamp
die **Schreibmaschine**, -n ▭	typewriter
die **Spülmaschine**, -n	dishwasher
die **Steckdose**, -n	(wall) socket
die **Stehlampe**, -n ▭	standard lamp
die **Stereoanlage**, -n	stereo (system)
die **Uhr**, -en ◊	clock
die **Waschmaschine**, -n	washing machine

die **Anrichte**, -n	dresser; sideboard
die **Einrichtung**	furnishings
die **Kommode**, -n	chest of drawers
die **Matratze**, -n	mattress
die **Nähmaschine**, -n	sewing machine
die **Satellitenantenne**, -n	satellite dish
die **Schublade**, -n ▭	drawer
die **Spedition**, -en	removal firm
die **Standuhr**, -en	grandfather clock
die **Strickmaschine**, -n	knitting machine
die **Tiefkühltruhe**, -n	freezer, deep freeze
die **Truhe**, -n	chest, trunk
die **Videokamera**, -s	video camera
die **Wäscheschleuder**, -n	spin dryer
die **Wiege**, -n	cradle

die **Antenne**, -n	aerial
die **Armlehne**, -n	armrest
die **Couch**, -en	couch
die **Fernbedienung**, -en	remote control
die **Gefriertruhe**, -n	freezer
die **Liege**, -n	divan (bed); couch
die **Schleuder**, -n	spin-dryer
die **Waage**, -n	(bathroom) scales
die **Wandlampe**, -n	wall lamp

das	**Bett,** -en	bed
das	**Bild,** -er ▢	picture; painting
das	**Bücherregal,** -e	bookcase, bookshelf
das	**Haus,** ̈er	house
das	**Klavier,** -e	piano
die	**Möbel** (*pl*)	furniture
das	**Möbelstück,** -e	piece of furniture
das	**Regal,** -e	(set of) shelves
das	**Sofa,** -s	settee, couch
das	**Telefon,** -e	telephone
das	**Transistorradio,** -s	transistor radio
das	**Videogerät,** -e	video (recorder)
das	**Zimmer,** –	room

das	**Bord,** -e	shelf
das	**Etagenbett,** -en	bunk bed
das	**Gemälde,** – ▢	painting, picture
das	**Gerät,** -e ◇	appliance
das	**Kinderbett,** -en	cot
das	**Rollo,** -s	(roller) blind
das	**schnurlose Telefon,** -n -e	cordless telephone
das	**Schubfach,** ̈er	drawer
das	**Tonbandgerät,** -e	tape recorder

die	**Gartenmöbel** (*pl*)	garden furniture
das	**Himmelbett,** -en	four-poster bed
das	**Klappbett,** -en	folding bed
das	**Radio,** -s	radio
das	**Sideboard,** -s	sideboard
das	**Sofabett,** -en	bed-settee, sofa bed

bequem *comfortable*
unbequem *uncomfortable*
in dem Zimmer ist es sehr eng *the room is very cramped*
ein möbliertes Zimmer *a furnished room*

GEOGRAPHICAL FEATURES

der	Berg, -e	mountain; hill
der	Erdteil, -e ⊞	continent
der	Fluß, ⁻sse	river
der	Kontinent, -e	continent
der	Ozean, -e	ocean
der	See, -n ◇	lake

der	Äquator	equator
der	Bach, ⁻e	stream, brook
der	Felsen, –	rock
der	Fjord, -e	fjord, fiord
der	Gipfel, – ⊞	summit, (mountain) top
der	Gletscher, – ⊞	glacier
der	Golf, -e ◇	gulf
der	Kanal, ⁻e ◇	canal
der	Nebenfluß, ⁻sse	tributary
der	Nordpol	North Pole
der	Pol, -e	pole
der	Strom, ⁻e ◇	(*large*) river
der	Südpol	South Pole
der	Sumpf, ⁻e	marsh, swamp

der	Abgrund, ⁻e	abyss
der	Archipel, -e	archipelago
der	Breitengrad, -e	(degree of) latitude
der	Dschungel, –	jungle
der	Eisberg, -e	iceberg
der	Erdrutsch, -e	landslide
der	Längengrad, -e	(degree of) longitude
der	Paß, ⁻sse ◇	(mountain) pass
der	Vulkan, -e	volcano
der	Wasserfall, ⁻e	waterfall

die nördliche/südliche Hemisphäre *the northern/southern hemisphere*
flußaufwärts/-abwärts *upstream/downstream*

GEOGRAPHICAL

ESSENTIAL WORDS (f)

die **Insel, -n**	island
die **See, -n** ◇	sea
die **Wüste, -n** ▯	desert

IMPORTANT WORDS (f)

die **Bergkette, -n**	(mountain) range
die **Ebene, -n**	plain
die **Halbinsel, -n**	peninsula
die **Klippe, -n**	cliff
die **Küste, -n**	coast; shore
die **Quelle, -n**	spring

USEFUL WORDS (f)

die **Bucht, -en**	bay
die **Düne, -n**	dune
die **Höhle, -n** ◇	cave
die **Lava**	lava
die **Meerenge, -n**	strait
die **Mündung, -en**	estuary
die **Oase, -n**	oasis
die **Schlucht, -en**	gorge, ravine
die **Spitze, -n** ◇	peak, top
die **Straße, -n** ◇	strait
die **Tropen** (*pl*)	tropics

ESSENTIAL WORDS (nt)

das **Delta, -s**	delta
das **Erdbeben, –**	earthquake
das **Gebirge, –**	mountains, mountain range
das **Tal, ̈-er** ▯	valley

USEFUL WORDS (nt)

das **Binnenmeer, -e**	inland sea
das **Hinterland**	hinterland
das **Kap, -s**	cape, headland
das **Moor, -e**	moor

GEOGRAPHICAL NAMES

die Alpen (*pl*)	the Alps
der Ärmelkanal	the English Channel
Athen	Athens
der Atlantik	the Atlantic (Ocean)
der Atlantische Ozean	the Atlantic (Ocean)
Basel (*nt*)	Basle
Bayern (*nt*)	Bavaria
Berlin (*nt*)	Berlin
der Bodensee	Lake Constance
die britischen Inseln (*pl*)	the British Isles
Brüssel (*nt*)	Brussels
Den Haag (*nt*)	The Hague
die Donau	the Danube
das Elsaß	Alsace
der Ferne Osten	the Far East
Genf (*nt*)	Geneva
der Genfer See	Lake Geneva
der Große Ozean	the Pacific Ocean
Hannover (*nt*)	Hanover
Kairo (*nt*)	Cairo
die Kanalinseln (*pl*)	the Channel Islands
Köln (*nt*)	Cologne
Korsika (*nt*)	Corsica
Kreta	Crete
Lissabon (*nt*)	Lisbon
London	London
Lothringen (*nt*)	Lorraine
Mailand (*nt*)	Milan
Mallorca (*nt*)	Majorca
das Mittelmeer	the Mediterranean (Sea)
die Mosel	Moselle
Moskau (*nt*)	Moscow
München (*nt*)	Munich
der Nahe Osten	the Middle East
die Nordsee	the North Sea
die Ostsee	the Baltic Sea
der Pazifik	the Pacific (Ocean)
der Pazifische Ozean	the Pacific (Ocean)
Peking (*nt*)	Peking
der Persische Golf	the Persian Gulf

GEOGRAPHICAL

die Pyrenäen (*pl*)	the Pyrenees
der Rhein	the Rhine
Rom (*nt*)	Rome
Sardinien	Sardinia
der Schwarzwald	the Black Forest
die Seine	the Seine
der Stille Ozean	the Pacific Ocean
die Themse	the Thames
Venedig (*nt*)	Venice
der Vesuv	Mount Vesuvius
Warschau (*nt*)	Warsaw
Wien (*nt*)	Vienna
die Wolga	the Volga
Zypern	Cyprus

Athener, -in *an Athenian*
Bas(e)ler, -in *a person from Basle*
Bayer, -in *a Bavarian*
Elsässer, -in *a person from Alsace, an Alsatian*
Friese, Friesin *a person from Frisia, a Frisian*
Hamburger, -in *a person from Hamburg*
Hannoveraner, -in *a person from Hanover, a Hanoverian*
Hesse, Hessin *a person from Hesse*
Indianer, -in *an (American) Indian*
Londoner, -in *a Londoner*
Moskauer, -in *a person from Moscow, a Muskovite*
Münch(e)ner, -in *a person from Munich*
Pariser, -in *a Parisian*
Preuße, Preußin *a Prussian*
Rheinländer, -in *a Rhinelander*
Römer, -in *a person from Rome, a Roman*
Sachse, Sächsin *a person from Saxony*
Schwabe, Schwäbin *a person from Swabia*
Tiroler, -in *a person from the Tyrol*
Venezianer, -in *a Venetian*
Westfale, Westfälin *a Westphalian*
Wiener, -in *a person from Vienna, a Viennese*

GREETINGS AND INTERJECTIONS

die Umarmung *embrace, hug*
der Händedruck *handshake*
jdm einen Kuß geben *to give sb a kiss*
jdm die Hand küssen/schütteln *to kiss/shake sb's hand*
sich küssen *to kiss each other*
(sich) vorstellen *to introduce (oneself)*
grüßen, begrüßen *to greet, welcome*
sich verabschieden *to say goodbye, take one's leave*
auf Wiedersehen! *goodbye*
auf Wiederhören! *goodbye (on phone)*
guten Morgen! *good morning*
guten Tag! *hello; good afternoon*
guten Abend! *good evening*
gute Nacht! *good night (when going to bed)*
bis später *see you later*
sehr angenehm *pleased to meet you*
bis morgen *see you tomorrow*
tschüs! *bye!*
wie geht's?; wie geht es Ihnen? *how are things?*
gut, danke; es geht mir gut, danke *very well, thank you*

POLITENESS

es tut mir leid *I'm sorry*
leider (nicht) *unfortunately (not)*
(wie) bitte? *(I beg your) pardon?*
es macht nichts *it doesn't matter*
bitte schön, bitte sehr *there you are*
mit Vergnügen *with pleasure*
entschuldigen Sie, Entschuldigung *excuse me; I'm sorry*
pardon *excuse me, I'm sorry*
verzeihen Sie, Verzeihung *(formal) I'm sorry, I beg your pardon*
machen Sie keine Umstände *don't go to any trouble*
keine Ursache *don't mention it*
bitte *please*
danke *thank you*
nein danke *no thank you*
danke schön, vielen Dank *thank you very much*

GREETINGS AND INTERJECTIONS — 2

frohe Ostern *happy Easter*
viele (liebe) Grüße *with lots of love* (at end of letter)
guten Appetit! *have a good meal, enjoy your meal*
gutes neues Jahr *happy New Year*
prost! *cheers!*
fröhliche Weihnachten *merry Christmas*
viel Glück *all the best; the best of luck*
alles Gute zum Geburtstag *happy birthday*
alles Gute zum Hochzeitstag *congratulations on your wedding day*
zum Wohl! *good health!*
Gesundheit! *bless you!* (after a sneeze)
hast du gut geschlafen? *did you sleep well?*
schlaf gut! *sleep well*
viel Spaß! *have a good time, enjoy yourself*
alles Gute *all the best, best wishes*
herzlichen Glückwunsch! *congratulations!*

SURPRISE

wie bitte? *what was that?*
das soll wohl ein Witz sein! *you must be joking!*
mein Gott! *good Lord!*
(ach) du lieber Himmel! *(good) heavens!*
so eine Frechheit! *what a nerve* or *cheek!*
aber wirklich! *well really!*
was ist los (mit dir)? *what's the matter (with you)?, what's wrong (with you)?*
ach du meine Güte *oh my goodness, oh dear*
na, so etwas! *you don't say!*
ach so! *oh I see!*
wie? *what?*
was für ein Glück! *what a piece of luck!*
so?, wirklich? *really?*
so, so! *well, well!*

3 — GREETINGS AND INTERJECTIONS

AGREEMENT

ich habe nichts dagegen *I don't mind or object*
desto besser *so much the better*
das ist mir gleich or ***egal*** *I don't mind*
schön *fine*
einverstanden! *agreed!*
genau, ganz recht *exactly*
na gut, also gut *O.K. then, all right then*
das stimmt *that's right*
ja *yes*
in Ordnung *O.K., all right*
nicht wahr? *isn't that right?*
natürlich *of course*
jawohl *yes indeed*
gut *good, O.K.*
prima! *great!*
klasse! *terrific!, marvellous!*

DISAGREEMENT

kümmern Sie sich um Ihren eigenen Kram! *mind your own business!*
nie!, um nichts in der Welt! *never!, not on your life!*
das stimmt nicht *that doesn't make sense*
im Gegenteil *on the contrary*
doch *yes (when contradictory)*
nein *no*
natürlich nicht *of course not*
du machst wohl Witze *you must be joking!*

ORDERS

beeil(e) dich! *hurry up!*
herein! *come in!*
raus! *get out!*
halt den Mund! *shut up!*
Ruhe! *be quiet!*
halt! *stop!*
Achtung! *watch out!*
Vorsicht! *be careful!*
paß auf! *look out!, watch out!*

GREETINGS AND INTERJECTIONS — 4

ich halte das nicht mehr aus *I can't stand it any more*
es ist mir peinlich *I'm embarrassed about it*
es geht mir auf die Nerven *it gets on my nerves*
es ärgert mich *it bothers me*
mein aufrichtiges Beileid *please accept my condolences*
jdm die letzte Ehre erweisen *to pay one's last respects to sb*
Hilfe! *help!*
ach je! *oh dear!*
geh mir aus dem Weg! *get out of my way!*
hau ab! *clear off!*
verflixt (nochmal)! *blow!, drat!, dash it!*
verflucht!, verdammt! *damn!*
wie ärgerlich! *what a nuisance!, how annoying!*
was soll ich tun? *what shall I do?*
ich kann ihn nicht ausstehen *I can't stand him*
ich habe es satt *I'm fed up with it*
armes Ding! *poor thing!*
das ist Pech *it's a shame, that's bad luck*

Sie wünschen? *can I help you?*
bitte machen Sie es sich bequem *please make yourself comfortable*
wenn doch endlich Ferien wären! *I can't wait for the holidays!*
schade! *(what a) shame!*
ich weiß da nicht Bescheid *I don't know (anything about it)*
ich weiß nicht genau *I don't know exactly*
machen Sie sich keine Sorgen *don't worry*
(ich habe) keine Ahnung *(I've) no idea*
ich weiß nicht *I don't know*
vielleicht *perhaps, maybe*
tu das nicht *don't do that*

ESSENTIAL WORDS (m)

der	**Apotheker, –**	(dispensing) chemist, pharmacist
der	**Arzt, ⸚e**	doctor; G.P.
der	**Atem**	breath
die	**Bauchschmerzen** (pl)	stomachache
der	**Durchfall**	diarrhoea
der	**Gips**	plaster; plaster of Paris
der	**Gipsverband, ⸚e**	plaster (cast)
die	**Halsschmerzen** (pl)	a sore throat
der	**Husten**	cough
die	**Kopfschmerzen** (pl)	headache
der	**Kranke*, -n**	patient; sick person
der	**Krankenschein, -e**	health insurance card
der	**Krankenwagen, –**	ambulance
der	**Kurort, -e** ▢	health resort
die	**Magenschmerzen** (pl)	stomachache
der	**Operationssaal, (-säle)**	operating theatre
der	**Patient, -en**	patient
der	**Schmerz, -en**	pain, ache
der	**Schnupfen**	cold (in the head)
der	**Schweiß**	sweat, perspiration
der	**Tod, -e**	death
die	**Tropfen** (pl)	drops
der	**Verband, ⸚e**	bandage, dressing
der	**Zahnarzt, ⸚e**	dentist
die	**Zahnschmerzen** (pl)	toothache

verletzt injured, hurt
es tut weh it hurts
verwundet wounded
sich übergeben to vomit, be sick
ich bin mit dem Auto verunglückt I've had an accident with the car
es blutet it's bleeding
was fehlt Ihnen? what's the matter with you?
können Sie mir helfen? can you help me?
sich erholen to recover
gute Besserung! get well soon!
untersuchen to examine

der	**Bazillus, (-len)**	germ
der	**Herzanfall, ̈-e**	heart attack
der	**Heuschnupfen**	hayfever
der	**Hitzschlag**	heatstroke
der	**HIV-Positive*, -n**	HIV-positive person
der	**Kratzer, –**	scratch
der	**Mumps**	mumps
der	**Puls**	pulse
der	**Rückfall, ̈-e**	relapse
der	**Schlaganfall, ̈-e**	stroke
der	**Schock**	shock
der	**Sonnenstich**	sunstroke
der	**Stich, -e** ⟡	sting
der	**Typhus**	typhoid

schwanger *pregnant*
im sechsten Monat (schwanger) *(over) five months pregnant*
ein Herzleiden haben *to have a heart condition*
im Koma sein *to be in a coma*
sich schwach fühlen *to feel weak*
hinfallen *to have a fall*
eine Kur machen *to take the waters (at a spa)*
eine Entziehungskur machen *to go/be on a cure for drug addiction/alcoholism*
eine Blutprobe entnehmen *to take a blood sample*
er fühlt sich heute etwas daneben *he's feeling a bit off-colour today*
jdn in ein Krankenhaus einweisen *to admit sb to a hospital*
ich fühle mich echt mies *I'm feeling really lousy*
sich schlechter/besser fühlen *to feel worse/better*
unter Quarantäne stellen *to put into quarantine*
aus der Flasche ernähren *to bottle-feed*
sich die Mandeln herausnehmen lassen *to have one's tonsils out*
das Bewußtsein verlieren *to lose consciousness*
sich den Fuß verstauchen *to sprain one's foot*
unter ärztlicher Aufsicht *under medical supervision*
anschwellen *to swell*

USEFUL WORDS (m)

der	Abstrich, -e	smear (test)
der	Alkoholmißbrauch	alcohol abuse
der	Antikörper, –	antibody
die	Augentropfen (*pl*)	eye drops
der	Balsam	balm, balsam
der	Beinbruch	broken leg
der	blaue Fleck, -n -en	bruise
der	Blutdruck	blood pressure
der	Bluter, –	haemophiliac
der	Brutkasten, ̈	incubator
der	Drogenmißbrauch	drug abuse
der	Eiter	pus
der	Fußpilz	athlete's foot
der	Gallenstein, -e	gallstone
der	Gehirntod	brain death
der	Haarausfall	hair loss
der	Hautkrebs	skin cancer
der	Herzinfarkt, -e	heart attack
der	HIV-Virus	HIV virus
der	Hüftbruch	hip fracture
der	Invalide, -n	disabled person
der	Kaiserschnitt	Caesarean (section)
der	Kehlkopfkrebs	cancer of the throat
der	Keuchhusten	whooping cough
der	Krebs ◊	cancer
der	Kriegsversehrte*, -n	disabled ex-serviceman
der	Kurgast, ̈-e	*person at a health resort or spa*
der	Leistenbruch	hernia, rupture
der	Lungenkrebs	lung cancer
der	Muskelriß, -sse	torn muscle
der	Muskelschwund	muscular atrophy
die	Nasentropfen (*pl*)	nose drops
der	Ohnmachtsanfall, ̈-e	fainting fit, blackout
der	Operationstisch, -e	operating table
der	Organspenderausweis, -e	donor card
der	Pfleger, –	male nurse
der	praktische Arzt, -n, ̈-e	general practitioner
der	Rollstuhl, ̈-e	wheelchair
die	Rückenschmerzen (*pl*)	backache

USEFUL WORDS (m) (cont)

der **Sanitäter, –**	ambulance man
der **Schädelbruch**	fractured skull
der **Scharlach**	scarlet fever
der **Schauder, –**	shudder
der **Schleim**	phlegm
der **Schluckauf**	hiccough(s)
der **Schnitt, -e**	cut
der **Schwindelanfall, ¨e**	dizzy spell
die **Seitenstiche** (*pl*)	stitch (*pain*)
der **Selbstmordversuch, -e**	suicide attempt
der **Streß**	stress
der **Stromschlag, ¨e**	electric shock
der **Tetanus**	tetanus
der **Todeskampf**	death throes
der **Tropf**	drip
der **Tumor, -en**	growth, tumour
der **Umschlag, ¨e** ◇	poultice
der **Virus, (-ren)**	virus
der **Vitaminmangel**	vitamin deficiency

verbinden *to bandage*
pflegen *to look after, nurse*
wiederbeleben *to resuscitate*
weitsichtig *long-sighted*
kurzsichtig *short-sighted*
heiser *hoarse*
der Arzt hat ihr Bettruhe verordnet *the doctor has ordered her to stay in bed*
abnehmen *to lose weight*
zunehmen *to put on weight*
mir ist heiß/kalt *I feel hot/cold*
leichtverletzt *slightly injured*
schwerverletzt *seriously injured*
ich habe mich verletzt *I have hurt myself*
ich habe mir die Hand verbrannt *I have burnt my hand*
ich habe Halsschmerzen/Zahnschmerzen/Kopfschmerzen *I've got a sore throat/toothache/a headache*

ESSENTIAL WORDS (f)

die	Allergie, -n	allergy
die	Ärztin	doctor; G.P.
die	Erkältung, -en	cold; chill
die	Erste Hilfe	first aid
die	Feuerwehr	fire brigade
die	Gesundheit	health
die	Grippe	flu, influenza
die	Klinik, -en	hospital, clinic
die	Kranke*, -n	patient; sick person
die	Krankenkasse, -n	health insurance company
die	Krankenschwester, -n	nurse
die	Krankheit, -en	illness
die	Kur, -en ⌐	(health) cure; treatment
die	Lebensgefahr	danger (to life)
die	Medizin	(science of) medicine
die	Operation, -en	operation
die	Patientin	patient
die	Pille, -n	pill
die	Ruhe ◇	rest
die	Sorge, -n	care, worry
die	Spritze, -n	syringe; injection
die	Tablette, -n	tablet, pill
die	Temperatur, -en	temperature
die	Untersuchung, -en ◇	(medical) examination, check-up
die	Verletzung, -en	injury
die	Verstopfung	constipation
die	Wunde, -n	wound
die	Zunge, -n	tongue

sterben to die
tot dead
atemlos breathless, out of breath
schwach weak
müde tired
schwindlig dizzy
krank ill
gesund healthy, well

IMPORTANT WORDS (f)

die	**Abmagerungskur, -en**	diet (*slimming*)
die	**Bandage, -n**	(elastic) bandage
die	**Blase, -n** ◇	blister; bladder
die	**Blinddarmentzündung**	appendicitis
die	**Blutübertragung, -en**	blood transfusion
die	**Diät, -en** ◇	(special) diet
die	**Droge, -n**	drug
die	**Epidemie, -n**	epidemic
die	**Genesung**	recovery, convalescence
die	**HIV-Positive*, -n**	HIV-positive person
die	**Kraft, ¨e**	strength, power
die	**Krücke, -n**	crutch
die	**Mandelentzündung**	tonsillitis
die	**Masern** (*pl*)	measles
die	**Migräne, -n**	migraine
die	**Narbe, -n**	scar
die	**Poliklinik, -en**	clinic (*for outpatients*)
die	**Röntgenaufnahme, -n**	X-ray
die	**Röteln** (*pl*)	German measles
die	**Salbe, -n**	ointment, cream
die	**Schiene, -n**	splint
die	**Schlinge, -n**	sling
die	**Station, -en** ◇	ward
die	**Trage, -n**	stretcher
die	**Übelkeit**	sickness, vomiting
die	**Watte**	cotton wool
die	**Windpocken** (*pl*)	chickenpox

USEFUL WORDS (f)

die	**Abtreibung, -en**	abortion
die	**Akne**	acne
die	**Ambulanz**	out-patient department
die	**Amputation, -en**	amputation
die	**Anstalt, -en**	home, institution
die	**Arthritis**	arthritis
die	**Arthrose**	osteoarthritis
die	**Bakterie, -n**	bacterium
die	**Behandlung**	treatment
die	**Behinderung, -en**	disability, handicap

USEFUL WORDS (f) (cont)

die	**Bindehautentzündung**	conjunctivitis
die	**Blasenentzündung**	cystitis
die	**Blindheit**	blindness
die	**Bluttransfusion, -en**	blood transfusion
die	**Blutung**	bleeding, haemorrhage
die	**Blutvergiftung**	blood poisoning
die	**Bronchitis**	bronchitis
die	**Chemotherapie**	chemotherapy
die	**Chirurgie**	surgery
die	**Depression, -en**	depression
die	**Diagnose, -n**	diagnosis
die	**Diphtherie**	diphtheria
die	**Dosierung, -en**	dosage
die	**Drüse, -n**	gland
die	**Elektroschocktherapie**	electric shock treatment
die	**Entbindung, -en**	delivery
die	**Entwöhnung**	weaning
die	**Epilepsie**	epilepsy
die	**Erholung**	recovery
die	**Euthanasie**	euthanasia
die	**Familienplanung**	family planning
die	**Fehlgeburt, -en**	miscarriage
die	**Fettleibigkeit**	obesity
die	**Frostbeulen** (*pl*)	frostbite
die	**Frühgeburt, -en**	premature baby
die	**Füllung, -en** ⟡	filling (*in tooth*)
die	**Galle**	bile
die	**Gänsehaut**	goose pimples
die	**Gebrauchsanweisung, -en**	directions for use
die	**Gegenanzeige, -n**	contra-indication
die	**Gehirnerschütterung**	concussion
die	**Geisteskrankheit, -en**	mental illness
die	**Gelbsucht**	jaundice
die	**Geschlechtskrankheit, -en**	venereal disease, VD
die	**Geschwulst, -e**	growth, tumour
die	**Gürtelrose**	shingles
die	**Halluzination, -en**	hallucination
die	**Hebamme, -n**	midwife
die	**Heilung**	healing; curing
die	**Herzverpflanzung, -en**	heart transplant

die	**Hirnhautentzündung**	meningitis
die	**Homöopathie**	homeopathy
die	**Hypnose**	hypnosis
die	**Hypnotherapie**	hypnotherapy
die	**Immunisierung**	immunization
die	**Impfung, -en**	vaccination
die	**In-vitro-Fertilisation**	in vitro fertilization
die	**Infektion, -en**	infection
die	**Injektion, -en**	injection
die	**Intensivstation, -en**	intensive care unit
die	**Kapsel, -n**	capsule
die	**Karies**	caries
die	**Kehlkopfentzündung**	laryngitis
die	**Krampfadern** (*pl*)	varicose veins
die	**Krankengeschichte, -n**	medical history
die	**Krätze**	scabies
die	**Krebsforschung**	cancer research
die	**künstliche Niere, -n -n**	kidney machine
die	**Lebenserwartung**	life expectancy
die	**Lebensmittelvergiftung**	food poisoning
die	**Lepra**	leprosy
die	**Leukämie**	leukaemia
die	**Liegekur**	rest cure
die	**Lungenentzündung**	pneumonia
die	**Magenverstimmung**	indigestion
die	**Magersucht**	anorexia
die	**Malaria**	malaria
die	**Mandeln** (*pl*) ◊	tonsils
die	**Mangelkrankheit, -en**	deficiency disease
die	**Massage, -n**	massage
die	**Menstruation**	menstruation
die	**Müdigkeit**	tiredness
die	**Mund-zu-Mund-Beatmung**	mouth-to-mouth resuscitation
die	**Narkose**	anaesthetic
die	**natürliche Geburt**	natural childbirth
die	**Neurose, -n**	neurosis
die	**Nikotinvergiftung**	nicotine poisoning
die	**Notaufnahme**	casualty department
die	**Ohrenentzündung, -en**	ear infection
die	**örtliche Betäubung**	local anaesthetic

die	**Pest**	plague
die	**Phobie, -n**	phobia
die	**Physiotherapie**	physiotherapy
die	**Plombe, -n**	filling (*in tooth*)
die	**Pocken**	smallpox
die	**Praxis, (-xen)**	surgery (*rooms*)
die	**Prothese, -n** ⬦	artificial limb; set of dentures
die	**Salmonellenvergiftung**	salmonella poisoning
die	**Scheinschwangerschaft**	phantom pregnancy
die	**Schirmbildunter-**	
	suchung, -en	X-ray examination
die	**Schlafmittelvergiftung**	barbiturate poisoning
die	**Schlaftablette, -n**	sleeping pill
die	**Schlankheitskur**	diet
die	**Schußverletzung, -en**	gunshot wound
die	**Schwangerschaft, -en**	pregnancy
die	**Schwindsucht**	consumption
die	**Seuche, -n**	plague
die	**Sprechstunde**	surgery
die	**Sucht, ¨e**	addiction
die	**Therapie, -n**	therapy
die	**Tollwut**	rabies
die	**Transplantation, -en**	transplant
die	**Tuberkulose**	tuberculosis, TB
die	**Ultraschallunter-**	
	suchung, -en	ultrasound (scan)
die	**Unfallstation, -en**	casualty department
die	**Unterkühlung**	hypothermia
die	**Verbrennung, -en**	burn
die	**Vergiftung**	poisoning
die	**Verrenkung**	dislocation
die	**Verschlimmerung**	worsening
die	**Verstauchung**	sprain
die	**Vollnarkose**	general anaesthetic
die	**Vorsorgeuntersuchung, -en**	medical check-up
die	**Wiederholungsimpfung, -en**	booster
die	**Zahnklinik, -en**	dental clinic
die	**Zerrung**	pulled ligament *or* muscle
die	**Zuckerkrankheit**	diabetes
die	**Zyste, -n**	cyst

USEFUL WORDS (m&f)

der/die **Alkoholiker(in)**, –	alcoholic
der/die **Augenarzt**, ⁻e/ **Augenärztin**	eye specialist
der/die **Augenoptiker(in)**, –	optician
der/die **Behinderte***, -n	handicapped or disabled person
der/die **Chirurg(in)**, -en	surgeon
der/die **Diabetiker(in)**, –	diabetic
der/die **Epileptiker(in)**, –	epileptic
der/die **Ersthelfer(in)**, –	first aid worker
der/die **Facharzt**, ⁻e/ **Fachärztin**	specialist
der/die **Fußpfleger(in)**, –	chiropodist
der/die **Gehirnchirurg(in)**, -en	brain surgeon
der/die **Gynäkologe**, -n/ **Gynäkologin**	gynaecologist
der/die **Hals-Nasen-Ohren- Arzt**, ⁻e/-**Ärztin**	ear, nose and throat specialist
der/die **Heroinsüchtige***, -n	heroin addict
der/die **Homöopath**, -en/ **Homöopathin**	homeopath
der/die **Kardiologe**, -n/ **Kardiologin**	cardiologist
der/die **Kinderarzt**, ⁻e/ **Kinderärztin**	paediatrician
der/die **Krebsspezialist(in)**, -en	cancer specialist
der/die **Leprakranke***, -n	leper
der/die **Opiumsüchtige***, -n	opium addict
der/die **Organspender(in)**, –	(organ) donor
der/die **Psychiater(in)**, –	psychiatrist
der/die **Psychoanalytiker(in)**, –	psychoanalyst
der/die **Psychopath(in)**, -en	psychopath
der/die **Schwerkranke***, -n	critically ill person
der/die **Schwerverletzte***, -n	severely injured person
der/die **Sterbende***, -n	dying person

schwitzen to sweat
niesen to sneeze
fallen, stürzen to fall

ESSENTIAL WORDS (nt)

das	**AIDS, Aids**	AIDS, aids
das	**Aspirin**	aspirin
das	**Blut**	blood
das	**Fieber**	fever, (high) temperature
das	**Heftpflaster**, –	sticking plaster
das	**Kopfweh**	headache
das	**Krankenhaus**, ⁻er	hospital
das	**Leiden**, –	complaint, condition
das	**Medikament**, -e	medicine
das	**Rezept**, -e ⇨	prescription
das	**Thermometer**, –	thermometer

IMPORTANT WORDS (nt)

das	**Altersheim**, -e	old people's home
das	**Antibiotikum**, (-ka)	antibiotic
das	**Erbrechen**	sickness, vomiting
das	**Gift**, -e 🕮	poison
das	**Sprechzimmer**, –	surgery, consulting room

ein Baby stillen/mit der Flasche ernähren to breast-feed/bottle-feed a baby
eine Wunde nähen to put stitches in a wound
ich habe meine Stimme verloren I've lost my voice
niedriger/hoher Blutdruck low/high blood pressure
Sodbrennen haben to have heartburn
einen Herzinfarkt/Schlaganfall haben to have a heart attack/stroke
Herzklopfen haben to have palpitations
geschwollene Drüsen haben to have swollen glands
Ohrensausen haben to have a buzzing (noise) in one's ears
schlechten Atem haben to have bad breath
unter Schlaflosigkeit leiden to suffer from insomnia
mir ist schwindlig I feel faint or dizzy
es ist ansteckend it's contagious
blaß pale
tödlich deadly, lethal
sich erkälten to catch cold
husten to cough
HIV-positiv/negativ HIV positive/negative

USEFUL WORDS (nt)

das	**Abführmittel, –**	laxative
das	**Anregungsmittel, –**	stimulant
das	**Asthma**	asthma
das	**Barbiturat, -e**	barbiturate
das	**Beruhigungsmittel, –**	sedative, tranquilliser
das	**Blutgerinnsel, –**	(blood)clot
das	**Desinfektionsmittel, –**	disinfectant
das	**Ekzem, -e**	eczema
das	**Elektrokardiogramm (EKG), -e**	electrocardiogram (ECG)
das	**Flaschenkind, -er**	bottle-fed baby
das	**Fluor**	fluorine
das	**Furunkel, –**	boil
das	**Gegenmittel, –**	antidote
das	**Geschwür, -e**	ulcer
das	**Heim, -e**	home
das	**Hörgerät, -e**	hearing aid
das	**Hühnerauge, -n**	corn
das	**Implantat, -e**	implant
das	**Jucken**	itching
das	**Kondom, -e**	condom
das	**Kribbeln**	pins and needles
das	**Nasenbluten**	nosebleed
das	**Nasenspray, -s**	nasal spray
das	**Nikotin**	nicotine
das	**Präservativ, -e**	condom
das	**Retortenbaby, -s**	test-tube baby
das	**Schlafmittel, –**	sleeping drug
das	**Schmerzmittel, –**	painkiller
das	**Sodbrennen**	heartburn
das	**Stillen**	breast-feeding
das	**Symptom, -e**	symptom
das	**Verhütungsmittel, –**	contraceptive
das	**Wachstum**	growth
das	**Wartezimmer, –**	waiting room
die	**Wechseljahre** (*pl*)	menopause

er hat Fieber *he has a temperature*
wo tut es Ihnen weh? *where does it hurt?*

ESSENTIAL WORDS (m)

der	**Aufenthalt**, -e	stay
der	**Aufzug**, ⸚e ⌑	lift
der	**Balkon**, -s ◇	balcony
der	**Blick**, -e	view
der	**Empfangschef**, -s ⌑	receptionist; head porter
der	**Farbfernseher**, –	colour television (set)
der	**Fernseher**, –	television set
der	**Feuerlöscher**, – ⌑	fire extinguisher
der	**Gast**, ⸚e	guest
der	**Gasthof**, ⸚e	inn, hotel
der	**Gepäckträger**, – ◇	porter
der	**Hotelier**, -s	hotelier, hotel-keeper
der	**Kellner**, –	waiter
der	**Koch**, ⸚e	chef; cook
der	**Koffer**, –	case, suitcase
der	**Lift**, -e	lift
der	**Notausgang**, ⸚e ⌑	emergency exit
der	**Prospekt**, -e	leaflet, brochure
der	**Reiseführer**, – ◇ ⌑	guidebook; travel guide (*person*)
der	**Reiseleiter**, – ⌑	travel courier
der	**Reisepaß**, ⸚sse	passport
der	**Schalter**, – ◇	switch
der	**Scheck**, -s	cheque
der	**Schlüssel**, –	key
der	**Stern**, -e	star
der	**Stock**, -werke ◇	floor
der	**Tag**, -e	day
der	**Weinkellner**, –	wine waiter
der	**Zuschlag**, ⸚e	extra charge

"Sie brauchen nur zu klingeln" *"just ring"*
"inklusive Bedienung" *"inclusive of service"*
"Zimmer frei" *"vacancies"*
Herr Ober! *waiter!*
"Bedienung inbegriffen" *"service included"*
ein 5-Sterne-Hotel *a 5-star hotel*
das Zimmer hat Aussicht or **Blick auf den Strand** *the room overlooks the beach*

HOTEL

163

IMPORTANT WORDS (m)

der	Brand, ⁼e	fire
der	Gastwirt, -e	owner; innkeeper; landlord
der	Ober	waiter
der	Oberkellner, –	head waiter

USEFUL WORDS (m)

der	Geschäftsführer, –	manager
der	Komfort	luxury; comfort
der	Luxus	luxury
der	Nachtportier, -s	night porter
der	Parkplatz, ⁼e	parking space; car park
der	Portier, -s	porter
der	Preis, -e ◇	price
der	Swimmingpool, -s	swimming pool
der	Zimmerservice	room service

USEFUL WORDS (f)

die	Beschwerde, -n	complaint
die	Decke, -n ◇	blanket
die	Gastfreundschaft	hospitality
die	Geschäftsführerin	manager
die	Quittung, -en	receipt
die	Reservierung, -en	reservation
die	Vermittlung	operator (*service*)
die	Zimmernummer, -n	room number

Fräulein! *excuse me, miss!*
im Erdgeschoß *on the ground floor, on ground level*
im ersten/zehnten Stock *on the first/tenth floor*
ich möchte hier übernachten *I'd like a room for the night*
ich möchte ein Zimmer mit Dusche/mit Bad
   I'd like a room with a shower/with a bath
sich in einem Hotel anmelden *to book in at a hotel*
ein Formular ausfüllen *to fill in a form*

ESSENTIAL WORDS (f)

die	**Anmeldung** 🕮	registration
die	**Antwort, -en**	answer, reply
die	**Aussicht, -en** 🕮	view
die	**Bar, -s**	bar
die	**Bedienung**	service; service charge
die	**Dusche, -n**	shower
die	**Empfangsdame, -n**	receptionist
die	**Garderobe, -n** ⇨	cloakroom
die	**Gaststätte, -n**	restaurant; pub
die	**Halbpension**	half board
die	**Kellnerin**	waitress
die	**Kneipe, -n**	pub
die	**Köchin**	chef; cook
die	**Mahlzeit, -en**	meal
die	**Mehrwertsteuer** 🕮	value added tax
die	**Nacht, ⸚e**	night
die	**Nummer, -n**	number
die	**Pension, -en**	guesthouse, boarding house
die	**Rechnung, -en** ⇨	bill
die	**Rezeption**	reception, reception desk
die	**Tasche, -n** ⇨	bag
die	**Terrasse, -n** ⇨	terrace
die	**Toilette, -n**	toilet
die	**Übernachtung mit Frühstück**	bed and breakfast
die	**Unterkunft, ⸚e**	accommodation
die	**Veranstaltung, -en**	organization
die	**Vollpension**	full board
die	**Woche, -n**	week

IMPORTANT WORDS (f)

die	**Gastwirtin**	owner; innkeeper; landlady
die	**Vorhalle, -n**	foyer

3 Tage bleiben *to stay for 3 days*
einpacken *to get packed*
auspacken *to get unpacked*
was kostet es?, wie teuer ist es? *how much is it?*
das ist ziemlich teuer *that is rather expensive*

das	**Abendessen**	evening meal, supper
das	**Badezimmer, –**	bathroom
das	**Café, -s**	café
das	**Doppelbett, -en**	double bed
das	**Doppelzimmer, –**	double room
das	**Einzelzimmer, –**	single room
das	**Erdgeschoß, -sse**	ground floor, ground level
das	**Farbfernsehen**	colour television
das	**Formular, -e** ▭	form
das	**Freibad, ̈-er**	open-air swimming pool
das	**Fremdenzimmer, –** ▭	guest room
das	**Frühstück**	breakfast
das	**Gasthaus, ̈-er**	inn, hotel
das	**Gepäck**	luggage
das	**Hotel, -s**	hotel
das	**Kleingeld**	small change
das	**Mittagessen**	lunch
das	**Restaurant, -s**	restaurant
das	**Speisezimmer, –**	dining room
das	**Telefon, -e**	telephone
das	**Treppenhaus, ̈-er**	staircase
das	**Wirtshaus, ̈-er**	inn
das	**Zimmer, –**	room
das	**Zimmermädchen, –**	chambermaid

das	**Foyer, -s**	foyer
das	**Schwimmbad, ̈-er**	swimming pool
das	**Stockwerk, -e**	floor
das	**Trinkgeld, -er** ▭	tip
das	**Zweibettzimmer, –**	twin-bedded room

das	**Bettlaken, –**	sheet
das	**Gästebuch, ̈-er**	register
das	**Handtuch, ̈-er**	towel
das	**Konferenzzimmer, –**	conference room
das	**Waschbecken, –**	washbasin

ESSENTIAL WORDS (m)

der	**Aufzug**, ¨e ▭	lift
der	**Balkon**, -s ◇	balcony
der	**Bezirk**, -e ▭	district
der	**Boden**, ¨ ◇	floor
der	**Bungalow**, -s	bungalow
der	**Dachboden**, ¨ ▭	attic, loft
der	**Einwohner**, –	inhabitant
der	**Flur**, -e ▭	(entrance) hall
der	**Fußboden**, ¨ ▭	floor
der	**Gang**, ¨e ◇ ▭	corridor
der	**Garten**, ¨	garden
der	**Haushalt**, -e ▭	household
der	**Hof**, ¨e	yard
der	**Kamin**, -e ▭	chimney; fireplace
der	**Keller**, –	cellar
der	**Mieter**, –	tenant
der	**Nachbar**, -n	neighbour
der	**Park**, -s	(public) park
der	**Parkplatz**, ¨e	parking space
der	**Rasen**	lawn; grass
der	**Raum**, ¨e ◇ ▭	room; space
der	**Schlüssel**, –	key
der	**Speisesaal**, (-säle)	dining room
der	**Stein**, -e ◇	stone
der	**Stock**, -werke ◇	floor, storey
der	**Vorort**, -e	suburb

IMPORTANT WORDS (m)

der	**Besitzer**, –	owner
der	**Hausmeister**, – ▭	caretaker
der	**Hauswirt**, -e	landlord
der	**Korridor**, -e	corridor
der	**Rauch**	smoke
der	**Schornstein**, -e ◇	chimney
der	**Treppenabsatz**, ¨e	landing
der	**Umzug**, ¨e ◇	removal
der	**Wintergarten**, ¨	conservatory
der	**Wohnblock**, -s	block of flats
der	**Zaun**, ¨e	fence

HOUSE

THE HOUSE – GENERAL — 2

USEFUL WORDS (m)

der	**Abstellraum,** ⸚e	storeroom
der	**Altbau,** -ten	old building
der	**Auszug**	move (*out*)
der	**Balken,** –	beam
der	**Blitzableiter,** –	lightning conductor
der	**Dachziegel,** –	roof tile
der	**Eingang,** ⸚e	doorway, entrance
der	**Einzug**	move (*in*)
der	**Giebel,** –	gable
der	**Hauseigentümer,** –	owner
der	**Häuserblock,** ⸚e	block (*of houses*)
der	**Hinterhof,** ⸚e	backyard
der	**Kurzschluß,** ⸚sse	short-circuit
der	**Landsitz,** -e	country seat
der	**Luftschacht,** ⸚e	ventilation shaft
der	**Müllschlucker,** –	refuse chute
der	**Neubau,** -ten	new building
der	**Riegel,** –	bolt
die	**Rolläden** (*pl*)	shutters
der	**Schlüsselbund,** -e	bunch of keys
der	**Speicher,** – ◇	loft, attic
der	**Spion,** -e ◇	spy-hole, peephole
der	**Stromausfall,** ⸚e	power cut
der	**Vermieter,** –	landlord
der	**Vorgarten,** ⸚	front garden
der	**Wohnungsmakler,** –	estate agent
der	**Wolkenkratzer,** –	skyscraper

im ersten/dritten Stock on the first/third floor
es klingelt somebody's ringing the bell
in der Stadt/auf dem Land wohnen to live in the town/in the country
mieten to rent
bauen to build
es klopft there's a knock at the door
besitzen to own
aufräumen to tidy up
eine Einzugsfete machen to have a house-warming party

ESSENTIAL WORDS (f)

die	**Adresse**, -n	address
die	**Anlage** 🕮	layout
die	**Aussicht**, -en 🕮	view
die	**Decke**, -n ◇	ceiling
die	**Dusche**, -n	shower
die	**Einwohnerin**	inhabitant
die	**Familie**, -n	family
die	**Garage**, -n	garage
die	**Gegend**, -en	district, area
die	**Hausfrau**, -en	housewife
die	**Haustür**, -en	front door
die	**Kohle** ◇	coal
die	**Küche**, -n ◇	kitchen; cooking
die	**Lage**, -n ◇ 🕮	position, situation
die	**Mauer**, -n 🕮	wall (*outside*)
die	**Miete**, -n 🕮	rent
die	**Nachbarin**	neighbour
die	**Stadt**, ̈e	town; city
die	**Straße**, -n ◇	street, road
die	**Telefonnummer**, -n	phone number
die	**Terrasse**, -n ◇	patio
die	**Toilette**, -n	toilet
die	**Treppe**, -n	stairs, staircase
die	**Tür**, -en	door
die	**Türklingel**, -n	doorbell
die	**Umgebung**	surroundings
die	**Wand**, ̈e	wall (*inside*)
die	**Wohnung**, -en	flat
die	**Zentralheizung**	central heating

*im **Erdgeschoß** on the ground floor, on ground level*
__einziehen__ to move in
__umziehen__ to move (house)
__sich einleben__ to settle down, settle in
__oben__ upstairs
__unten__ downstairs
__zu Hause, daheim__ at home

IMPORTANT WORDS (f)

die **Allee, -n**	avenue
die **Antenne, -n**	aerial
die **Einrichtung**	furnishings
die **Etagenwohnung, -en**	flat
die **Fensterläden** (pl)	shutters
die **Fensterscheibe, -n**	window pane
die **Fliese, -n**	tile
die **Gasse, -n**	lane (in town), alley
die **Hecke, -n**	hedge
die **Hütte, -n** ◇ ▭	cottage
die **Jalousie, -n**	venetian blind
die **Kachel, -n**	(wall) tile
die **Kellerwohnung, -en**	basement flat
die **Mansarde, -n**	attic
die **Putzfrau, -en**	cleaner, cleaning woman
die **Rumpelkammer, -n**	boxroom, junk room
die **Siedlung, -en** ▭	housing estate
die **Stube, -n**	room
die **Stufe, -n**	step
die **Veranda, (-den)**	veranda
die **Wohnsiedlung, -en**	housing estate

USEFUL WORDS (f)

die **Beleuchtung**	lighting
die **Belüftung**	ventilation
die **Dachrinne, -n**	gutter (roof)
die **Dreizimmerwohnung, -en**	three-room flat
die **Einzimmerwohnung, -en**	one-room flat
die **Etage, -n**	floor, storey
die **Fensterbank, ⁻e**	window sill or ledge
die **Ferienwohnung, -en**	holiday home
die **Hauptwohnung**	main home
die **Hauseigentümerin**	owner
die **Hypothek, -en**	mortgage
die **Junggesellenwohnung, -en**	bachelor flat
die **Kacheln** (pl)	tiles, tiling
die **Kammer, -n**	small room; boxroom
die **Kanalisation**	sewerage system
die **Klimaanlage**	air conditioning

USEFUL WORDS (f) (cont)

die	**Kochnische, -n**	kitchenette
die	**Maisonettewohnung, -en**	maisonette
die	**Markise, -n**	canopy
die	**möblierte Wohnung, -n -en**	furnished flat
die	**Nachbarschaft**	neighbourhood
die	**Nische, -n**	recess, alcove
die	**Schallisolierung**	soundproofing
die	**Sozialwohnung, -en**	council flat *or* house
die	**Speisekammer, -n**	larder, pantry
die	**Sprechanlage, -n**	intercom
die	**Spülküche, -n**	scullery
die	**Täfelung**	panelling
die	**Trennwand, ̈-e**	partition
die	**Vermieterin**	landlady
die	**Villa, (-len)**	villa
die	**Waschküche, -n**	laundry room, utility room
die	**Wendeltreppe, -n**	spiral staircase
die	**Wohnküche, -n**	kitchen-cum-living-room
die	**Zweitwohnung, -en**	second home
die	**Zweizimmerwohnung, -en**	two-room flat

USEFUL WORDS (nt)

das	**Bauernhaus, ̈-er**	farmhouse
die	**Doppelfenster** (*pl*)	double glazing
das	**Einzelhaus, ̈-er**	detached house
das	**Fachwerkhaus, ̈-er**	half-timbered house
das	**Fundament, -e**	foundations
das	**Geländer, –**	railing, handrail
das	**Glasdach, ̈-er**	glass roof
das	**Kinderzimmer, –**	children's room; nursery
das	**Linoleum**	linoleum
das	**Maklerbüro, -s**	estate agency
das	**Mietshaus, ̈-er**	block of (rented) flats
das	**möblierte Zimmer, -n –**	furnished room, bedsit
das	**Rohr, -e ◇**	pipe
das	**Schlüsselloch, ̈-er**	keyhole
das	**Souterrain, -s**	basement
das	**Wohnhaus, ̈-er**	residential building
das	**Zwischengeschoß, -sse**	mezzanine (floor)

ESSENTIAL WORDS (nt)

das Bad, ⁻er ◇	bathroom
das Badezimmer, –	bathroom
das Dach, ⁻er	roof
das Doppelhaus, ⁻er	semi-detached (house)
das Dorf, ⁻er	village
das Einfamilienhaus, ⁻er	detached house
das Erdgeschoß, -sse	ground floor
das Eßzimmer, –	dining room
das Fenster, –	window
das Gebäude, – ▭	building
das Gebiet, -e ▭	area
das Haus, ⁻er	house
das Hochhaus, ⁻er ▭	multi-storey building
das Klo, -s	toilet, loo
die Möbel (pl)	furniture
das Möbelstück, -e	piece of furniture
das Parkett, -e ◇	wooden or parquet floor
das Reihenhaus, ⁻er	terraced house
das Schlafzimmer, –	bedroom
das Schloß, ⁻sser ◇	lock
das Tor, -e ◇	gate
das Treppenhaus ▭	staircase
das Wohnzimmer, –	lounge, living room
das Zentrum, (-tren)	centre
das Zimmer, –	room

IMPORTANT WORDS (nt)

das Arbeitszimmer, –	study
das Dachfenster, –	skylight
das Fenstersims, -e	window sill
das Gästezimmer, –	spare room, guest room
das Kaminsims, -e	mantelpiece
das Kellergeschoß, -sse	basement
das Oberlicht, -er	skylight
das Stockwerk, -e	floor, storey

muffig riechen to smell musty
verfallen, baufällig dilapidated

---

der Abfall, ⸚e ◇	rubbish, refuse
der Aschenbecher, –	ashtray
der Briefkasten, ⸚ ◇	letterbox
der Fernsehapparat, -e	television set
der Fön, -e ▭	hair dryer
der Hahn, ⸚e ◇ ▭	tap
der Hausputz	house cleaning
der Kamm, ⸚e	comb
der Knopf, ⸚e	knob, button
der Kühlschrank, ⸚e	fridge, refrigerator
der Rasierapparat, -e	razor
der Schalter, – ◇	switch
der Schrank, ⸚e	cupboard
der Spiegel, –	mirror
der Teppich, -e	carpet
der Topf, ⸚e	pot
der Vorhang, ⸚e ▭	curtain
der Wasserhahn, ⸚e	tap
der Wecker, –	alarm clock

IMPORTANT WORDS (m)

der Besen, –	broom
der Bettvorleger, –	bedside rug
der Deckel, –	lid
der Eimer, –	bucket, pail
der Griff, -e	handle (*of door etc*)
der Handfeger, –	brush
der Heizkörper, –	radiator
der Henkel, –	handle (*of jug etc*)
der Kachelofen, ⸚	tiled stove
der Kessel, –	kettle
der Kleiderbügel, –	coat hanger
der Krug, ⸚e	jug
der Mixer, –	(electric) blender
der Müll ▭	rubbish, refuse
der Mülleimer, –	dustbin
der Papierkorb, ⸚e	waste paper basket
der Pinsel, –	(paint)brush
der Rasierpinsel, –	shaving brush

HOUSE

173

IMPORTANT WORDS (m) (cont)

der	**Schmutz** 🗀	dirt
der	**Schneebesen,** –	whisk, egg beater
der	**Schwamm,** ⁝e	sponge
der	**Staub**	dust
der	**Staubsauger,** –	vacuum cleaner, Hoover ®
der	**Toaster,** –	toaster
der	**Ziergegenstand,** ⁝e	ornament

USEFUL WORDS (m)

der	**Abfalleimer,** –	rubbish bin
der	**Bettbezug,** ⁝e	duvet *or* quilt cover
der	**Bettkasten,** ⁝	bed base
der	**Blumenkasten,** ⁝	window box
der	**Feuerlöscher,** –	fire extinguisher
der	**Haken,** –◇	hook
der	**Handtuchhalter,** –	towel rail
der	**Kamin, -e**	fireplace
der	**Kerzenhalter,** –	candlestick
der	**Kerzenleuchter,** –	candlestick
der	**Kleiderhaken,** –	coat hook
der	**Kleiderschrank,** ⁝e	wardrobe
der	**Kopfkissenbezug,** ⁝e	pillowslip, pillowcase
der	**Läufer,** –◇	rug
der	**Putzlappen,** –	floorcloth
der	**Staubwedel,** –	feather duster
der	**Trockenautomat, -en**	tumble dryer
der	**Türpfosten,** –	doorpost
der	**Wandschrank,** ⁝e	wall cupboard

die Tür aufmachen or *öffnen to open the door*
die Tür zumachen or *schließen to close the door*
sein eigenes Zimmer haben to have a room of one's own
das Zimmer betreten to go into the room
die Hausarbeit machen to do the housework
duschen to have a shower
aufwecken to wake (up)
baden to have a bath
fernsehen to watch television

ESSENTIAL WORDS (f)

die **Badewanne**, -n	bath
die **Bettdecke**, -n	blanket, cover
die **Bettwäsche**	bed linen
die **Birne**, -n ⌂	(light) bulb
die **Bratpfanne**, -n ⌸	frying pan
die **Bürste**, -n	brush
die **Decke**, -n ⌂	blanket; cover
die **Dusche**, -n	shower
die **Elektrizität**	electricity
die **Farbe**, -n ⌂	paint; colour
die **Gardine**, -n	curtain
die **Hausarbeit**	housework
die **Kanne**, -n	jug; pot
die **Kerze**, -n ⌸	candle
die **Lampe**, -n	lamp
die **Pflanze**, -n	plant
die **Seife**, -n	soap
die **Zahnbürste**, -n	toothbrush
die **Zahncreme**, -s	toothpaste
die **Zahnpasta**, (-ten)	toothpaste

IMPORTANT WORDS (f)

die **Brücke**, -n ⌂	(narrow) rug or mat
die **Daunendecke**, -n	eiderdown
die **Fußmatte**, -n	doormat
die **Heizdecke**, -n	electric blanket
die **Kaffeemühle**, -n	coffee grinder
die **Leiter**, -n ⌂	ladder
die **Matte**, -n	mat
die **Nackenrolle**, -n	bolster
die **Rasierklinge**, -n	razor blade
die **Röhre**, -n	pipe
die **Rührmaschine**, -n	(electric) mixer
die **Satellitenantenne**, -n	satellite dish
die **Steppdecke**, -n	(continental) quilt
die **Tapete**, -n	wallpaper
die **Vase**, -n	vase
die **Waage**, -n	(set of) scales
die **Wäscheschleuder**, -n	spin dryer

USEFUL WORDS (f)

die	**Mottenkugel,** -n	mothball
die	**Mülltonne,** -n	dustbin
die	**Nähmaschine,** -n	sewing machine
die	**Scheuerbürste,** -n	scrubbing brush
die	**Schüssel,** -n	bowl; basin
die	**Seifenschale,** -n	soapdish
die	**Sicherung,** -en	fuse
die	**Tagesdecke,** -n	bedspread
die	**Türangel,** -n	hinge (*of door*)
die	**Türmatte,** -n	doormat
die	**Wärmflasche,** -n	hot-water bottle
die	**Wäscheklammer,** -n	clothes peg

USEFUL WORDS (nt)

das	**Becken,** – ◇	basin
das	**Bettlaken,** –	sheet
das	**Bettzeug**	bedding
das	**Bidet,** -s	bidet
das	**Bügeln**	ironing
das	**Heißwassergerät,** -e	water heater
das	**Kehrblech,** -e	shovel
das	**Küchengerät,** -e	kitchen utensil; kitchen appliance
das	**Reinigungsmittel,** –	cleansing agent
das	**Set,** -s	table mat
das	**Silber**	silverware
das	**Spannbettuch,** ¨-er	fitted sheet

putzen *to clean*
waschen *to wash*
bürsten *to brush*
bügeln *to iron*
staubsaugen *to hoover*
Staub putzen *to dust*
etw in der Pfanne braten *to fry sth in a frying-pan*
sein Zimmer aufräumen *to tidy one's room*
seine Sachen herumliegen lassen *to leave one's things lying around*

ESSENTIAL WORDS (nt)

das Bild, -er 📖	picture; painting
das Federbett, -en	(continental) quilt
das Feuer	fire
das Gas	gas
das Geschirr ◇	dishes; crockery; pots and pans
das Handtuch, ⁻er	towel
das Kissen, –	cushion; pillow
das Kopfkissen, – 📖	pillow
das Licht, -er	light
das Poster, –	poster
das Rezept, -e ◇	recipe
das Shampoo, -s	shampoo
das Spülbecken, –	sink
das Tablett, -s	tray
das Waschbecken, –	washbasin
das Wasser	water

IMPORTANT WORDS (nt)

das Abwaschtuch, ⁻er	dishcloth
das Brett, -er ◇	tray
das Bügelbrett, -er	ironing board or table
das Bügeleisen, –	iron
das Gemälde, – 📖	painting, picture
das Geschirrtuch, ⁻er	tea towel
das Polster, –	cushion; pillow
das Rohr, -e ◇	pipe
das Staubtuch, ⁻er	duster
das Waschpulver, –	washing powder

Platten/Kassetten/Radio hören *to listen to records/tape cassettes/the radio*
im Fernsehen/Radio *on television/on the radio*
das Fernsehen einschalten/ausschalten *to switch on/off the TV*
spülen *to do the dishes*
abwaschen *to do the dishes*
einstöpseln/ausstöpseln *to plug in/to unplug*

THE HUMAN BODY

ESSENTIAL WORDS (m)

der **Arm**, -e	arm
der **Atem**	breath
der **Bauch**, ⸚e ⟡	stomach
der **Daumen**, –	thumb
der **Finger**, –	finger
der **Fuß**, ⸚e	foot
der **Hals**, ⸚e	neck; throat
der **Kopf**, ⸚	head
der **Körper**, –	body
der **Körperteil**, -e	part of the body
der **Magen**, ⸚	stomach
der **Mund**, ⸚er	mouth
der **Rücken**, –	back
der **Zahn**, ⸚e	tooth
der **Zeigefinger**, –	forefinger, index finger

IMPORTANT WORDS (m)

der **Ell(en)bogen**, –	elbow
der **Hintern**, –	bottom
der **Kiefer**, – ⟡	jaw
der **Knöchel**, –	knuckle; ankle
der **Knochen**, – ▢	bone
der **Muskel**, -n	muscle
der **Nacken**, –	nape of the neck
der **Nagel**, ⸚	nail
der **Nerv**, -en	nerve
der **Schenkel**, –	thigh

(mit der Hand) winken to wave
jdm die Hand geben to shake hands with sb
auf etwas zeigen to point to something
den Kopf schütteln to shake one's head
mit dem Kopf nicken to nod one's head
von Kopf bis Fuß from head to foot, from top to toe
berühren to touch
riechen to smell

HUMAN BODY

USEFUL WORDS (m)

der	**Backenzahn, ⸚e**	molar
der	**Bizeps**	biceps
der	**blaue Fleck, -n -en**	bruise
der	**Brustumfang**	bust *or* chest measurement
der	**Dickdarm**	large intestine
der	**Dünndarm**	small intestine
der	**Eckzahn, ⸚e**	canine (tooth), eye tooth
der	**Embryo, -s**	embryo
der	**Fötus, (-ten)**	foetus
der	**Gaumen, –**	palate
der	**Gefühlssinn**	sense of touch
der	**Geruchssinn**	sense of smell
der	**Geschmackssinn**	sense of taste
der	**Handteller, –**	palm
der	**kleine Finger, -n – –**	little finger
der	**Knorpel**	cartilage
der	**Körperbau**	build
der	**Krampf, ⸚e**	cramp
der	**Kratzer, –**	scratch
der	**Leberfleck, -e**	mole
der	**Milchzahn, ⸚e**	milk tooth
der	**Mittelfinger, –**	middle finger
der	**Nabel, –**	navel
der	**Ohrenschmalz**	earwax
der	**Pickel, – ⬦**	spot, pimple
der	**Puls**	pulse
der	**Ringfinger, –**	ring finger
der	**Schädel, –**	skull
der	**Schneidezahn, ⸚e**	incisor
der	**Schweiß**	sweat, perspiration
der	**Unterarm, -e**	forearm
der	**Unterleib**	abdomen
der	**Weisheitszahn, ⸚e**	wisdom tooth
der	**Zahnstein**	tartar (*on teeth*)

sehen *to see*
hören *to hear*
fühlen *to feel*
schmecken *to taste*

ESSENTIAL WORDS (f)

die	Bewegung, -en 📖	movement, motion
die	Büste, -n	bust
die	Hand, ¨e	hand
die	Lippe, -n	lip
die	Nase, -n	nose
die	Schulter, -n	shoulder
die	Seite, -n ◇	side
die	Stimme, -n ◇	voice
die	Zunge, -n	tongue

IMPORTANT WORDS (f)

die	Ader, -n	vein
die	Arterie, -n	artery
die	Augenbraue, -n	eyebrow
die	Brust, ¨e	breast; chest
die	Faust, ¨e	fist
die	Ferse, -n	heel
die	Figur, -en ◇	figure
die	Form, -en	shape, figure
die	Fußsohle, -n	sole of foot
die	Gestalt, -en	figure, form, shape
die	Geste, -n	gesture
die	große Zehe, -n -n	big toe
die	Haut 📖	skin
die	Hüfte, -n	hip
die	Kehle, -n	throat
die	Leber	liver
die	Lunge, -n	lung
die	Niere, -n	kidney
die	Pupille, -n	pupil (of eye)
die	Rippe, -n	rib
die	Schläfe, -n	temple
die	Schlagader, -n	artery
die	Stirn, -en 📖	forehead
die	Taille, -n	waist
die	Wade, -n	calf (of leg)
die	Wange, -n	cheek
die	Wimpern (pl)	eyelashes
die	Zehe, -n	toe

USEFUL WORDS (f)

die **Achselhöhle**, -n	armpit
die **Aorta**	aorta
die **Atmung**	breathing
die **Blase** ◇	bladder
die **Bronchien** (*pl*)	bronchial tubes
die **Brustwarze**, -n	nipple
die **Falte**, -n ◇	wrinkle
die **Frostbeule**, -n	chilblain
die **Genetik**	genetics
die **Gliedmaßen** (*pl*)	limbs
die **Hüftweite**	hip measurement
die **Kniescheibe**, -n	kneecap
die **Leiste**, -n	groin
die **Mandeln** (*pl*) ◇	tonsils
die **Milz**	spleen
die **Muskulatur**	muscle structure
die **Narbe**, -n	scar
die **Nebenhöhle**, -n	sinus
die **plastische Chirurgie**	plastic surgery
die **Prothese**, -n ◇	denture(s), false teeth; artificial limb
die **Regel** ◇	(menstrual) period
die **Schürfwunde**, -n	graze
die **Sehne**, -n	tendon, sinew
die **Taillenweite**	waist measurement
die **Vene**, -n	vein
die **Warze**, -n	wart; verruca
die **Wirbelsäule**	spinal column

blind *blind*
stumm *dumb*
taub *deaf*
geistig behindert *mentally handicapped*
körperbehindert *physically handicapped*
barfuß gehen *to go* or *walk barefoot*
zu Fuß *on foot*
mein Arm/Bein tut weh *my arm/leg hurts*
auf die Figur achten *to watch one's figure*

ESSENTIAL WORDS (nt)

das	**Auge**, -n	eye
das	**Bein**, -e	leg
das	**Blut**	blood
das	**Fleisch** ⟡	flesh
das	**Gesicht**, -er	face
das	**Haar**, -e	hair
das	**Herz**, -en ⟡	heart
das	**Knie**, –	knee
das	**Ohr**, -en	ear

*einen steifen **Nacken haben*** to have a stiff neck
*ich habe mir den **Arm/das Bein gebrochen*** I've broken my arm/leg
ich ruhe mich aus I'm resting or having a rest
biegen to bend
*ich habe mir den **Knöchel verstaucht*** or **verrenkt** I've sprained my ankle
strecken to stretch
bewegen to move (part of the body)
*sich **bewegen*** to move (one's self)
knien to kneel (down)
unfit unfit
fit fit
stürzen to fall
verletzen, verwunden to injure
müde tired
*sich die **Nase putzen*** to blow one's nose
neben mir at my side
*die **linke/rechte Körperseite*** the left-hand/right-hand side of the body
*eine **leise/laute Stimme haben*** to have a soft/loud voice
*jdm auf die **Schulter klopfen*** to tap sb on the shoulder
*sein **Herz klopfte*** his heart was beating
*sich **legen*** to lie down
sitzen to sit, be sitting
*sich **setzen*** to sit down
stehen to stand
leise/laut sprechen to speak softly/loudly
*ich lasse mir die **Haare schneiden*** I'm having my hair cut
*auf den **Knien*** on one's knees

IMPORTANT WORDS (nt)

das	**Augenlid**, -er	eyelid
das	**Blutgefäß**, -e	blood vessel
das	**Gehirn**, -e 🕮	brain
das	**Gelenk**, -e	joint
das	**Genick**, -e	nape of the neck
das	**Glied**, -er	limb
das	**Handgelenk**, -e	wrist
das	**Kinn**, -e	chin
das	**Lid**, -er	lid
die	**Maße** (pl)	measurements
das	**Rückgrat**, -e	spine
das	**Skelett**, -e	skeleton

USEFUL WORDS (nt)

das	**Band**, ¨-er ◇	ligament
das	**Becken**, – ◇	pelvis
das	**Doppelkinn**, -e	double chin
die	**Eingeweide** (pl)	entrails, innards
das	**Gehör**	hearing
das	**Gen**, -e	gene
das	**Gesäß**, -e	bottom, buttocks
das	**Jochbein**, -e	cheekbone
das	**Muttermal**, -e	birthmark
das	**Nasenloch**, ¨-er	nostril
das	**Ohrläppchen**, –	earlobe
das	**Organ**, -e	organ
das	**Rückenmark**	spinal cord
das	**Schienbein**, -e	shin(bone)
das	**Schlüsselbein**	collarbone, clavicle
das	**Schulterblatt**, ¨-er	shoulder blade
das	**Trommelfell**	eardrum
das	**Zahnfleisch**	gum(s)

sich das Gesicht liften lassen to have a facelift
rülpsen to belch
bei jdm Maß nehmen to take sb's measurements
meine Finger sind steif vor Kälte my fingers are numb with cold

INFORMATION AND SERVICES

der **Absender**, –	sender
der **Anruf**, -e	telephone call
der **Anschluß**, ¨sse ◇	(telephone) extension
der **Bescheid** ◇	information; directions
der **Brief**, -e	letter
der **Briefkasten**, ¨ ◇	postbox, pillar box
der **Briefträger**, –	postman
der **Fehler**, –	fault; mistake, error
der **Groschen**, –	10-pfennig piece
der **Hörer**, - ◇ ▭	(telephone) receiver
der **Kugelschreiber**, – ▭	ballpoint (pen), Biro ®
der **Kurs**, -e ◇ ▭	rate
der **Luftpostbrief**, -e	airmail letter
der **Name**, -n	name
der **Personalausweis**, -e	identity card
der **Polizist**, -en	policeman
der **Postbeamte***, -n	counter clerk
der **Preis**, -e ◇	price, cost
der **Reisepaß**, ¨sse	passport
der **Reisescheck**, -s	traveller's cheque
der **Schalter**, – ◇	counter
der **Scheck**, -s	cheque
der **Schilling**, -e	schilling
der **Telefonhörer**, – ▭	(telephone) receiver
der **Telefonist**, -en	telephonist
der **Termin**, -e	(*doctor's etc*) appointment
der **Umschlag**, ¨e ◇	envelope
der **Vorname**, -n	first name, Christian name
der **Zeuge**, -n ▭	witness
der **Zuname**, -n	surname

wieviel Geld willst du wechseln? *how much money do you want to change?*
ich habe kein Kleingeld *I don't have any change*
können Sie mir fünfzig Mark wechseln? *can you give me change of 50 marks?*
ich möchte Pfund in Mark umtauschen *I'd like to change some pounds into marks*

IMPORTANT WORDS (m)

der **Einschreibebrief**, -e	registered letter
der **Empfänger**, –	addressee
der **Stempel**, –	postmark

USEFUL WORDS (m)

der **Abonnent**, -en	subscriber
der **Dauerauftrag**, ¨e	standing order
der **Geldautomat**, -en	cash dispenser
der **Kontoauszug**, ¨e	bank statement
der **Prospekt**, -e	leaflet, brochure
der **Wechselkurs**, -e	exchange rate

jdn anrufen, mit jdm telefonieren to phone or call sb
bleiben Sie am Apparat hold on, please
einen Augenblick, ich verbinde Sie just a minute, I'll put you through
kann ich (mit) Peter sprechen? could I speak to Peter?
hallo, hier ist ... hello, this is ...
besetzt engaged
eine Nachricht hinterlassen to leave a message
den Hörer abheben to lift the receiver
die Nummer heraussuchen/wählen to look up/dial the number
wie lautet die Vorwahlnummer? what is the dialling code?
ein R-Gespräch führen to make a reverse-charge call
wer ist am Apparat? who's speaking?
das Telefon läutet the phone rings or is ringing
Sie sind falsch verbunden you've got the wrong number
ich rufe Sie zurück I'll call you back
danke für den Anruf thank you for calling
die Verbindung ist sehr schlecht it's a bad line
ich habe mich verwählt I dialled the wrong number
den Hörer auflegen or **einhängen** to replace the receiver
soll ich Ihnen das buchstabieren? shall I spell that for you?
ich möchte einen Scheck einlösen I'd like to cash a cheque
ein Scheck über 100 Pfund a cheque for £100
bar bezahlen to pay in cash

ESSENTIAL WORDS (f)

die **Adresse, -n**	address
die **Anschrift, -en** ▭	address
die **Ansichtskarte, -n**	(picture) postcard
die **Auskunft** ◇	information; directory enquiries
die **Bank, -en** ◇	bank
die **Banknote, -n**	banknote
die **Beschreibung, -en** ▭	description
die **Bezahlung, -en**	payment
die **Briefmarke, -n**	(postage) stamp
die **Brieftasche, -n**	wallet
die **Einladung, -en** ▭	invitation
die **Geldstrafe, -n** ▭	fine
die **Kasse, -n** ◇	cash desk; check-out; till
die **Leerung, -en** ▭	collection (*of mail*)
die **Luftpost**	airmail
die **Mark, –**	mark
die **Münze, -n**	coin
die **Nummer, -n**	number
die **Polizei**	police
die **Polizeiwache, -n**	police station
die **Polizistin**	policewoman
die **Post, -en** ◇	post, mail; post office
die **Postbeamtin**	counter clerk
die **Postgebühr, -en** ▭	postage
die **Postkarte, -n**	postcard
die **Rückgabe, -n** ▭	return
die **Scheckkarte, -n**	cheque card
die **Sparkasse, -n**	savings bank
die **Tasche, -n** ◇	bag
die **Taste, -n** ◇ ▭	(push-)button
die **Telefonistin**	telephonist
die **Telefonnummer, -n**	phone number
die **Telefonzelle, -n**	callbox, telephone box
die **Unterschrift, -en** ▭	signature
die **Verbindung, -en**	line, connection
die **Vorwahlnummer, -n** ▭	dialling code
die **Währung, -en** ▭	currency
die **Wechselstube, -n**	bureau de change

IMPORTANT WORDS (f)

die	**Belohnung, -en**	reward
die	**Blockschrift**	block capitals
die	**Drucksache, -n**	printed matter
die	**Handtasche, -n**	handbag
die	**Heimat, -en** 🕮	home (*town/country etc*)
die	**Kaution, -en**	deposit
die	**Paketpost**	parcel post
die	**Postanweisung, -en**	postal order
die	**Postleitzahl, -en** 🕮	postcode
die	**Reparatur, -en**	repair; repairing
die	**Steuer, -n** ◊	tax
die	**Verabredung, -en** 🕮	appointment

USEFUL WORDS (f)

die	**Abhebung, -en**	withdrawal
die	**Abkürzung, -en** ◊	abbreviation
die	**Abonnentin**	subscriber
die	**Einzahlung, -en**	payment; deposit
die	**Fernsehgebühr, -en**	TV licence fee
die	**Gebrauchsanweisung, -en**	directions for use
die	**Gelben Seiten** (*pl*)	Yellow Pages
die	**Gutschrift, -en**	credit note
die	**Initialen** (*pl*)	initials
die	**Kreditkarte, -n**	credit card
die	**Lautsprecheranlage, -n**	PA system
die	**Postüberweisung, -en**	Giro transfer
die	**Telefongebühr, -en**	telephone rental
die	**Überweisung, -en**	transfer

---

drücken to press
außer Betrieb out of order
links/rechts abbiegen to turn left/right
2 Kilometer nördlich der Stadtmitte 2 kilometres north of the town centre
die dritte Straße rechts the third street on the right
die erste Straße links the first street on the left
beschreiben to describe

ESSENTIAL WORDS (nt)

das	Bargeld	cash, ready money
das	Briefpapier	writing paper
das	Ferngespräch, -e ▫	trunk call
das	Formular, -e ▫	form
das	Fundbüro, -s	lost-property office
das	Geschlecht, -er ▫	sex
das	Kleingeld	small change
das	Mißverständnis, -se	misunderstanding
das	Ortsgespräch, -e	local call
das	Päckchen, –	package, (small) parcel
das	Paket, -e	parcel, package
das	Pfund (Sterling)	pound (sterling)
das	Portemonnaie, -s	purse
das	Postamt, ̈er	post office
das	Postwertzeichen, – ▫	postage stamp
das	Problem, -e	problem
das	R-Gespräch, -e	reverse charge call
das	Scheckheft, -e	chequebook
das	Telefon, -e	telephone
das	Telefonbuch, ̈er	telephone directory
das	Telefongespräch, -e	phone call
das	Telegramm, -e	telegram, cable
das	Verkehrsamt, ̈er	tourist information office

ich habe meine Tasche verloren, hat jemand sie gefunden? *I've lost my bag, has anyone found it?*
liegenlassen *to leave behind*
weißt du hier Bescheid? *do you know this place (well)?*
wie komme ich zum Bahnhof? *how do I get to the station?*
ein Paket abgeben *to hand in a parcel*
ein Formular ausfüllen *to fill in a form*
wie schreibt man das? *how do you spell that?*
verstehen *to understand*
könnten Sie das bitte wiederholen? *could you repeat that please?*
was heißt das auf deutsch? *what's that in German?*
sprechen Sie Englisch? *do you speak English?*
"Unzutreffendes bitte streichen" *"delete as appropriate"*
ich wäre Ihnen sehr dankbar, wenn Sie ... *I would be most grateful if you ...*

das	**Branchenverzeichnis**	Yellow Pages
das	**Konto, (-ten)** 📖	account
das	**Packpapier**	brown paper, wrapping paper
das	**Porto**	postage

das	**Amtszeichen**	dialling tone
das	**Autotelefon, -e**	car phone
das	**Besetztzeichen**	engaged tone
das	**drahtlose Telefon, -n -e**	cordless phone
das	**Freizeichen**	ringing tone
das	**Paßfoto, -s**	passport photograph

mit Luftpost *by airmail*
portofrei *postage paid*
postlagernd *poste restante*
bekommen, erhalten *to get, receive*
einen Brief schreiben *to write a letter*
einige Briefmarken kaufen *to buy some stamps*
was ist das Porto für einen Brief nach Schottland? *how much is a letter to Scotland?*
den Brief einwerfen *to post the letter* (in postbox)
ist Post für mich da? *is there any mail for me?*
3 Briefmarken zu einer Mark *3 one-mark stamps*
zur Post gehen *to go to the post office*
senden, schicken *to send*
Liebe Bettina! *Dear Bettina*
Sehr geehrter Herr X! *Dear Mr X*
Sehr geehrte Damen und Herren! *Dear Sir or Madam*
Hochachtungsvoll *Yours faithfully/sincerely*
Viele Grüße *Best wishes*
Mit freundlichen Grüßen *Yours faithfully/sincerely*

PRONUNCIATION GUIDE

When you are talking on the phone or giving details to someone you are
often asked to spell something out. This is how you go about it in German.

	Pronounced as		*Pronounced as*
A	ah	N	en
B	bay	O	oh
C	tsay	P	pay
D	day	Q	koo
E	ay	R	air
F	ef	S	ess
G	gay	T	tay
H	hah	U	oo
I	ee	V	fow
J	yot	W	vay
K	kah	X	eeks
L	el	Y	ew-pseelon
M	em	Z	tset

PUNCTUATION

der	**Akzent**	accent
die	**Anführungszeichen** (*pl*)	inverted commas
die	**Auslassungspunkte** (*pl*)	suspension points
das	**Ausrufezeichen**	exclamation mark
der	**Bindestrich**	hyphen
die	**eckigen Klammern** (*pl*)	square brackets
das	**Eszett**	the 'ß'
das	**Fragezeichen**	question mark
der	**Gedankenstrich**	dash
die	**Klammern** (*pl*)	brackets
das	**Komma**	comma
der	**Punkt**	full stop
die	**runden Klammern** (*pl*)	round brackets
das	**Satzzeichen**	punctuation mark
der	**Schrägstrich**	oblique, slash
das	**Semikolon**	semicolon
das	**Sternchen**	asterisk
der	**Umlaut**	umlaut

THE TELEPHONE ALPHABET

A	**wie Anton**	A	for Andrew
B	**wie Berta**	B	for Benjamin
C	**wie Cäsar**	C	for Charlie
D	**wie Dora**	D	for David
E	**wie Emil**	E	for Edward
F	**wie Friedrich**	F	for Frederick
G	**wie Gustav**	G	for George
H	**wie Heinrich**	H	for Harry
I	**wie Ida**	I	for Isaac
J	**wie Jerusalem**	J	for Jack
K	**wie Kaufmann**	K	for King
L	**wie Ludwig**	L	for Lucy
M	**wie Martha**	M	for Mike
N	**wie Nordpol**	N	for Nelly
O	**wie Otto**	O	for Oliver
P	**wie Paula**	P	for Peter
Q	**wie Quelle**	Q	for Queen
R	**wie Richard**	R	for Robert
S	**wie Samuel**	S	for Sugar
T	**wie Theodor**	T	for Tommy
U	**wie Ulrich**	U	for Uncle
V	**wie Viktor**	V	for Victor
W	**wie Wilhelm**	W	for William
X	**wie Xanthippe**	X	for Xmas
Y	**wie Ypsilon**	Y	for Yellow
Z	**wie Zacharias**	Z	for Zebra

IN THE KITCHEN

der **Backofen**, ¨	oven
der **Eßlöffel**, –	tablespoon
der **Herd**, -e ⌑	cooker
der **Kochtopf**, ¨e	saucepan
der **Kühlschrank**, ¨e	fridge, refrigerator
der **Löffel**, –	spoon
der **Schrank**, ¨e	cupboard
der **Teelöffel**, –	teaspoon
der **Teller**, –	plate

IMPORTANT WORDS (m)

der **Behälter**, –	container
der **Dessertteller**, –	dessert plate
der **Dosenöffner**, –	tin-opener
der **Eierbecher**, –	egg cup
der **Elektroherd**, -e	electric cooker
der **Gasherd**, -e	gas cooker
der **Kartoffelschäler**, –	potato peeler
der **Kartoffelstampfer**, –	potato masher
der **Mikrowellenherd**, -e	microwave (oven)
der **Pfefferstreuer**, –	pepperpot, pepper shaker
der **Salzstreuer**, –	salt cellar
der **Suppenteller**, –	soup plate
der **Tisch**, -e	table

USEFUL WORDS (m)

der **Bratspieß**, -e	roasting spit
der **Entsafter**, –	juice extractor
der **Flaschenöffner**, –	bottle-opener
der **Fleischwolf**, ¨e	(meat) mincer
der **Kaffeefilter**, –	coffee filter
der **Korkenzieher**, –	corkscrew
der **Nußknacker**, –	nutcracker
der **Schaumlöffel**, –	skimmer
der **Schneebesen**, –	whisk, egg beater
der **Toaster**, –	toaster
der **Tortenboden**, ¨	flan case
der **Tortenheber**, –	cake slice

ESSENTIAL WORDS (f)

die **Gabel**, -n	fork
die **Gefriertruhe**, -n	freezer
die **Kaffeekanne**, -n	coffeepot
die **Pfanne**, -n	frying pan
die **Schüssel**, -n	bowl; basin
die **Spüle**, -n	sink
die **Tasse**, -n	cup
die **Teekanne**, -n	teapot
die **Untertasse**, -n	saucer

IMPORTANT WORDS (f)

die **Bratpfanne**, -n	frying pan
die **Herdplatte**, -n	hotplate
die **Kaffeemaschine**, -n	coffee machine
die **Kuchengabel**, -n	pastry fork
die **Küchenmaschine**, -n	food processor
die **Reibe**, -n	grater
die **Salatschüssel**, -n	salad bowl
die **Suppenschüssel**, -n	(soup) tureen
die **Zitronenpresse**, -n	lemon squeezer
die **Zuckerdose**, -n	sugar bowl

USEFUL WORDS (f)

die **Alufolie**	tinfoil
die **Auflaufform**, -en	ovenproof dish
die **Butterdose**, -n	butter dish
die **Eieruhr**, -en	egg timer
die **Friteuse**, -n	chip pan
die **Grillpfanne**, -n	grill pan
die **Kasserolle**, -n	saucepan; casserole
die **Knoblauchpresse**, -n	garlic press
die **Kuchenform**, -en	cake tin
die **Küchenrolle**, -n	kitchen roll
die **Obstschale**, -n	fruit dish *or* bowl
die **Pastetenform**, -en	pie dish
die **Sauciere**, -n	sauceboat; gravy boat
die **Schöpfkelle**, -n	ladle
die **Warmhalteplatte**, -n	hot plate

IN THE KITCHEN — 3

das **Besteck** ▭	cutlery
das **Gefrierfach**, ¨-er	freezer compartment
das **Geschirr** ◇	dishes; crockery; pots and pans
das **Glas**, ¨-er ◇	glass
das **Küchengerät**, -e	kitchen utensil; kitchen appliance
das **Küchenmesser**, –	kitchen knife
das **Messer**, –	knife

das **Geschirrtuch**, ¨-er	tea towel
das **Milchkännchen**, –	milk jug
das **Sieb**, -e	sieve; strainer
das **Spültuch**, ¨-er	dishcloth

das **Geschirrspülmittel**	washing-up liquid
das **Hackbrett**, -er	chopping board
das **Hackmesser**, –	chopping knife
das **Kochsalz**	cooking salt
das **Nudelholz**, ¨-er	rolling pin
das **Reinigungsmittel**, –	cleansing agent
das **Tablett**, -s	tray
das **Waffeleisen**, –	waffle iron

kneten *to knead*
vorheizen *to preheat*
(das Geschirr) spülen *to do the dishes*
abtrocknen *to do the drying-up*

ESSENTIAL WORDS (m)

der	**Ausweis, -e**	identity card
der	**Bandit, -en**	bandit
der	**Demonstrant, -en**	demonstrator
der	**Detektiv, -e**	detective
der	**Dieb, -e** ⌓	thief
der	**Diebstahl, ⸚e**	theft
der	**Gangster, –**	gangster
der	**Hijacker, –**	hijacker
die	**Notdienste** (*pl*)	emergency services
der	**Polizist, -en**	policeman
der	**Privatdetektiv, -e**	private detective
der	**Reisescheck, -s**	traveller's cheque
der	**Retter, –**	rescuer
der	**Revolver, –**	revolver
der	**Rowdy, -s**	hooligan
der	**Scheck, -s**	cheque
der	**Sicherheitsbeamte*, -n**	security guard
der	**Streit, -e** ◇	argument, dispute
der	**Taschendieb, -e** ⌓	pickpocket
der	**Terrorist, -en**	terrorist
der	**Tote*, -n**	dead man
der	**Überfall, ⸚e**	raid; attack
der	**Unfall, ⸚e**	accident
der	**Zeuge, -n** ⌓	witness

retten *to rescue*
entkommen *to escape*
die Polizei kommen lassen *to send for the police*
bestrafen *to punish*
demonstrieren *to demonstrate*
entführen *to kidnap, abduct*
verschwinden *to disappear*
hijacken *to hijack*
eine Bank überfallen *to rob a bank*
ins Gefängnis kommen *to go to jail*
verhaften *to arrest*
schuldig *guilty*
sind Sie versichert? *are you insured?*
verunglücken *to have an accident*

IMPORTANT WORDS (m)

der Anwalt, ⸚e	lawyer, barrister
der Beweis, -e	evidence
der Brand, ⸚e	fire
der Einbrecher, – ▭	burglar
der Einbruch, ⸚e	burglary, break-in
der Entführer, –	abductor, kidnapper; hijacker
der Feind, -e	enemy
der Gefangene*, -n	prisoner
der Gefängniswärter, –	prison warder
der Gerichtshof, ⸚e	law court
der Mord, -e	murder
der Mörder, –	murderer, killer
der Notruf	emergency call
der Prozeß, -sse	trail, lawsuit
der Raub	robbery
der Räuber, –	robber
der Raubüberfall, ⸚e	robbery with violence
der Rechtsanwalt, ⸚e	lawyer, barrister
der Spion, -e ◇	spy
der Verbrecher, –	criminal
der Verdächtige*, -n	suspect

ein Gebäude (in die Luft) sprengen to blow up a building
erschießen to shoot (dead)
ermorden to murder
töten to kill
unschuldig innocent
betrunken drunk
verwundet wounded
jdn überfahren to run sb over
rauben to rob
stehlen to steal
Angst haben to be afraid
klauen to pinch
Hilfe! help!
haltet den Dieb! stop thief!
Hände hoch! hands up!

USEFUL WORDS (m)

der	**Betrug**	swindle; fraud
der	**Bundesgerichtshof**	German Supreme Court
der	**Drogenhandel**	drug trafficking
der	**Durchsuchungsbefehl, -e**	search warrant
der	**Eid**	oath
der	**elektrische Stuhl**	electric chair
der	**Fall, ⸚e** ◊	case
der	**Fingerabdruck, ⸚e**	fingerprint
der	**Flüchtling, -e** ◊	fugitive, runaway
der	**Fluchtversuch, -e**	escape bid
der	**Freispruch, ⸚e**	acquittal
der	**Galgen, –**	gallows
der	**Gerichtsdiener, –**	bailiff
der	**Gewalttäter, –**	violent criminal
der	**Gummiknüppel, –**	truncheon
der	**Haftbefehl, -e**	warrant for arrest
der	**Häftling, -e**	prisoner
der	**Hausarrest**	house arrest
der	**Henker, –**	executioner
der	**Justizirrtum, ⸚er**	miscarriage of justice
der	**Meineid**	perjury
der	**Schmuggel**	smuggling
der	**Spitzel, –**	(police) informant
der	**Staatsanwalt, ⸚e**	public prosecutor
der	**Sträfling, -e**	convict, prisoner
der	**Totschlag**	manslaughter
der	**Vergewaltiger, –**	rapist
der	**Voyeur, -e**	peeping Tom
der	**Zeugenstand, ⸚e**	witness box

---

vorbestraft sein *to have a criminal record*
jdn wegen Verleumdung verklagen *to sue sb for slander*
ein Verbrechen begehen *to commit a crime*
verurteilt zu 5 Monaten (Gefängnis) mit Bewährung *given a 5 month suspended (prison) sentence*
"Sie sind verhaftet" *"You're under arrest"*
auf frischer Tat *in the act, red-handed*

ESSENTIAL WORDS (f)

die	**Armee**, -n	army
die	**Atomwaffe**, -n	atomic weapon
die	**Auskunft**, ⁻e ◇	information; particulars
die	**Ausweiskarte**, -n	identity card
die	**Bande**, -n	band, gang
die	**Bank**, -en ◇	bank
die	**Beschreibung**, -en ▭	description
die	**Bombe**, -n	bomb
die	**Brieftasche**, -n	wallet
die	**Demonstrantin**	demonstrator
die	**Demonstration**, -en	demonstration
die	**Diebin** ▭	thief
die	**Droge**, -n	drug
die	**Erlaubnis**, -se ▭	permission; permit
die	**Gefahr**, -en ▭	danger, risk
die	**Geldstrafe**, -n ▭	fine
die	**Pflicht**, -en	duty
die	**Pistole**, -n	pistol, gun
die	**Polizei**	police
die	**Polizistin**	policewoman
die	**Rettung**, -en	rescue
die	**Tasche**, -n ◇	bag
die	**Terroristin**	terrorist
die	**Tote***, -n	dead woman
die	**Untersuchung**, -en ◇	inquiry, investigation
die	**Zeugin** ▭	witness

jdn gegen Kaution freilassen *to release sb on bail*
unter Bewährung stehen *to be on probation; to be on parole*
verletzt *injured*
unter Hausarrest *under house arrest*
das Gesetz brechen *to break the law*
jdn ins Kreuzverhör nehmen *to cross-examine sb*
dem Gesetz Geltung verschaffen *to enforce the law*
jdn beschatten *to shadow sb*
lebenslänglich bekommen *to get life*
in ein Haus einbrechen *to break into a house*

IMPORTANT WORDS (f)

die	**Alarmanlage, -n**	burglar alarm
die	**Anwältin**	lawyer, barrister
die	**Belohnung, -en**	reward
die	**Festnahme, -n**	arrest
die	**Flucht, -en**	escape
die	**Gefangene*, -n**	prisoner
die	**Haft**	custody
die	**Handschellen** (*pl*)	handcuffs
die	**Justiz**	judiciary
die	**Leiche, -n**	corpse, body
die	**Mörderin**	murderer, killer
die	**Polizeiwache, -n**	police station
die	**Regierung, -en** ⌒	government
die	**Schuld** ◇	guilt; fault
die	**Spionin**	spy
die	**Unschuld**	innocence
die	**Verdächtige*, -n**	suspect
die	**Verhaftung, -en**	arrest
die	**Versicherungspolice, -n**	insurance policy

USEFUL WORDS (f)

die	**Amnestie**	amnesty
die	**Aussage, -n**	testimony, evidence
die	**Befragung, -en**	questioning
die	**Berufung**	appeal
die	**Beschlagnahmung**	confiscation
die	**Beschwerde, -n**	complaint
die	**Bestechung**	bribery
die	**Bewährung**	probation
die	**Brandstiftung**	arson
die	**Durchsuchung, -en**	(police) search
die	**eidesstattliche Erklärung, -n -en**	affidavit, solemn statement
die	**Einzelheiten** (*pl*)	particulars
die	**Entführung, -en**	abduction, kidnapping; hijack(ing)
die	**Entschädigung, -en**	compensation
die	**Erpressung**	blackmail
die	**Fälschung, -en**	fake, forgery

USEFUL WORDS (f) (cont)

die **Geisel**, -n	hostage
die **Geiselnahme**	hostage-taking
die **Geldfälschung**	counterfeiting
die **Gewalttat**, -en	act of violence
die **Hehlerei**	receiving (*stolen goods*)
die **Jugendkriminalität**	juvenile delinquency
die **Korruption**	corruption
die **Rechtshilfe**	legal aid
die **Rekonstruktion**	reconstruction
die **Spionage**	espionage
die **Steuerhinterziehung**	tax evasion
die **Strafe**, -n ⟡	sentence; punishment
die **Todesstrafe**	death penalty
die **Unterschlagung**	embezzlement
die **Unterwelt**	underworld
die **Verfügung**, -en	decree
die **Vergewaltigung**, -en	rape
die **Verhandlung**, -en	hearing
die **Verleumdung**, -en	slander; libel
die **Verschwörung**, -en	conspiracy
die **Vorstrafe**, -n	previous conviction
die **Zelle**, -n	cell
die **Zwangsjacke**, -n	straitjacket

unter Mordanklage stehen *to be on a murder charge*
jdn/etw vor Gericht bringen *to take sb/sth to court*
in Untersuchungshaft bleiben *to be remanded in custody*
begnadigen *to pardon*
entlassen *to release*
einen Eid leisten *to take an* or *the oath*
das ist nicht meine Schuld *it's not my fault*
als vermißt gemeldet sein *to be reported missing*

USEFUL WORDS (m&f)

der/die	**Angeklagte***, -n	accused; defendant
der/die	**Attentäter(in)**, –	assassin
der/die	**Erpresser(in)**, –	blackmailer
der/die	**Fälscher(in)**, –	forger
der/die	**Geldfälscher(in)**, –	counterfeiter, forger
der/die	**Hehler(in)**, –	receiver (*of stolen goods*)
der/die	**Informant(in)**, -en	informant
der/die	**Jurist(in)**, -en	jurist
der/die	**Kidnapper(in)**, –	kidnapper
der/die	**Killer(in)**, –	killer
der/die	**Kommissar(in)**, -e	(police) superintendent
der/die	**Komplize**, -n/ **Komplizin**	accomplice
der/die	**Minderjährige***, -n	minor
der/die	**Rechtsbrecher(in)**, –	lawbreaker, criminal
der/die	**Richter(in)**, –	judge
der/die	**Schmuggler(in)**, –	smuggler
der/die	**Schöffe**, -n/**Schöffin**	juror
der/die	**Täter(in)**, –	perpetrator
der/die	**Volljährige***, -n	major
der/die	**Wiederholungstäter(in)**, –	second offender; persistent offender

IMPORTANT WORDS (nt)

das	**Gefängnis**, -se	prison, jail
das	**Gesetz**, -e	law
das	**Gewehr**, -e	gun, rifle
das	**Rauschgift**, -e	drug
das	**Todesurteil**, -e	death sentence
das	**Urteil**, -e	verdict; sentence
das	**Verbrechen**, –	crime
das	**Zuchthaus**, ̈-er ▢	(top-security) prison

das	**Bargeld**	cash, ready money
das	**Fundbüro, -s**	lost-property office
das	**Geld**	money
das	**Gericht, -e** ◇	court
das	**Gold**	gold
das	**Portemonnaie, -s**	purse
das	**Recht, -e**	the law; right
das	**Silber**	silver

USEFUL WORDS (nt)

das	**Alibi, -s**	alibi
das	**Attentat, -e**	assassination
das	**Berufungsgericht**	Court of Appeal
das	**Bestechungsgeld, -er**	bribe (*money*)
das	**Delikt, -e**	(criminal) offence
das	**Erhängen**	hanging
das	**Gerichtsverfahren, –**	legal proceedings
das	**Geständnis, -se**	confession
das	**Gnadengesuch, -e**	plea for clemency
das	**Indiz, -ien**	clue; piece of evidence
das	**Jugendgericht, -e**	juvenile court
das	**Kapitalverbrechen, –**	serious crime; capital crime
das	**Kreuzverhör**	cross-examination
das	**Notzuchtverbrechen, –**	indecent assault; rape
das	**Opfer, –**	victim
das	**Phantombild, -er**	Identikit ® picture
das	**Plädoyer, -s**	address to the jury, summing up
das	**Polizeipräsidium**	police headquarters
das	**Schafott, -e**	scaffold
das	**Schiedsgericht, -e**	magistrate's court
das	**Schmerzensgeld**	damages
das	**Schöffengericht, -e**	court (*with jury*)
das	**Strafgericht, -e**	criminal court
das	**Strafgesetzbuch**	penal code

ESSENTIAL WORDS (m)

der **Aufkleber**, –	sticker, label
der **Fleck**, -en 🕮	mark, spot
der **Gips**	plaster; plaster of Paris
der **Jeansstoff**	denim
der **Kaugummi**, -s	chewing gum
der **Klebstoff**, -e	glue
der **Kord**	cord, corduroy
der **Kunststoff**, -e	synthetic material *or* substance
der **Polyester**	polyester
der **Stahl**	steel
der **Stein**, -e ⟡	stone; rock
der **Stoff**, -e	cloth, material

IMPORTANT WORDS (m)

der **Backstein**, -e	brick
der **Beton** 🕮	concrete
der **Bindfaden**, ¨	string
der **Draht**, ¨e	wire
der **Faden**, ¨	thread
der **Kalk**	lime
der **Karton**, -s	cardboard; cardboard box
der **Kautschuk**	(india) rubber (*substance*)
der **Marmor**	marble
der **Pelz**, -e	fur
der **Samt**	velvet
der **Satin**	satin
der **Schaumgummi**	foam rubber
der **Tesafilm** ®	Sellotape ®
der **Ton** ⟡	clay, earthenware
der **Tweed**	tweed
der **Zement**	cement
der **Ziegelstein**, -e	brick
der **Zustand**, ¨e	condition

ein Holzstuhl (m) *a wooden chair*
ein Seidenschal (m) *a silk scarf*
ein Strohhut (m) *a straw hat*

MATERIALS — 2

USEFUL WORDS (m)

der	**Asphalt**	asphalt
der	**Bast**	raffia
der	**Bimsstein**	pumice stone
der	**Edelstein, -e**	precious stone
der	**Filz**	felt
der	**Granit**	granite
der	**Jaspis**	jasper
der	**Kitt**	putty
der	**Korb** ⬦	wicker
der	**Kork**	cork
der	**Mörtel**	mortar
der	**Musselin**	muslin
der	**Rost**	rust
der	**rostfreie Stahl**	stainless steel
der	**Sandstein**	sandstone
der	**Schwefel**	sulphur
der	**Smaragd, -e**	emerald
der	**Velours**	velours

eine Baumwollbluse *a cotton blouse*
ein Pappkarton (m) *a cardboard box*
echt *real, genuine*
kostbar *precious; costly, expensive*
silbern, Silber- *silver*
marmorn, Marmor- *marble*
golden, Gold- *gold, golden*
eisern, Eisen- *iron*
hölzern, Holz- *wooden*
etw chemisch reinigen *to dry-clean sth*
in gutem/schlechtem Zustand *in good/bad condition*
"vor Nässe schützen" *"keep dry"*
die Strickwaren (pl) *knitwear*
eine Ledertasche *a leather bag*
die Tasche ist aus Leder *the bag is made of leather*
ein Lammfellmantel (m) *a sheepskin coat*

die	**Baumwolle**	cotton
die	**Bronze**	bronze
die	**Gebrauchsanweisung, -en**	directions for use
die	**Seide**	silk

die	**Flüssigkeit, -en**	liquid
die	**Kohle** ◇	coal
die	**Leinwand** ◇	canvas
die	**Pappe** ▭	cardboard
die	**Plastikfolie**	clingfilm
die	**Schnur, ¨e** ◇	string; cord
die	**Spitze, -n** ◇	lace
die	**Watte**	cotton wool
die	**Wolle**	wool

die	**Alufolie**	tinfoil
die	**Emaille**	enamel
die	**Gaze**	gauze
die	**Glasfaser**	fibreglass
die	**Jade**	jade
die	**Legierung, -en**	alloy
die	**Schurwolle**	new wool

eine Vase aus Ton *an earthenware vase*
die Vase ist aus Ton *the vase is made of earthenware*
ein Pelzmantel (m) *a fur coat*
ein Wollpullover (m) *a woollen jumper*
die Gummistiefel (pl) *wellington boots*

MATERIALS — 4

das	**Aluminium**	aluminium
das	**Benzin**	petrol
das	**Blei**	lead
das	**Dieselöl**	diesel oil
das	**Gas, -e**	gas
das	**Glas** ✿	glass
das	**Gold**	gold
das	**Gummi**	rubber; gum; elastic
das	**Gummiband, ¨-er**	rubber band; elastic
das	**Holz**	wood
das	**Leder**	leather
das	**Material, -ien**	material, cloth; material(s)
das	**Metall, -e**	metal
das	**Nylon**	nylon
das	**Öl**	oil
das	**Papier**	paper
das	**Petroleum**	paraffin
das	**Plastik**	plastic
das	**Seidenpapier**	tissue paper
das	**Silber**	silver
das	**Silberpapier**	silver paper
das	**Stroh**	straw
das	**Vinyl**	vinyl
das	**Wildleder**	suede

das	**Blech**	tin
das	**Eisen**	iron
das	**Fell, -e**	fur
das	**Kristall**	crystal
das	**Kupfer**	copper
das	**Leinen**	linen
das	**Messing**	brass
das	**Porzellan**	porcelain, china
das	**Segeltuch**	sailcloth, canvas
das	**Stanniolpapier**	tinfoil
das	**Steingut**	stoneware
das	**Wachs**	wax
das	**Zinn**	pewter; tin

USEFUL WORDS (nt)

das	**Acryl**	acrylic
das	**Alteisen**	scrap iron
das	**Ebenholz**	ebony
das	**Eisenerz**	iron ore
das	**Elfenbein**	ivory
das	**Erz, -e**	ore
das	**Frottee**	(terry) towelling
das	**Gewebe, –**	fabric, material
das	**Gußeisen**	cast iron
das	**Kunstleder**	imitation leather
das	**Mahagoni**	mahogany
das	**Mineral, -ien**	mineral
das	**Perlmutt**	mother-of-pearl
das	**Platin**	platinum
das	**Quecksilber**	mercury
das	**Rohr** ◇	cane, wicker
das	**Schaffell**	sheepskin
das	**Schmiedeeisen**	wrought iron
das	**Schmirgelpapier**	sandpaper
das	**Schweinsleder**	pigskin
das	**Seil, -e**	rope
das	**Soda**	soda
das	**Sperrholz**	plywood
das	**Styropor**	polystyrene
das	**Wachstuch**	oilcloth
das	**Wellblech**	corrugated iron

klebrig *sticky*
rauh *rough*
widerstandsfähig *hard-wearing*
seidig *silky*
vergoldet *gold-plated*
versilbert *silver-plated*

MEDIA

der **Hörer**, – ◇	listener (*radio*)
der **Journalist**, -en	journalist
der **Reporter**, –	reporter
der **Zuschauer**, – ◇	viewer

IMPORTANT WORDS (m)

der **Artikel**, –	article
der **Bestseller**, –	best-seller
der **Empfang**	reception
der **Fernsehfilm**, -e	TV film
der **Kanal**, ⁻e ◇	channel
der **Korrespondent**, -en	correspondent
der **Kritiker**, –	critic
der **Leitartikel**, –	leading article, editorial
der **Videorekorder**, –	video recorder
der **Werbespot**, -s	commercial

USEFUL WORDS (m)

der **Bestsellerautor**, -en	best-selling author
der **Conférencier**, -s	compère
der **Dokumentarfilm**, -e	documentary
der **Exklusivbericht**, -e	scoop, exclusive
der **Groschenroman**, -e	cheap novel
der **Kolumnist**, -en	columnist
der **Leitartikler**, –	leader *or* editorial writer
der **Moderator**, -en	presenter
der **Nachdruck**, -e	reprinting; reprint
der **Nachruf**, -e	obituary
der **Piratensender**, –	pirate (radio) station
der **Pressezar**, -e	press baron
der **Slogan**, -s	slogan
der **Sponsor**, -en	sponsor

senden to broadcast
einschalten to switch on
ausschalten to switch off

MEDIA

ESSENTIAL WORDS (f)

die **Hörerin**	listener (*radio*)
die **Illustrierte**, -n ▭	magazine
die **Journalistin**	journalist
die **Nachrichten** (*pl*) ▭	news
die **Presse**	press
die **Reportage**, -n	report; (live) commentary
die **Reporterin**	reporter
die **Schlagzeile**, -n ▭	headline
die **Sendung**, -en ▭	transmission; programme, broadcast
die **Titelseite**, -n	front page
die **Zeitschrift**, -en	magazine; periodical
die **Zeitung**, -en	newspaper
die **Zuschauerin**	viewer

IMPORTANT WORDS (f)

die **Abendzeitung**, -en	evening paper
die **Anzeige**, -n ▭	advertisement
die **Boulevardzeitung**, -en	tabloid
die **Kleinanzeigen** (*pl*)	classified ads
die **Korrespondentin**	correspondent
die **Kritik**, -en	criticism; review
die **Kritikerin**	critic
die **Kurzmeldung**, -en	news flash
die **Kurznachrichten** (*pl*)	news headlines
die **Livesendung**, -en	live broadcast
die **Nachrichtenagentur**, -en	news agency
die **Presseagentur**, -en	news agency
die **Pressekonferenz**, -en	press conference
die **Redaktion**	editorial staff; editorial office
die **Reklame** ▭	advertisements; advertising
die **Seite**, -n ◇	page
die **Serie**, -n	series
die **Sonntagszeitung**, -en	Sunday paper
die **Störung**, -en	interference
die **Tageszeitung**, -en	daily (paper)
die **Werbung** ▭	advertising
die **Wiederholung**, -en ▭	repeat (*programme*)

USEFUL WORDS (f)

die	**Antenne**, -n	aerial
die	**Auflage**	circulation
die	**Aufzeichnung**, -en	recording; pre-recorded programme
die	**Bestsellerautorin**	best-selling author
die	**Einschaltquote**, -n	viewing figures
die	**Filmkritik**, -en	film review
die	**Fortsetzung**, -en	sequel
die	**Kolumnistin**	columnist
die	**Kurzwelle (KW)**	short wave
die	**Langwelle (LW)**	long wave
die	**Leitartiklerin**	leader or editorial writer
die	**Lokalzeitung**, -en	local or regional newspaper
die	**Mittelwelle (MW)**	medium wave
die	**Moderatorin**	presenter
die	**Monatszeitschrift**, -en	monthly (magazine)
die	**Morgenzeitung**, -en	morning paper
die	**Neuausgabe**, -n	new edition
die	**Parabolantenne**	satellite dish
die	**Plakatwand**, ¨-e	hoarding
die	**Pressefreiheit**	freedom of the press
die	**Presseveröffentlichung**, -en	press release
die	**Rubrik**, -en	column
die	**Spalte**, -n	column
die	**Sportseite**, -n	sports page
die	**Tantiemen** (pl)	royalties
die	**Theaterkritik**, -en	theatre review
die	**Ultrakurzwelle (UKW)**	FM
die	**Videothek**, -en	video shop
die	**Wochenzeitschrift**, -en	weekly (magazine)
die	**Zensur** ◊	censorship

im Fernsehen/Radio on television/(the) radio
täglich daily
wöchentlich weekly
monatlich monthly
vierteljährlich quarterly

ESSENTIAL WORDS (nt)

das **Fernsehen**	television
das **Magazin, -e**	magazine
die **Massenmedien** *(pl)*	mass media
das **Programm, -e** ◇	programme
das **Radio**	radio

IMPORTANT WORDS (nt)

das **Exemplar, -e**	copy
das **Farbfernsehen**	colour television
das **Kabelfernsehen**	cable television
das **Nachrichtenmagazin, -e**	news magazine
das **Satellitenfernsehen**	satellite television
das **Schwarzweißfernsehen**	black and white television
das **Studio, -s**	studio
das **Video, -s**	video

USEFUL WORDS (nt)

das **Abonnement, -s**	subscription
das **Interview, -s**	interview
das **Popvideo, -s**	pop video
das **Poster, –**	poster

anspruchsvoll *up-market*
nicht anspruchsvoll *down-market*
zur Hauptsendezeit *in prime time*

MILITARY MATTERS

der **Angriff**, -e 📖	attack
der **Ersatzdienst** 📖	alternative *or* community service
der **Kampf**, ⸚e 📖	fight, fighting
der **Krieg**, -e	war
der **Militärdienst**	military service
der **Soldat**, -en	soldier

IMPORTANT WORDS (m)

der **Alarm**	alarm
der **Befehlshaber**, –	commander
der **Bombenangriff**, -e	bomb attack
der **Bomber**, –	bomber (*plane*)
der **Deserteur**, -e	deserter
der **Einberufungsbescheid**, -e	call-up papers
der **Fallschirmjäger**, –	paratrooper
der **Feind**, -e	enemy
der **Freiwillige***, -n	volunteer
der **Frieden** 📖	peace
der **Hinterhalt**, -e	ambush
die **Invasoren** (*pl*)	invaders
der **Kriegsausbruch**	outbreak of war
der **Kriegsgefangene***, -n 📖	prisoner of war
der **Luftalarm**, -e	air-raid alarm
der **Luftangriff**, -e	air raid
der **Luftschutzbunker**, –	bomb shelter
der **Panzer**, - ◇ 📖	armoured car; tank
der **Stützpunkt**, -e	base; stronghold
der **Waffenstillstand**	armistice
der **Wehrdienst** 📖	military service
der **Wehrdienstverweigerer**, –	conscientious objector
der **Wehrpflichtige***, -n	conscript
der **Zivilist**, -en	civilian

USEFUL WORDS (m)

der	**Abzug**, ⁻e ⋄	trigger
der	**Adjutant**, -en	adjutant
der	**Admiral**, ⁻e	admiral
der	**Atomsprengkopf**, ⁻e	nuclear warhead
der	**Beobachtungsposten**, –	look-out post
der	**Bombenkrater**, –	bomb crater
der	**Bombenräumexperte**, -n	bomb disposal expert
der	**Brigadegeneral**, ⁻e	brigadier
der	**Dolch**, -e	dagger
der	**Feldmarschall**, ⁻e	field marshal
der	**Feldwebel**, –	sergeant
der	**Flammenwerfer**, –	flame-thrower
der	**Friedensvertrag**, ⁻e	peace treaty
der	**Gefreite***, -n	private
der	**General**, ⁻e	general
der	**Generalangriff**, -e	general attack
der	**Generalfeldmarschall**, ⁻e	field marshal
der	**Generalleutnant**, -s	lieutenant general; air marshal
der	**Generalmajor**, -e	major general; air vice-marshal
der	**Generalstab**, ⁻e	general staff
der	**Grenadier**, -e	grenadier
der	**Guerillakämpfer**, –	guerrilla
der	**Guerillakrieg**, -e	guerrilla warfare
der	**Infanterist**, -en	infantryman
der	**Kapitän**, -e	captain
der	**Kavallerieoffizier**, -e ⌐	cavalry officer
der	**Kavallerist**, -en	cavalryman
der	**Kommandant**, -en	commander
der	**Korporal**, -e	corporal
der	**Krieger**, –	warrior
der	**Kriegsbeschädigte***, -n	war disabled person
der	**Kriegsteilnehmer**, –	combatant
der	**Kundschafter**, –	scout
der	**Legionär**, -e	legionnaire
der	**Leutnant**, -s	lieutenant
der	**Major**, -e	major
der	**Obergefreite***, -n	lance-corporal
der	**Oberst**, -e	colonel

der	**Offizier, -e**	officer
der	**Raketenwerfer, –**	missile launcher
der	**Rang, ̈e**	rank
der	**Rekrut, -en**	recruit
der	**Revolver, –**	revolver
der	**Scharfschütze, -n**	marksman, sharpshooter
der	**Schütze, -n**	gunner; private
der	**Söldner, –**	mercenary
der	**Speer, -e**	spear
der	**Streifen, –**	stripe
der	**Torpedo, -s**	torpedo
der	**Trupp, -s**	squad
der	**Unteroffizier, -e**	non-commissioned officer (NCO)
der	**Veteran, -en**	ex-serviceman
der	**Wachtturm, ̈e**	watchtower

die	**Admiralität**	admirals; admirality
die	**Atombombe, -n**	atom *or* atomic bomb
die	**Ausgangssperre**	curfew
die	**Befestigungen** (*pl*)	fortifications
die	**Belagerung, -en**	siege
die	**Besatzungsmacht, ̈e**	occupying forces
die	**Fregatte, -n**	frigate
die	**Fremdenlegion**	Foreign Legion
die	**Garnison, -en**	garrison
die	**Generalität**	generals
die	**Kriegsverletzung, -en**	war wound
die	**Legion, -en**	legion
die	**Miliz, -en**	militia
die	**Musterung, -en**	inspection; medical examination
die	**Parade, -n**	parade
die	**Patrone, -n**	cartridge
die	**Schwadron, -en**	squadron (*army*)
die	**Staffel, -n**	squadron (*air force*)
die	**Wache, -n**	sentry

ESSENTIAL WORDS (f)

die	**Armee, -n**	army
die	**Bombe, -n**	bomb
die	**Bundeswehr** 🕮	German armed forces
die	**Granate, -n**	shell
die	**Luftwaffe**	air force
die	**Marine, –**	navy
die	**Uniform, -en**	uniform
die	**Verteidigung** 🕮	defence
die	**Waffe, -n**	weapon

IMPORTANT WORDS (f)

die	**Berufsarmee, -n**	regular army
die	**Brigade, -n**	brigade
die	**Einziehung**	enlistment
die	**Festung, -en**	fortress; fortified castle
die	**Feuerpause, -n**	ceasefire
die	**Flotte, -n**	navy, fleet
die	**Infanterie**	infantry
die	**Invasion, -en**	invasion
die	**Kanone, -n**	cannon
die	**Kapitulation**	surrender
die	**Kaserne, -n** 🕮	barracks
die	**Kavallerie**	cavalry
die	**Kriegserklärung, -en**	declaration of war
die	**Kugel, -n** ◇	bullet
die	**Maschinenpistole, -n**	submachine gun
die	**Munition**	ammunition
die	**Offensive, -n**	offensive
die	**Pistole, -n**	pistol, gun
die	**Vergeltung**	reprisals, retaliation
die	**Zivilistin**	civilian

vor ein Kriegsgericht gestellt werden *to be court-martialled*
sich zur Armee melden *to enlist in the army*
zum Angriff übergehen *to go into the attack*
sich zurückziehen *to withdraw*

MILITARY MATTERS — 5

das **Gefecht**, -e 📖	skirmish
das **Gewehr**, -e	rifle
das **Kampfflugzeug**, -e	fighter (*plane*)
das **Maschinengewehr**, -e	machine gun

das **Bombardement**, -s	bombing
das **Feuergefecht**, -e	gun fight
das **Kriegsgericht**, -e	court-martial
das **Manöver**, –	exercise; manoeuvre

das **Aufklärungsflugzeug**, -e	reconnaissance plane
das **Bataillon**, -e	batallion
das **Bombenräumkommando**, -s	bomb disposal squad
das **Dynamit**	dynamite
das **Exekutionskommando**, -s	firing squad
das **Geschwader**, –	squadron (*navy*)
das **Kasino**, -s	mess
das **Kriegsopfer**, –	war victim
das **Lager**, – ⇨	camp
das **Offizierskasino**, -s	officers' mess
das **Regiment**, -er	regiment
das **Schwert**, -er	sword
das **Torpedoboot**, -e	torpedo boat
das **Tränengas**	teargas
das **Ziel**, -e ⇨	target

Posten stehen to stand *guard*
er ist dienstuntauglich he is unfit for *service*

MUSIC

ESSENTIAL WORDS (m)

der **Chor**, ⸚e	choir; chorus
der **Jazz**	jazz
der **Musiker**, –	musician
der **Zuhörer**, –	listener; (*pl*) audience

IMPORTANT WORDS (m)

der **Akkord**, -e	chord
der **Dirigent**, -en	conductor
der **Dudelsack**, ⸚e	bagpipes
der **Flügel**, – ◇	grand piano
der **Kontrabaß**, ⸚sse	double bass
der **Konzertsaal**, (-säle)	concert hall
der **Solist**, -en	soloist
der **Taktstock**, ⸚e	(conductor's) baton
der **Ton**, ⸚e ◇	note
der **Triangel**, –	triangle

USEFUL WORDS (m)

der **Bariton**, -e	baritone
der **Bassist**, -en	(double) bass player; bass (*singer*)
der **Bogen**, ⸚ ◇	bow
der **CD-Spieler**, –	CD *or* compact disc player
der **Impresario**, -s	impresario
der **Instrumentenbauer**, –	instrument maker
der **Lautsprecher**, –	speaker
der **Plattenspieler**, –	record player
der **Plattenteller**, –	turntable
der **Refrain**, -s	refrain, chorus
der **Schlagzeuger**, –	drummer
der **Synthesizer**, –	synthesizer
der **Tenor**, ⸚e	tenor
der **Text**, -e ◇	lyrics
der **Verstärker**, –	amplifier

Klavier/Gitarre spielen *to play the piano/the guitar*
Noten lesen *to read music*

ESSENTIAL WORDS (f)	

die	**Blaskapelle, -n**	brass band
die	**Blockflöte, -n**	recorder
die	**Flöte, -n**	flute
die	**Geige, -n**	violin, fiddle
die	**Gitarre, -n**	guitar
die	**Gruppe, -n**	group
die	**Kapelle, -n** ◇	band, orchestra
die	**Klarinette, -n**	clarinet
die	**klassische Musik**	classical music
die	**Musik**	music
die	**Musikerin**	musician
die	**Note, -n** ◇	note
die	**Oboe, -n**	oboe
die	**Popmusik**	pop music
die	**Taste, -n** ◇ ▢	(piano) key
die	**Trompete, -n**	trumpet

IMPORTANT WORDS (f)	

die	**Blasmusik**	brass band music
die	**Dirigentin**	conductor
die	**Harfe, -n**	harp
die	**Mundharmonika, -s**	mouth organ, harmonica
die	**Musikkapelle, -n**	band
die	**Oper, -n**	opera; opera house
die	**Orgel, -n**	organ
die	**Posaune, -n**	trombone
die	**Querflöte, -n**	flute
die	**Saite, -n**	string
die	**Solistin**	soloist
die	**Tastatur, -en**	keyboard
die	**Tonart, -en**	(musical) key
die	**Trommel, -n**	drum
die	**Violine, -n**	violin
die	**Ziehharmonika, -s**	concertina; accordion

zerkratzt *scratched* (record)
Musik hören *to listen to music*
richtig/falsch singen *to sing in tune/out of tune*

USEFUL WORDS (f)

die **Altistin**	(contr)alto
die **Arie, -n**	aria
die **Aufnahme, -n** ⟡	recording
die **Ballade, -n**	ballad
die **Baßgitarre, -n**	bass guitar
die **Compact Disc (CD), – -s**	compact disc, CD
die **E-Musik (ernste Musik)**	serious music
die **Hi-fi-Anlage, -n**	hi-fi
die **Langspielplatte (LP), -n**	long-playing record, LP
die **Melodie, -n**	melody; tune
die **Operette, -n**	operetta
die **Partitur, -en**	score
die **Plattenhülle, -n**	record sleeve
die **Popmusik**	pop music
die **Single, -s**	single
die **Sopranistin**	soprano
die **Tonleiter**	scale
die **Tournee, -n**	tour (*of artist*)
die **U-Musik** (Unterhaltungsmusik)	light music

USEFUL WORDS (m&f)

der/die **Akkordeonist(in), -en**	accordionist
der/die **Cellist(in), -en**	cellist, cello player
der/die **Flötist(in), -en**	flute player, flautist
der/die **Geiger(in), –**	violinist
der/die **Gitarrist(in), -en**	guitarist
der/die **Klarinettist(in), -en**	clarinettist
der/die **Komponist(in), -en**	composer
der/die **Künstler(in), –** ⟡	performer
der/die **Leadsänger(in), –**	lead singer
der/die **Liedermacher(in), –**	singer-songwriter
der/die **Musikliebhaber(in), –**	music lover
der/die **Organist(in), -en**	organist
der/die **Pianist(in), -en**	pianist
der/die **Sänger(in), –**	singer
der/die **Violinist(in), -en**	violinist, violin player
der/die **Virtuose, -n/ Virtuosin**	virtuoso

das	**Akkordeon**, -s	accordion
das	**Bügelhorn**, ¨er	bugle
das	**Cello**, -s	cello
das	**Horn**, ¨er	horn
das	**Instrument**, -e	(musical) instrument
das	**Klavier**, -e	piano
das	**Konzert**, -e ◇	concert; concerto
das	**Musikinstrument**, -e	musical instrument
das	**Orchester**, –	orchestra; band
das	**Saxophon**, -e	saxophone
das	**Schlagzeug**, -e	drums
das	**Xylophon**, -e	xylophone

das	**Becken**, – ◇	cymbals
das	**Fagott**, -e	bassoon
das	**Jagdhorn**, ¨er	bugle; hunting horn
das	**Opernhaus**, ¨er	opera house
das	**Streichorchester**, –	string orchestra
das	**Tamburin**, -e	tambourine
das	**Violoncello**, -s	violoncello
das	**Waldhorn**, ¨er	French horn

das	**Cembalo**, -s	harpsichord
das	**Duo**, -s	duet
das	**Grammophon**, -e	gramophone
das	**Lied**, -er	song
das	**Mikrofon**, -e	microphone
das	**Musical**, -s	musical
das	**Playback**	miming
das	**Potpourri**, -s	potpourri, medley
das	**Quartett**, -e	quartet(te)
das	**Quintett**, -e	quintet(te)
das	**Rockkonzert**, -e	rock concert
das	**Sextett**, -e	sextet(te)
das	**Solo**, (Soli)	solo
das	**Terzett**, -e	trio

NUMBERS AND QUANTITIES

CARDINAL NUMBERS		

nought	0	null
one	1	eins
two	2	zwei
three	3	drei
four	4	vier
five	5	fünf
six	6	sechs
seven	7	sieben
eight	8	acht
nine	9	neun
ten	10	zehn
eleven	11	elf
twelve	12	zwölf
thirteen	13	dreizehn
fourteen	14	vierzehn
fifteen	15	fünfzehn
sixteen	16	sechzehn
seventeen	17	siebzehn
eighteen	18	achtzehn
nineteen	19	neunzehn
twenty	20	zwanzig
twenty-one	21	einundzwanzig
twenty-two	22	zweiundzwanzig
twenty-three	23	dreiundzwanzig
thirty	30	dreißig
thirty-one	31	einunddreißig
thirty-two	32	zweiunddreißig
forty	40	vierzig
fifty	50	fünfzig
sixty	60	sechzig
seventy	70	siebzig
eighty	80	achtzig
ninety	90	neunzig
ninety-nine	99	neunundneunzig
a (or one) hundred	100	(ein)hundert
a hundred and one	101	hunderteins
a hundred and two	102	hundertzwei
a hundred and ten	110	hundertzehn
a hundred and eighty-two	182	hundertzweiundachtzig

NUMBERS AND QUANTITIES — 2

two hundred	200	zweihundert
two hundred and one	201	zweihunderteins
two hundred and two	202	zweihundertzwei
three hundred	300	dreihundert
four hundred	400	vierhundert
five hundred	500	fünfhundert
six hundred	600	sechshundert
seven hundred	700	siebenhundert
eight hundred	800	achthundert
nine hundred	900	neunhundert
a (or one) thousand	1000	(ein)tausend
a thousand and one	1001	tausendeins
a thousand and two	1002	tausendzwei
two thousand	2000	zweitausend
ten thousand	10000	zehntausend
a (or one) hundred thousand	100000	hunderttausend
a (or one) million	1000000	eine Million
two million	2000000	zwei Millionen

ein Millionär a millionaire
zum zigsten Male for the umpteenth time
0,4 (Null Komma vier) 0.4 (nought point four)
gerade/ungerade Zahlen even/odd numbers
50 Prozent 50 per cent
1994 neunzehnhundertvierundneunzig
pro Dutzend/Hundert/Tausend per dozen/hundred/thousand
die Flasche war dreiviertel leer the bottle was three-quarters empty
dutzendweise, im Dutzend by the dozen
etwa dreitausend around three thousand
ein Löffelvoll Honig a spoonful of honey

ORDINAL NUMBERS

These can be masculine, feminine or neuter, and take the appropriate endings.

first	1	der erste
second	2	der zweite
third	3	der dritte
fourth	4	der vierte
fifth	5	der fünfte
sixth	6	der sechste
seventh	7	der siebte
eighth	8	der achte
ninth	9	der neunte
tenth	10	der zehnte
eleventh	11	der elfte
twelfth	12	der zwölfte
thirteenth	13	der dreizehnte
fourteenth	14	der vierzehnte
fifteenth	15	der fünfzehnte
sixteenth	16	der sechzehnte
seventeenth	17	der siebzehnte
eighteenth	18	der achtzehnte
nineteenth	19	der neunzehnte
twentieth	20	der zwanzigste
twenty-first	21	der einundzwanzigste
twenty-second	22	der zweiundzwanzigste
thirtieth	30	der dreißigste
thirty-first	31	der einunddreißigste
fortieth	40	der vierzigste
fiftieth	50	der fünfzigste
sixtieth	60	der sechzigste
seventieth	70	der siebzigste
eightieth	80	der achzigste
ninetieth	90	der neunzigste
hundredth	100	der hundertste
hundred and first	101	der hunderterste
hundred and tenth	110	der hundertzehnte
two hundredth	200	der zweihundertste

ORDINAL NUMBERS (cont)

three hundredth	300	der dreihundertste
four hundredth	400	der vierhundertste
five hundredth	500	der fünfhundertste
six hundredth	600	der sechshundertste
seven hundredth	700	der siebenhundertste
eight hundredth	800	der achthundertste
nine hundredth	900	der neunhundertste
thousandth	1000	der tausendste
two thousandth	2000	der zweitausendste
millionth	1000000	der millionste
two millionth	2000000	der zweimillionste

FRACTIONS

a half	½	halb, die Hälfte
one and a half kilos	1½	eineinhalb Kilo, anderthalb Kilo
two and a half kilos	2½	zweieinhalb Kilo
a third	⅓	ein Drittel (*nt*)
two thirds	⅔	zwei Drittel
a quarter	¼	ein Viertel (*nt*)
three quarters	¾	drei Viertel
a sixth	⅙	ein Sechstel (*nt*)
five and five sixths	5⅚	fünf fünf Sechstel
an eighth	⅛	ein Achtel (*nt*)
a twelfth	1/12	ein Zwölftel (*nt*)
a twentieth	1/20	ein Zwanzigstel (*nt*)
a hundredth	1/100	ein Hundertstel (*nt*)
a thousandth	1/1000	ein Tausendstel (*nt*)
a millionth	1/1000000	ein Millionstel (*nt*)

der Becher ⇨ **(Joghurt)** *pot (of yoghurt)*
ein bißchen *a little (bit of)*
die Büchse ⇨ *tin, can*

das Deziliter decilitre
das Dutzend dozen
Dutzende von dozens of
etwas Zucker a little (bit of) sugar
das Faß barrel
die Flasche (Wein) bottle (of wine)
das Glas ⬦ *(Milch)* glass (of milk)
das Glas ⬦ *Marmelade* jar or pot of jam
eine Halbe a half (litre of beer etc)
ein halbes Dutzend/Pfund a half dozen/pound
ein halbes Kilo/Liter half a kilo/litre
die Handvoll (Münzen) handful (of coins)
der Haufen heap, pile
hundert Gramm Käse a hundred grams of cheese
Hunderte von hundreds of
die Kanne (Kaffee) pot (of coffee)
das Kilo(gramm) kilo(gram)
ein Kleines a half pint (of beer etc)
das Liter litre
die Menge ⬦ quantity; heaps of
der Meter (Stoff) metre (of cloth)
das Paar ⬦ *(Schuhe)* pair (of shoes)
das Päckchen packet
die Packung Keks/Zigaretten packet of biscuits/cigarettes
das Pfund (Kartoffeln) pound (of potatoes)
die Portion (Eis) portion or helping (of ice cream)
der Riegel Schokolade bar of chocolate
die Schachtel box; packet (of cigarettes)
die Scheibe (Brot) slice (of bread)
die Schüssel bowl, dish
der Stapel pile
das Stück ⬦ *Kuchen* piece or slice of cake
das Stück ⬦ *Papier* bit or piece of paper
das Stück ⬦ *Zucker* lump of sugar
die Tafel ⬦ *Schokolade* bar of chocolate
die Tasse cup
Tausende von thousands of
der Teller plate
das Viertel(pfund) ⬦ quarter(-pound)
ein wenig a little (bit) of
das Wollknäuel ball of wool
der Zuckerwürfel lump of sugar

PERSONAL ITEMS

ESSENTIAL WORDS (m)

der **Artikel**, –	article
der **Ehering**, -e	wedding ring
der **Juwel**, -en	jewel
der **Kamm**, ¨e	comb
der **Ohrring**, -e	earring
der **Rasierapparat**, -e 📖	razor
der **Ring**, -e	ring
der **Schlüsselring**, -e	key ring
der **Schmuck**	jewellery
der **Schönheitssalon**, -s	beauty salon
der **Spiegel**, –	mirror

IMPORTANT WORDS (m)

der **Anhänger**, – ◇	pendant
der **Edelstein**, -e	gem, precious stone
der **Lidschatten**	eyeshadow
der **Lippenstift**, -e	lipstick
der **Lockenwickler**, –	curler; roller
der **Manschettenknopf**, ¨e	cufflink
der **Nagellack**, -e	nail varnish, nail polish
der **Nagellackentferner**, –	nail varnish remover
der **Schwamm**, ¨e	sponge
der **Trauring**, -e	wedding ring
der **Waschbeutel**, –	toilet bag
der **Waschlappen**, –	face flannel, facecloth

USEFUL WORDS (m)

der **Diamant**, -en	diamond
der **Eyeliner**	eyeliner
der **Glücksbringer**, –	lucky charm
der **Körperpuder**	talc, talcum powder
der **Kulturbeutel**, –	toilet bag, sponge bag
der **Make-up-Entferner**	make-up remover
der **Rubin**, -e	ruby
der **Saphir**, -e	sapphire
der **Siegelring**, -e	signet ring
der **Tampon**, -s	tampon
der **Teddy**, -s	teddy (bear)

die	**Armbanduhr, -en**	(wrist)watch
die	**Bürste, -n**	brush
die	**Gesichtscreme, -s**	face cream
die	**Halskette, -n**	necklace
die	**Kette, -n** ◇	chain
die	**Kosmetik**	cosmetics
die	**Perle, -n**	pearl; bead
die	**Perlenkette, -n**	beads, string of beads
die	**Rasiercreme, -s**	shaving cream
die	**Sache, -n** ◇	thing
die	**Schönheit**	beauty
die	**Seife, -n**	soap
die	**Zahnbürste, -n**	toothbrush
die	**Zahnpasta, (-ten)**	toothpaste

die	**Brosche, -n**	brooch
die	**Frisur, -en**	hairstyle
die	**Krawattennadel, -n**	tie-pin
die	**Perücke, -n**	wig
die	**Puderdose, -n**	(powder) compact
die	**Schminke, -n**	make-up
die	**Wimperntusche, -n**	mascara

die	**Damenbinde, -n**	sanitary towel
die	**Handtasche, -n**	handbag
die	**Nagelschere, -n**	nail scissors
die	**Pinzette, -n**	tweezers
die	**Rasierklinge, -n**	razor blade
die	**Sachen** (*pl*)	gear, things
die	**Schatulle, -n**	case, box (*for silver, jewels*)
die	**Spardose, -n**	moneybox
die	**Wertsachen** (*pl*)	valuables

PERSONAL ITEMS — 3

das Armband, ⁝er	bracelet
das Deodorant, -s	deodorant
das Gesichtspuder	face powder
das Gold	gold
das Haarwaschmittel, – ⌑	shampoo
das Handtuch, ⁝er	towel
das Make-up	foundation; make-up
das Parfüm, -s	perfume, scent
das Rasierwasser, –	aftershave
das Shampoo, -s	shampoo
das Silber	silver
das Taschengeld	pocket money
das Toilettenwasser, –	toilet water

das After-shave	aftershave
das Brillenetui, -s	glasses case
das Haarspray	hair spray
das Kondom, -e	condom
das Plüschtier, -e	soft toy, fluffy animal
das Sparschwein, -e	piggy bank
das Tagebuch, ⁝er	diary

kämmen to comb
bürsten to brush
duschen to have a shower
baden to have a bath
sich rasieren to shave
Erinnerungswert haben to have sentimental value
wertvoller Schmuck precious jewellery
sich waschen to get washed
sich anziehen to get dressed
sich die Zähne putzen to brush one's teeth

der	Baum, ⁻e	tree
der	Blumentopf, ⁻e	flower pot
der	Boden, ⁻ ◇	ground, soil, earth
der	Busch, ⁻e	bush, shrub
der	Garten, ⁻	garden
der	Gärtner, –	gardener
der	Gemüsegarten, ⁻	vegetable garden
der	Grund ◇	ground
der	Krokus, -se	crocus
der	Obstgarten, ⁻	orchard
der	Pfad, -e	path
der	Rasen	lawn; turf
der	Regen	rain
der	Schatten	shadow; shade
der	Sonnenschein	sunshine
der	Stamm, ⁻e ◇	trunk
der	Stein, -e ◇	stone; rock
der	Steingarten, ⁻	rockery, rock garden
der	Weg, -e ◇	path
der	Wurm, ⁻er	worm

der	Ast, ⁻e ▯	branch
der	Baumstamm, ⁻e	tree trunk
der	Blumenstrauß, ⁻e	bunch *or* bouquet of flowers
der	Dorn, -en	thorn
der	Duft, ⁻e	perfume, scent
der	Efeu	ivy
der	Flieder	lilac
der	Gartenschlauch, ⁻e	garden hose
der	Goldlack	wallflower
der	Halm, -e	stalk, blade
der	Löwenzahn	dandelion
der	Mohn	poppy
der	Rasenmäher, –	lawnmower
der	Rosenstock, ⁻e	rose bush
der	Samen, –	seed(s)
der	Schmetterling, -e ▯	butterfly
der	Schubkarren, –	wheelbarrow

PLANTS AND GARDENS — 2

IMPORTANT WORDS (m) (cont)

der Stachel, -n ✿	thorn
der Stengel, –	stalk, stem
der Stiel, -e	stem
der Strauch, ⁻er	bush, shrub
der Strauß, ⁻e ✿	bunch (of flowers)
der Tau ✿	dew
der Weiher, –	pond
der Wintergarten, ⁻	conservatory
der Zaun, ⁻e	fence
der Zweig, -e	branch

USEFUL WORDS (m)

der Ableger, –	cutting
der Enzian	gentian
der Estragon	tarragon
der Farn, -e	fern
der Ginster	broom; gorse
der Hopfen, –	hop
der Kies	(loose) gravel
der Klee	clover
der Kompost	compost
der Komposthaufen, –	compost heap
der Küchengarten, ⁻	kitchen garden
der Landschaftsgärtner, –	landscape gardener
der Lavendel	lavender
der Lorbeer	laurel; bayleaf
der Majoran	marjoram
der Maschendraht	wire netting
der Nutzgarten, ⁻	kitchen garden
der Pilz, -e	mushroom; fungus
der Rosengarten, ⁻	rose garden
der Rotdorn	hawthorn
der Sand	sand
der Schotter	(loose) gravel
der Schrebergarten, ⁻	allotment, plot
der Vorgarten, ⁻	front garden
der Wacholder	juniper
der Weißdorn	hawthorn
der Ziergarten, ⁻	ornamental garden

ESSENTIAL WORDS (f)

die	**Bank,** ⁅e ◇	bench
die	**Biene,** -n	bee
die	**Blume,** -n	flower
die	**Chrysantheme,** -n	chrysanthemum
die	**Dahlie,** -n	dahlia
die	**Erde** ◇	earth, soil
die	**Gartentür,** -en	garden gate
die	**Hütte,** -n ◇ ▢	hut, shed
die	**Hyazinthe,** -n	hyacinth
die	**Lilie,** -n	lily
die	**Orchidee,** -n	orchid
die	**Pflanze,** -n	plant
die	**Rose,** -n	rose
die	**Sonne**	sun
die	**Sonnenblume,** -n	sunflower
die	**Tulpe,** -n	tulip
die	**Wespe,** -n	wasp

IMPORTANT WORDS (f)

die	**Beere,** -n	berry
die	**Blüte,** -n	blossom
die	**Butterblume,** -n	buttercup
die	**Gartenwicke,** -n	sweet pea
die	**Gießkanne,** -n	watering can
die	**Hacke,** -n	hoe
die	**Harke,** -n	rake
die	**Hecke,** -n	hedge
die	**Heckenschere,** -n	hedge-cutters; garden shears
die	**Hortensie,** -n	hydrangea
die	**Knospe,** -n	bud
die	**Leiter,** -n ◇	ladder
die	**Margerite,** -n	daisy
die	**Narzisse,** -n	narcissus, daffodil
die	**Nelke,** -n	carnation
die	**Osterglocke,** -n	daffodil
die	**Primel,** -n	primrose
die	**Rabatte,** -n	border, flower bed
die	**Walze,** -n	roller
die	**Wurzel,** -n	root

die	**Baumschule,** -n	nursery (*for trees*)
die	**Brennessel,** -n	(stinging) nettle
die	**Distel,** -n	thistle
die	**Gartenschau,** -en	horticultural show
die	**Gärtnerin**	gardener
die	**Geranie,** -n	geranium
die	**Gladiole,** -n	gladiolus
die	**Hagebutte,** -n	rosehip
die	**Hummel,** -n	bumble-bee
die	**Iris,** –	iris
die	**Kapuzinerkresse**	nasturtium
die	**Kornblume,** -n	cornflower
die	**Landschaftsgärtnerin**	landscape gardener
die	**Laube,** -n	bower, arbour
die	**Magnolie,** -n	magnolia
die	**Mimose,** -n	mimosa
die	**Minze**	mint
die	**Mistel,** -n	mistletoe
die	**Pforte,** -n	(garden) gate
die	**Rinde,** -n	bark
die	**Seerose,** -n	water lily

die Hecke schneiden to cut the hedge
Unkraut jäten to do the weeding
die Blätter zusammenharken to rake up the leaves
hier duftet es (gut) what a nice smell there is here
allerlei Pflanzen all kinds of plants
schattig shady
umzäunt fenced in
sonnig sunny
Ableger nehmen to take cuttings
beschneiden to prune
verblüht faded
stachelig prickly
umtopfen to repot
aussetzen to plant out
pflücken to pick
gießen to water

ESSENTIAL WORDS (nt)

das	**Blatt, ¨er** ⬦	leaf
das	**Gartenhaus, ¨er**	summerhouse
das	**Gärtnern**	gardening
das	**Gemüse, –**	vegetable(s)
das	**Gras**	grass
das	**Laub**	leaves
das	**Unkraut**	weed(s)
das	**Werkzeug, -e**	tool

IMPORTANT WORDS (nt)

das	**Blumenbeet, -e**	flowerbed
das	**Gänseblümchen, –**	daisy
das	**Geißblatt**	honeysuckle
das	**Gewächshaus, ¨er**	greenhouse
das	**Maiglöckchen, –**	lily of the valley
das	**Schneeglöckchen, –**	snowdrop
das	**Stiefmütterchen, –**	pansy
das	**Veilchen, –**	violet
das	**Vergißmeinnicht, -e**	forget-me-not

USEFUL WORDS (nt)

das	**Gartenfest, -e**	garden party
das	**Grün**	greenery
das	**Heidekraut**	heather
das	**Immergrün**	periwinkle
das	**Löwenmäulchen, –**	snapdragon
das	**Moos**	moss
das	**Rhododendron, (-dren)**	rhododendron
das	**Treibhaus, ¨er**	greenhouse
das	**Unkrautvertilgungsmittel, –**	weedkiller

ein Strauß Rosen/Veilchen *a bunch of roses/violets*
Blumen pflanzen *to plant flowers*
im Schatten eines Baumes *in the shade of a tree*
den Garten umgraben *to dig the garden*
den Rasen mähen *to mow the lawn*
in voller Blüte *in full bloom*

POLITICS AND CURRENT AFFAIRS

der	Aufschwung	(economic) recovery
der	Bund	federation
der	Bundeskanzler ▭	(federal) chancellor
der	Bundespräsident	(federal) president
der	Bundestag ▭	German parliament
der	Bürger, –	citizen
der	Landtag	regional German parliament
der	Minister, –	minister
der	Politiker, –	politician
der	Premierminister, –	prime minister, premier
der	Regierungschef, -s	head of government
der	Staat, -en	state
der	Staatsbürger, –	citizen
der	Wähler, –	voter
der	Wahlkampf, ⸚e	election campaign
der	Wahlkreis, -e	constituency

der	Aufstand, ⸚e	insurrection, revolt
der	Faschismus	fascism
der	Geheimdienst, -e	secret service
der	Kapitalismus	capitalism
der	Regierungssturz	overthrow (*of government*)
der	Rücktritt, -e	resignation
der	Staatsstreich, -e	coup
der	Streit, -e ⬦	controversy
der	Terrorismus	terrorism
der	Volksentscheid, -e	referendum

für etw sein/stimmen *to be/vote in favour of sth*
links(gerichtet) *left-wing*
rechts(gerichtet) *right-wing*
verstaatlichen *to nationalize*
privatisieren *to privatize*

POLITICS

USEFUL WORDS (m)

der **Belagerungszustand**	state of siege
der **Bombenanschlag, ¨-e**	bomb attack
der **Drogenhandel**	drug trafficking
der **Export, -e**	export
der **Flüchtling, -e** ▷	refugee
der **Import, -e**	import
der **König, -e**	king
der **Mittelstand**	middle classes
der **Nazi, -s**	Nazi
der **Neonazi, -s**	neo-Nazi
der **politische Gefangene, -n -n**	political prisoner
der **Polizeistaat, -en**	police state
der **Staatsdienst**	civil service
der **Staatsmann, ¨-er**	statesman
die **Straßenkämpfe** (*pl*)	street fighting
der **Streik, -s**	strike
der **Totalitarismus**	totalitarianism
der **Verfassungsfeind, -e**	enemy of the constitution
der **Verfassungsschutz**	(office for the) defence of the constitution
der **Völkermord**	genocide
der **Waffenhandel**	arms dealing
der **Wohlfahrtsstaat**	welfare state

demonstrieren to demonstrate
von der Sozialhilfe leben to live off social security
die Vertrauensfrage stellen to ask for a vote of confidence
Sanktionen verhängen gegen to impose sanctions on
im In- und Ausland at home and abroad
ein ausländischer Staatsangehöriger a foreign national
den Notstand verhängen to declare a state of emergency

ESSENTIAL WORDS (f)

die	**Außenpolitik**	foreign affairs
die	**Bevölkerung, -en** ▭	population
die	**Bundesrepublik Deutschland (BRD)** ▭	Federal Republic of Germany (FRG)
die	**Bundestagswahl, -en**	general election
die	**Bürgerin**	citizen
die	**Debatte, -n**	debate
die	**Demokratie**	democracy
die	**Diktatur, -en**	dictatorship
die	**Freiheit, -en**	freedom
die	**Gewerkschaft, -en** ▭	trade union
die	**Herrschaft**	reign
die	**Inflation**	inflation
die	**Inflationsrate, -n**	rate of inflation
die	**Innenpolitik**	domestic policy
die	**Koalition, -en**	coalition
die	**Landtagswahl, -en**	regional election
die	**Mehrheit, -en**	majority
die	**Meinungsfreiheit**	freedom of thought
die	**Minderheit, -en**	minority
die	**Ministerin**	minister
die	**Monarchie**	monarchy
die	**öffentliche Meinung**	public opinion
die	**Opposition**	opposition
die	**Partei, -en**	party
die	**Politik** ◇	politics
die	**Politikerin**	politician
die	**Premierministerin**	prime minister, premier
die	**Regierung, -en** ▭	government
die	**Republik, -en**	republic
die	**Rezession, -en**	recession
die	**Staatsbürgerin**	citizen
die	**Stimme, -n** ◇	vote
die	**Verfassung, -en** ▭	constitution
die	**Verhandlungen** (*pl*)	talks, negotiations
die	**Wahl, -en** ◇ ▭	election
die	**Wählerin**	voter
die	**Weltpolitik**	world politics

IMPORTANT WORDS (f)

die	**Abstimmung, -en**	ballot; vote
die	**Allgemeinheit**	general public
die	**Arbeiterklasse**	working class
die	**Ausländerfeindlichkeit**	hostility towards foreigners
die	**Botschaft, -en** ◇	embassy
die	**CDU** ▭	Christian Democratic Union
die	**Demonstration, -en**	demonstration
die	**Einheit**	unity
die	**Europäische Gemeinschaft (EG)**	European Community (EC)
die	**FDP** ▭	Free Democratic Party
die	**Kabinettsumbildung, -en**	cabinet reshuffle
die	**Krise, -n**	crisis
die	**Meinungsumfrage, -n**	opinion poll
die	**Nachwahl, -en**	by-election
die	**Nation, -en**	nation
die	**Neutralität**	neutrality
die	**Polizei**	police
die	**Rede, -n** ▭	speech
die	**Reform, -en**	reform
die	**Revolution, -en**	revolution
die	**SPD** ▭	the Social Democrats
die	**Staatsbürgerschaft**	citizenship
die	**Steuer, -n** ◇	tax
die	**Supermacht, ¨e**	superpower
die	**Wählerschaft**	electorate
die	**Wirtschaft** ◇ ▭	economy
die	**wirtschaftliche Lage**	economic situation
die	**Wirtschaftskrise, -n**	economic crisis

USEFUL WORDS (f)

die	**Affäre, -n**	affair
die	**Amtszeit**	term of office
die	**arbeitende Bevölkerung**	working population
die	**Arbeitslosenhilfe**	unemployment benefit
die	**Arbeitsniederlegung, -en**	stoppage (*of work*)
die	**Armut**	poverty
die	**Auswanderung**	emigration
die	**Briefwahl**	postal vote

---

die	**Diäten** (*pl*) ⬦	parliamentary allowance
die	**Diskriminierung**	discrimination
die	**Dritte Welt**	Third World
die	**Einkommenssteuer**	income tax
die	**Einwanderung**	immigration
die	**Folter**	torture
die	**Forderung, -en**	claim, demand
die	**Friedensbewegung**	peace movement
die	**Geiselnahme, -n**	hostage-taking
die	**Gesetzesvorlage, -n**	(government) bill
die	**Hungersnot, ⁻e**	famine
die	**Kommunalwahl, -en**	municipal election
die	**Königin**	queen
die	**Lebenshaltungskosten** (*pl*)	cost of living
die	**Legislaturperiode, -n**	parliamentary term
die	**Mafia**	Mafia
die	**Marionettenregierung, -en**	puppet government
die	**Mietbeihilfe, -n**	rent allowance
die	**NATO**	NATO
die	**Privatisierung, -en**	privatization
die	**Protestbewegung, -en**	protest movement
die	**Rassentrennung**	racial segregation
die	**Repression, -en**	repression
die	**Selbstbestimmung**	self-determination
die	**Sozialhilfe**	social security
die	**Sterblichkeitsrate, -n**	mortality rate
die	**Stimmenauszählung**	counting the votes
die	**Überbevölkerung**	overpopulation
die	**Unabhängigkeit**	independence
die	**UNO**	UN
die	**Vereinten Nationen**	the United Nations
die	**Verstaatlichung, -en**	nationalization
die	**Volkszählung, -en**	census
die	**Wahlkabine, -n**	polling booth
die	**Wahlurne, -n**	ballot box

IMPORTANT WORDS (m&f)

der/die	**Abgeordnete***, -n 🕮	M.P., Member of Parliament
der/die	**Arbeitslose***, -n	unemployed man/woman
der/die	**Beamte***, -n/	
	Beamtin 🕮	civil servant
der/die	**Botschafter(in)**, –	ambassador
der/die	**Christdemokrat(in)**, -en	Christian Democrat
der/die	**Demonstrant(in)**, -en	demonstrator
der/die	**Faschist(in)**, -en	fascist
der/die	**Gegner(in)**, –	opponent
der/die	**Grüne***, -n	Green
der/die	**Kandidat(in)**, -en	candidate
der/die	**Kommunist(in)**, -en	communist
der/die	**Konservative***, -n	conservative
der/die	**Liberale***, -n	liberal
der/die	**Linksextremist(in)**, -en	left-wing extremist
der/die	**Parteivorsitzende***, -n	party leader
der/die	**Präsident(in)**, -en	president
der/die	**Rechtsextremist(in)**, -en	right-wing extremist
der/die	**Sozialdemokrat(in)**, -en	social democrat
der/die	**Sozialist(in)**, -en	socialist
der/die	**Sprecher(in)**, –	spokesman/-woman
der/die	**Steuerzahler(in)**, –	taxpayer
der/die	**Terrorist(in)**, -en	terrorist
der/die	**Volksvertreter(in)**, –	elected representative
der/die	**Wahlberechtigte***, -n	person entitled to vote

USEFUL WORDS (m&f)

der/die	**Asylbewerber(in)**, –	asylum seeker
der/die	**Aussiedler(in)**, –	emigrant
der/die	**Bürgermeister(in)**, –	mayor(ess)
der/die	**Diktator(in)**, -en	dictator
der/die	**Drogenabhängige***, -n	drug addict
der/die	**Einwanderer**, -/	
	Einwanderin	immigrant
der/die	**Herrscher(in)**, –	ruler
der/die	**Obdachlose***, -n	homeless person
der/die	**Prominente***, -n	prominent citizen, VIP
der/die	**Stadtrat**, ¨e/	
	Stadträtin	town councillor

---

das	Gesetz, -e	law
das	Kabinett, -e	cabinet
das	Mehrparteiensystem	multi-party system
das	Parlament, -e	parliament
das	Staatsoberhaupt, ̈-er	head of state
das	Volk, ̈-er ▭	people
das	Wahlrecht	right to vote
das	Zweiparteiensystem	two-party system

das	Außenministerium	Foreign Office
die	Bürgerrechte (pl)	civil rights
das	Innenministerium	Home Office
das	Land, ̈-er ◇	country; state (within FRG)
das	Mißtrauensvotum, (-ten)	vote of no confidence
das	Oberhaus	House of Lords
das	Referendum, (-den)	referendum
das	Regime, -(s)	regime
das	Unterhaus	House of Commons

das	Bruttosozialprodukt	gross national product
das	Einkommen, –	income
das	Finanzamt, ̈-er	tax office
das	Kindergeld	child benefit
das	Mehrheitswahlrecht	first-past-the-post system
die	Menschenrechte (pl)	human rights
das	Mutterschaftsgeld	maternity benefit
das	politische Asyl	political asylum
das	Verbrechen, –	crime
das	Verhältniswahlrecht	proportional representation
das	Wettrüsten	arms race
das	Wohngeld	housing benefit

der	**Agnostiker, –**	agnostic
der	**Anhänger, –** ◇	follower
der	**Atheist, -en**	atheist
der	**Geistliche*, -n** ⌑	clergyman; priest; minister
der	**Glaube** ⌑	faith; belief
	Gott	God
der	**Gott, ¨er**	god
	Jesus (Christus)	Jesus (Christ)
der	**Philosoph, -en**	philosopher

	Allah	Allah
der	**Altar, ¨e**	altar
der	**Apostel, –**	apostle, disciple
der	**Bischof, ¨e**	bishop
der	**Buddha**	Buddha
der	**Buddhismus**	Buddhism
der	**Buddhist, -en**	Buddhist
der	**Christ, -en**	Christian
der	**Geist** ◇	ghost; spirit
der	**Gläubige*, -n**	believer; (*pl*) the faithful
der	**Gottesdienst, -e** ⌑	service
der	**Heide, -n** ◇	pagan, heathen
der	**Himmel** ◇	heaven
der	**Hindu, -s**	Hindu
der	**Hinduismus**	Hinduism
der	**Islam**	Islam
der	**Jesuit, -en**	Jesuit
der	**Judaismus**	Judaism
der	**Jude, -n**	Jew
der	**Katholik, -en**	(Roman) Catholic
der	**Katholizismus**	(Roman) Catholicism
der	**Methodist, -en**	Methodist
der	**Mönch, -e**	monk
der	**Moslem, -s**	Muslim, Moslem
der	**Papst, ¨e** ⌑	pope
der	**Protestant, -en**	Protestant
der	**Teufel**	devil
der	**Zionismus**	Zionism

RELIGION

USEFUL WORDS (m)	

der **Abt**, ̈-e	abbot
der **Ajatollah**, -s	ayatollah
der **Anglikaner**, –	Anglican
der **Ästhet**, -en	aesthete
der **Beichtstuhl**, ̈-e	confessional
der **Beichtvater**, ̈-	father confessor
der **Besessene***, -n	person possessed
der **Denker**, –	thinker
der **Engel**, –	angel
der **Erzbischof**, ̈-e	archbishop
der **Erzengel**, –	archangel
der **Freimaurer**, –	freemason
der **Fundamentalismus**	fundamentalism
der **Fundamentalist**, -en	fundamentalist
der **Garten Eden**	Garden of Eden
der **Heilige Geist**	Holy Spirit
der **Heiligenschein**, -e	halo
der **Hellseher**, –	clairvoyant
der **Hexer**, –	sorcerer
der **Jünger**, –	disciple
der **Kirchenchor**, ̈-e	church choir
der **Kleriker**, –	cleric
der **Klerus**	clergy
der **Kommunikant**, -en	communicant
der **Konfirmand**, -en	candidate for confirmation
der **Konformist**, -en	conformist
der **Pastor**, -en	parish priest; vicar; minister
der **Pfarrer**, –	minister, clergyman
der **Pilger**, –	pilgrim
der **Prediger**, –	preacher
der **Priester**, –	priest
der **Psalm**, -en	psalm
der **Rabbiner**, –	rabbi
der **Ritus**, (-ten)	rite
der **Rosenkranz**, ̈-e	rosary
der **Tempel**, –	temple
der **Utopist**, -en	Utopian
der **Vikar**, -e	curate
die **Zeugen Jehovas** (*pl*)	Jehovah's Witnesses

ESSENTIAL WORDS (f)

die	**Agnostikerin**	agnostic
die	**Anhängerin**	follower
die	**Atheistin**	atheist
die	**Bibel, -n**	Bible
die	**Geistliche*, -n** ▢	priestess; minister
die	**Göttin**	goddess
die	**Heidin**	pagan, heathen
die	**Kirche, -n**	church
die	**Philosophie, -n**	philosophy
die	**Philosophin**	philosopher

IMPORTANT WORDS (f)

die	**Auferstehung**	resurrection
die	**Beichte, -n** ▢	confession
die	**Buddhistin**	Buddhist
die	**Christin**	Christian
die	**Gemeinde, -n**	parish; congregation
die	**Gläubige*, -n**	believer
die	**Heilige Schrift**	Holy Scriptures
die	**Hölle**	hell
die	**Jüdin**	Jew, Jewess
die	**Katholikin**	(Roman) Catholic
die	**Kreuzigung**	crucifixion
die	**Messe, -n** ◇	mass
die	**Methodistin**	Methodist
die	**Moschee, -n**	mosque
die	**Nonne, -n**	nun
die	**Predigt, -en**	sermon
die	**Protestantin**	Protestant
die	**Sekte, -n**	sect
die	**Sünde, -n** ▢	sin
die	**Synagoge, -n**	synagogue

den Rosenkranz beten to say the rosary
Geistlicher werden to join the clergy
das Wort Gottes the Word of God
beten to pray
(gegen Gott) sündigen to sin (against God)

USEFUL WORDS (f)

die **Äbtissin**	abbess
die **Anglikanerin**	Anglican
die **Ästhetin**	aesthete
die **Aufklärung**	Age of Enlightenment
die **Basilika, (-ken)**	basilica
die **Besessene*, -n**	person possessed
die **Erlösung**	redemption
die **Fastenzeit**	fast (*period*)
die **Freimaurerei**	freemasonry
die **Fundamentalistin**	fundamentalist
die **Glaubensfreiheit**	freedom of worship
die **Heilige Jungfrau**	Blessed Virgin
die **Hellseherei**	clairvoyance
die **Hellseherin**	clairvoyant
die **Hexe, -n**	witch
die **Hexerei**	witchcraft
die **Hostie, -n**	host
die **Indoktrination**	indoctrination
die **Kapelle, -n** ⟡	chapel
die **Kerze, -n**	candle
die **Kollekte, -n**	collection
die **Kommunikantin**	communicant
die **Kommunion**	(Holy) Communion
die **Konfession, -en**	denomination
die **Konfessionsschule, -n**	denominational school
die **Konfirmandin**	candidate for confirmation
die **Konfirmation**	confirmation
die **Madonna**	Madonna
die **Pastorin**	parish priest; vicar; minister
die **Pfarrei, -en**	parish
die **Pfarrerin**	minister, clergywoman
die **Pilgerin**	pilgrim
die **Priesterin**	priestess
die **Reformation**	Reformation
die **Theologie**	theology
die **Todsünde, -n**	deadly sin
die **Utopistin**	Utopian
die **Wallfahrt, -en**	pilgrimage
die **Wiedergeburt**	rebirth; reincarnation

IMPORTANT WORDS (nt)

das	**Alte Testament**	Old Testament
das	**Christentum**	Christianity
das	**Evangelium, (-ien)**	gospel
das	**Kloster, ¨**	monastery; convent
das	**Kreuz, -e** ◇	cross
das	**Kruzifix, -e**	crucifix
das	**Neue Testament**	New Testament
das	**Wunder, –** ▱	miracle

USEFUL WORDS (nt)

die	**Almosen** (*pl*)	alms
das	**Beichtgeheimnis**	seal of the confessional
das	**Bistum, ¨er**	bishopric
das	**Episkopat**	episcopate
das	**Fegefeuer**	purgatory
das	**Gemeindemitglied, -er**	parishioner
das	**Horoskop, -e**	horoscope
das	**Kirchenlied, -er**	hymn
das	**Omen**	omen
das	**Paradies**	paradise
das	**Räucherfaß, ¨sser**	censer, thurible
das	**Ritual, -e**	ritual
das	**Tabu, -s**	taboo
das	**Taufbecken, –**	font
das	**Weihwasser**	holy water

Herr Pfarrer *Vicar* (address)
jdm die Karten lesen *to read sb's cards*
jdn verzaubern *to cast a spell over sb*
den Zauber lösen *to break the spell*
sich reinwaschen *to redeem o.s.*
die (römisch-)katholische Kirche *the (Roman) Catholic Church*
die anglikanische Kirche *the Church of England, the Anglican Church*
katholisch *Catholic*
protestantisch *Protestant*
evangelisch *Protestant*
anglikanisch *Anglican*

ESSENTIAL WORDS (m)

der	**Abstand**, ¨e 🕮	distance
der	**Autofahrer**, –	motorist, driver
der	**Blinker**, –	indicator
der	**Chauffeur**, -e	chauffeur
der	**Dachgepäckträger**, –	roof rack
der	**Fahrer**, –	motorist, driver
der	**Fahrlehrer**, –	driving instructor
der	**Fahrschüler**, –	learner driver
der	**Firmenwagen**, –	company car
der	**Führerschein**, -e	driving licence
der	**Fußgänger**, – 🕮	pedestrian
der	**Gang**, ¨e ◊ 🕮	gear
der	**Kilometer**, –	kilometre
der	**Koffer**, –	case, suitcase
der	**Kofferraum**, ¨e	boot
der	**Lastkraftwagen**, – 🕮	lorry, truck
der	**Lastwagenfahrer**, –	lorry driver
der	**Liter**, –	litre
der	**LKW**, -s 🕮	lorry, truck
der	**Parkplatz**, ¨e	parking space; car park
der	**Parkschein**, -e	parking permit
der	**Passagier**, -e	passenger
der	**Personenkraftwagen**, –	private car
der	**PKW**, -s 🕮	private car
der	**Polizist**, -en	policeman
der	**Reifen**, –	tyre
der	**Scheinwerfer**, –	headlight
der	**Sicherheitsgurt**, -e 🕮	seat belt
der	**Stau**, -e 🕮	(traffic) jam
der	**Tod**, -e	death
der	**Tramper**, –	hitch-hiker
der	**Umweg**, -e	detour
der	**Unfall**, ¨e	accident
der	**Verkehr**	traffic
der	**Verkehrspolizist**, -en	traffic warden
der	**Verkehrsunfall**, ¨e	road accident
der	**Verletzte***, -n	casualty
der	**Weg**, -e ◊	road; way
der	**Wohnwagen**, –	caravan
der	**Zusammenstoß**, ¨e	collision, crash

ROAD

IMPORTANT WORDS (m)

der	**Abschleppwagen,** –	breakdown van
der	**Anhänger,** –◇	trailer
der	**Anlasser,** –	starter
der	**Ersatzreifen,** –	spare tyre
der	**Fußgängerüberweg,** -e	pedestrian crossing
der	**Kreisverkehr,** -e ▭	roundabout
der	**Leerlauf**	neutral (*gear*)
der	**Mechaniker,** –	mechanic; engineer
der	**Mittelstreifen,** –	central reservation
der	**Motorschaden,** ¨	engine trouble
der	**Rasthof,** ¨e ▭	service station
der	**Rastplatz,** ¨e ▭	lay-by
der	**Reifendruck**	tyre pressure
der	**Rückspiegel,** –	rear-view *or* driving mirror
der	**Scheibenwischer,** –	windscreen wiper
der	**Sportwagen,** –◇	sports car
der	**Strafzettel,** –	(parking) ticket
der	**Tachometer,** – ▭	speedometer
der	**Verkehrsrowdy,** -s	road hog
der	**Wagenheber,** –	jack

USEFUL WORDS (m)

der	**Auspufftopf,** ¨e	silencer
der	**Autoknacker,** –	car burglar
der	**Benzinkanister,** –	petrol can
der	**Brennstoff,** -e	(*motor*) fuel
der	**Bürgersteig,** -e	pavement
der	**Choke,** -s	choke
der	**Defroster,** –	de-icer
der	**Diesel,** –	diesel
der	**Gebrauchtwagen,** –	used car
der	**Geisterfahrer,** –	person driving in the wrong direction
der	**Hubraum**	cubic capacity
der	**Kaltstart,** -s	cold start
der	**Katalysator,** -en	catalytic converter
der	**Keilriemen,** –	fanbelt
der	**Kilometerstein,** -e	milestone

USEFUL WORDS (m) (cont)

der	**Kindersitz, -e**	child seat
der	**Kotflügel, –**	wing
der	**Kraftfahrzeugbrief, -e**	registration document, logbook
der	**Kraftfahrzeugschein, -e**	registration document
der	**Kühler, –**	radiator
der	**Motor, -en**	engine
der	**Ölmeßstab, ˶e**	dipstick
der	**Pannendienst, -e**	breakdown service
der	**Promillemesser, –**	Breathalyser ®
der	**Radkranz, ˶e**	(wheel) rim
der	**Rückstau, -s**	tailback
der	**Rückwärtsgang**	reverse gear
der	**Schadenfreiheitsrabatt**	no-claims bonus
der	**Schaltknüppel, –**	gear stick
der	**Seitenstreifen, –**	verge; hard shoulder
der	**Sonntagsfahrer, –**	Sunday driver
der	**Stoßdämpfer, –**	shock absorber
der	**Tank, -s**	tank
der	**Unfallwagen, –**	car involved in an accident
der	**Vergaser, –**	carburettor
der	**Zigarettenanzünder, –**	cigar lighter
der	**Zusammenprall, -e**	minor collision

prüfen *to check*
in ein Auto fahren *to bump into a car*
sperren *to block*
das Auto reparieren lassen *to have the car repaired*
100 Kilometer pro Stunde machen *to do 100 kilometres an hour*
schnell *fast*
langsam *slowly*
kaputt *broken*
gefährlich *dangerous*
ankommen *to arrive*
trampen, per Anhalter fahren *to hitch-hike*
"Anlieger frei" *"residents only"*
"Parken verboten" *"no parking"*
beschleunigen, Gas geben *to accelerate*
eine rote Ampel überfahren *to go through a red light*

ESSENTIAL WORDS (f)

die	**Ampel, -n**	traffic lights
die	**Ausfahrt, -en**	exit; drive; slip road
die	**Autobahn, -en**	motorway
die	**Autofahrerin**	motorist, driver
die	**Autoschlange, -n** 🕮	line of cars
die	**Autowäsche, -n** 🕮	car wash
die	**Bahn, -en** ✧	road, way; lane
die	**Batterie, -n**	battery
die	**Bremse, -n** ✧	brake
die	**Ecke, -n**	corner
die	**Einbahnstraße, -n** 🕮	one-way street
die	**Fahrerin**	motorist, driver
die	**Fahrlehrerin**	driving instructress
die	**Fahrprüfung, -en**	driving test
die	**Fahrschule, -n**	driving school
die	**Fahrschülerin**	learner driver
die	**Fahrstunde, -n**	driving lesson
die	**Fahrt, -en** ✧	journey; trip; drive
die	**Garage, -n**	garage
die	**Gebühr, -en** ✧	toll
die	**Gefahr, -en**	danger, risk
die	**Geldstrafe, -n** 🕮	fine
die	**Geschwindigkeit, -en**	speed
die	**Grenze, -n**	border, frontier
die	**grüne Karte**	green card
die	**Hauptstraße, -n**	main road; main street
die	**Hauptverkehrszeit**	rush hour
die	**Kreuzung, -en**	crossroads
die	**Kurve, -n**	bend, corner
die	**Landkarte, -n**	map
die	**Maschine, -n** ✧ 🕮	engine
die	**Notbremsung, -en**	emergency stop
die	**Panne, -n**	breakdown
die	**Parkuhr, -en**	parking meter
die	**Polizei**	police
die	**Polizistin**	policewoman
die	**Querstraße, -n**	intersection
die	**Raststätte, -n**	service area
die	**Reifenpanne, -n**	puncture
die	**Reise, -n**	journey

ESSENTIAL WORDS (f) (cont)

die	**Reiseroute, -n**	route, itinerary
die	**Reparatur, -en**	repair; repairing
die	**Reparaturwerkstatt, ¨en**	garage, workshop
die	**Richtung, -en**	direction
die	**Ringstraße, -n**	ring road
die	**SB-Tankstelle, -n**	self-service petrol station
die	**Selbstbedienung** ▯	self-service
die	**Straße, -n** ◇	road, street
die	**Straßenkarte, -n**	road map
die	**Straßenverkehrsordnung**	Highway Code
die	**Tankstelle, -n**	petrol station, garage
die	**Tiefgarage, -n** ▯	underground garage
die	**Umleitung, -en**	diversion
die	**Verkehrsampel, -n**	traffic lights
die	**Verkehrspolizistin**	(female) traffic warden
die	**Verkehrsstauung, -en** ▯	traffic jam
die	**Verletzte*, -n**	casualty
die	**Versicherung** ▯	insurance
die	**Vorfahrt** ▯	right of way
die	**Vorsicht**	caution, care
die	**Warnung, -en** ▯	warning
die	**Werkstatt, ¨en**	garage, workshop
die	**Windschutzscheibe, -n**	windscreen

IMPORTANT WORDS (f)

die	**Abzweigung, -en**	junction
die	**Auffahrt, -en**	slip road
die	**Beleuchtung**	lights, lighting
die	**Biegung, -en**	bend, curve
die	**Gasse, -n** ▯	lane (*in town*), alley
die	**Geschwindigkeits-**	
	begrenzung	speed limit
die	**Hupe, -n**	horn
die	**Kupplung, -en**	clutch
die	**Marke, -n** ◇	make (*of car*)
die	**Motorhaube, -n**	bonnet
die	**Politesse, -n** ▯	(female) traffic warden
die	**Stoßstange, -n**	bumper
die	**Versicherungspolice, -n**	insurance policy

USEFUL WORDS (f)

die **Antenne**, -n	aerial
die **Autobahnraststätte**, -n	motorway services
die **Autokolonne**, -n	line of cars
die **Autovermietung**, -en	car hire
die **Beschilderung**	signposting
die **Diebstahlssicherung**, -en	anti-theft device
die **Fußgängerin**	pedestrian
die **Gabelung**, -en	fork (*in road*)
die **Geschwindigkeits-überschreitung**	speeding
die **grüne Welle**	phased traffic lights
die **Handbremse**, -n	handbrake
die **Hängebrücke**, -n	suspension bridge
die **Heizung**	heating
die **Karambolage**, -n	collision, crash
die **Kindersicherung**, -en	childproof safety catch
die **Kopfstütze**, -n	headrest
die **Landstraße**, -n	country road; B road
die **Leitplanke**, -n	crash barrier
die **Limousine**, -n	saloon
die **Nebelschlußleuchte**, -n	rear fog light
die **Nebenstraße**, -n	side street; minor road
die **Notrufsäule**, -n	emergency telephone
die **Parkkralle**, -n	wheel clamp
die **Radkappe**, -n	hub cap
die **Scheibenwaschanlage**, -n	windscreen washer
die **Sonntagsfahrerin**	Sunday driver
die **Steuerplakette**, -n	(road) tax disc
die **Straßenlage**	roadholding
die **Überführung**, -en	flyover
die **Umgehungstraße**, -n	ring road; bypass
die **Unfallstelle**, -n	scene of the/an accident
die **Verkehrssicherheit**	road safety
die **Zapfsäule**, -n	petrol pump
die **Zündkerze**, -n	spark(ing) plug
die **Zündung**	ignition

unter Alkoholeinfluß *under the influence of alcohol*
ins Röhrchen blasen *to be breathalysed*

ESSENTIAL WORDS (nt)

das	**Auto,** -s	car
das	**Autobahndreieck,** -e ▭	motorway junction
das	**Autobahnkreuz,** -e ▭	motorway intersection
das	**Benzin**	petrol
das	**Dieselöl**	diesel (oil)
das	**Fahrzeug,** -e ▭	vehicle
das	**Gepäck**	luggage
das	**Mietauto,** -s	hired car
das	**Normalbenzin**	2-star (petrol)
das	**Öl**	oil.
das	**Parken**	parking
das	**Parkhaus,** ¨er	multi-storey car park
das	**Parkverbot,** -e	parking ban
das	**Rad,** ¨er ◇	wheel
das	**Reserverad,** ¨er	spare wheel
das	**Straßenschild,** -er	road sign
das	**Super**	4-star (petrol)
das	**Trampen**	hitch-hiking
das	**Wasser**	water
das	**Wohngebiet,** -e ▭	built-up area

IMPORTANT WORDS (nt)

das	**Armaturenbrett,** -er ◇	dashboard
das	**Ersatzteil,** -e	spare part
das	**Getriebe,** –	gearbox
das	**Kat-Auto,** -s	car with a catalytic converter
das	**Lenkrad,** ¨er	steering wheel
das	**Nummernschild,** -er	number plate
das	**polizeiliche Kennzeichen,** -n –	registration number
das	**Steuerrad,** ¨er	steering wheel
das	**Todesopfer,** –	fatality
das	**Verdeck,** -e	hood
das	**Verkehrsdelikt,** -e	traffic offence
das	**Warndreieck,** -e	warning triangle

Ihre Papiere, bitte *your identification/documentation please*

USEFUL WORDS (nt)

das	**Auspuffrohr, -e**	exhaust pipe
das	**Automatikmodell, -e**	automatic
das	**Autoradio, -s**	car radio
das	**Autotelefon, -e**	car phone
das	**Fahrrad, ¨er**	bicycle
das	**Frostschutzmittel, –**	antifreeze
das	**Hecktürmodell, -e**	hatchback (*car*)
das	**Hinterrad, ¨er**	rear wheel
das	**Mofa, -s**	small moped
das	**Moped, -s**	moped
das	**Motorrad, ¨er**	motorbike, motorcycle
das	**Schiebedach, ¨er**	sunroof
das	**Standlicht, -er**	sidelight
das	**Starthilfekabel, –**	jump leads
das	**Verkehrszeichen, –**	road sign
das	**Vorderrad, ¨er**	front wheel

sich verfahren to get lost, take the wrong road
(voll)tanken to fill up (with petrol)
sich anschnallen to put on one's seat belt
aussteigen to get out
einsteigen to get in
parken to park
abbiegen to turn off
halten to stop
sich einordnen to get into lane
abstellen to park; to switch off
bremsen to brake
schalten to change gear
überholen to overtake
hupen to sound or toot the horn
die Lichthupe betätigen to flash one's headlights
einen Platten haben to have a flat (týre)
zurücksetzen to reverse
abschleppen to tow
den Motor abstellen to switch off the engine
eine Panne haben to break down, have a breakdown

SCHOOL AND OFFICE EQUIPMENT

der **Aktenschrank**, ¨e	filing cabinet
die **Büroartikel** (*pl*)	office supplies
der **Computer**, –	computer
der **Fotokopierer**, –	photocopier
der **Kopierer**, –	(photo)copier
der **Notizblock**, ¨e	notepad
der **Ordner**, – ▭	folder
der **Rechner**, – ▭	calculator; computer
der **Schreibtisch**, -e	desk (*office*)

IMPORTANT WORDS (m)

der **Bleistift**, -e	pencil
der **Bleistiftspitzer**, –	pencil sharpener
der **Briefumschlag**, ¨e	envelope
der **Drucker**, – ◇	printer
der **Filzstift**, -e	felt-tip (pen)
der **Füller**, –	fountain pen
der **Hefter**, –	stapler
der **Kalender**, –	calendar
der **Kugelschreiber**, – ▭	ballpoint (pen), Biro ®
der **Locher**, –	punch
der **Markierstift**, -e	marker pen
der **Monitor**, -e	monitor
der **Radiergummi**, -s	rubber
der **Schwamm**, ¨e	sponge
der **Taschenrechner**, –	pocket calculator
der **Terminkalender**, –	(appointments) diary
der **Umschlag**, ¨e ◇	envelope
der **Videorekorder**, –	video recorder

USEFUL WORDS (m)

der **Briefbeschwerer**, –	paperweight
der **Globus**, -se	globe
der **Tintenradiergummi**, -s	ink eraser
der **Zirkel**, –	pair of compasses

SCHOOL

ESSENTIAL WORDS (f)

die **Akte**, -n ▭	file
die **Schreibmaschine**, -n ▭	typewriter
die **Tafel**, -n ◇	blackboard

IMPORTANT WORDS (f)

die **Aktentasche**, -n ▭	briefcase
die **Büroklammer**, -n	paper clip
die **Diskette**, -n	floppy disk
die **Heftklammer**, -n	staple
die **Kartei**, -en	card index
die **Karteikarte**, -n	index card
die **Kreide**	chalk
die **Maus**, ¨e	mouse
die **Schultasche**, -n	school bag, satchel
die **Tastatur**, -en	keyboard
die **Tinte**	ink

USEFUL WORDS (f)

die **Kladde**, -n	rough book
die **Landkarte**, -n	map
die **Lupe**, -n	magnifying glass

verstellbar *adjustable*
selbstklebend *self-adhesive*
etw an die Tafel schreiben *to write sth on the blackboard*
einen Brief tippen *to type a letter*

das **Buch**, ⸚er	book
das **Heft**, -e	exercise book, jotter
das **Lineal**, -e	ruler
das **Notizbuch**, ⸚er	notebook
das **Papier**, -e	paper

das **Lexikon**, (-ka)	encyclopaedia; dictionary
das **Schreibmaschinenpapier**	typing paper
das **Schulheft**, -e	exercise book
das **Wörterbuch**, ⸚er ▭	dictionary

das **Adreßbuch**, ⸚er	address book
das **Briefpapier (mit Briefkopf)**	(headed) writing paper
das **Durchschlagpapier**	copy paper; carbon paper
das **Fach**, ⸚er ⋄	pigeonhole
das **Federmäppchen**, –	pencil case
das **Klassenbuch**, ⸚er	class register
das **Lesezeichen**, –	bookmark
das **Löschpapier**	blotting paper
das **Mikroskop**, -e	microscope
das **Pauspapier**	tracing paper
das **Pult**, -e	desk (*school*)
das **Rechenpapier**	squared paper
das **Schmierheft**, -e	rough notebook
das **Schmierpapier**	rough paper
das **Textverarbeitungssystem**, -e	word processor
das **Tipp-Ex** ®	Tipp-Ex ®
das **Zeichendreieck**, -e	set square

der	**Anker**, –	anchor
der	**Ausflug**, ⁻e	trip, outing
der	**Badeanzug**, ⁻e	swimming *or* bathing costume
der	**Badende***, -n	bather, swimmer
der	**Bikini**, -s	bikini
der	**Dampfer**, –	steamer
der	**Fahrgast**, ⁻e ▭	passenger
der	**Fisch**, -e	fish
der	**Fischer**, –	fisherman
der	**Hafen**, ⁻	port, harbour
der	**Horizont**	horizon
der	**Meeresboden**	bottom of the sea
der	**Ozean**, -e	ocean
der	**Passagier**, -e	passenger
der	**Rettungsring**, -e	lifebelt
der	**Rettungsschwimmer**, –	lifeguard
der	**Sand**	sand
der	**Schwimmer**, –	swimmer
der	**Seehafen**, ⁻	seaport
der	**Seemann**, (-leute)	sailor, seaman
der	**Segler**, –	sailor, yachtsman
der	**Sonnenschein**	sunshine
der	**Spaziergang**, ⁻e	walk
der	**Stein**, -e ◇	stone; rock
der	**Strand**, ⁻e	shore; beach
der	**Urlauber**, –	holiday-maker

der	**Jachthafen**, ⁻	marina
der	**Kahn**, ⁻e	(small) boat
der	**Kai**, -s	quay, quayside
der	**Kieselstein**, -e	pebble
der	**Krebs**, -e ◇	crab
der	**Leuchtturm**, ⁻e	lighthouse
der	**Liegestuhl**, ⁻e	deck chair
der	**Pier**	pier
der	**Schiffbruch**, ⁻e	shipwreck
der	**Seetang**	seaweed
der	**Sonnenstich**	sunstroke

SEASIDE

AT THE SEASIDE — 2

USEFUL WORDS (m)	

der **Anlegeplatz**, ¨e	mooring
der **Ball**, ¨e ◊	ball
der **Eimer**, –	bucket, pail
der **Ertrinkende***, -n	drowning man
der **Mast**, -en	mast
der **Matrose**, -n	sailor
der **Prospekt**, -e	leaflet, brochure
der **Sandstrand**, ¨e	sandy beach
der **Schatten**	shade
der **Schaum**	foam
der **Schornstein**, -e ◊	funnel
der **Seeigel**, –	sea urchin
der **Sonnenschirm**, -e	parasol, sunshade
der **Spaten**, –	spade
der **Strandkorb**, ¨e	wicker beach chair
der **Strandräuber**, –	beachcomber

USEFUL WORDS (f)	

die **Düne**, -n	dune
die **Ertrinkende***, -n	drowning woman
die **Flutwelle**, -n	tidal wave
die **Gezeiten** (*pl*)	tides
die **Gischt**	sea spray
die **Hängematte**, -n	hammock
die **Koralle**, -n	coral
die **Küstenwacht**	coastguards
die **Lagune**, -n	lagoon
die **Qualle**, -n	jellyfish
die **Strandpromenade**, -n	promenade
die **Woge**, -n	wave

an Bord gehen *to go on board*
eine Bootsfahrt machen *to go on a boat trip*
einen Sonnenstich bekommen *to get sunstroke*
braun werden *to get a tan*
untergehen *to go under*
seekrank werden *to get seasick*

ESSENTIAL WORDS (f)

die	**Ansichtskarte, -n**	(picture) postcard
die	**Badehose, -n**	swimming _or_ bathing trunks
die	**Badende*, -n**	bather, swimmer
die	**Fähre, -n** ▢	ferry (boat)
die	**Flagge, -n**	flag
die	**Hafenstadt, ¨e**	port
die	**Insel, -n**	island
die	**Küste, -n**	coast; shore; seaside
die	**Luftmatratze, -n**	Lilo ®, air bed
die	**Mannschaft, -en** ◇	crew
die	**Schwimmerin**	swimmer
die	**See, -n** ◇	sea
die	**Seekrankheit**	seasickness
die	**Seeluft**	sea air
die	**Seglerin**	sailor, yachtswoman
die	**Sonne**	sun
die	**Sonnenbrille, -n**	(pair of) sunglasses
die	**Sonnencreme, -s**	sun(tan) cream
die	**Überfahrt, -en**	crossing
die	**Urlauberin**	holiday-maker
die	**Vergnügungsfahrt, -en**	pleasure cruise

IMPORTANT WORDS (f)

die	**Boje, -n**	buoy
die	**Bucht, -en**	bay
die	**Ebbe** ▢	low tide
die	**Flut** ◇ ▢	high tide
die	**Jacht, -en**	yacht
die	**Klippe, -n**	cliff
die	**Kreuzfahrt, -en**	cruise
die	**Last, -en**	load, cargo
die	**Möwe, -n** ▢	seagull
die	**Mündung, -en**	mouth (_of river_), estuary
die	**Muschel(schale), -n (-n)**	shell
die	**Sandburg, -en**	sandcastle
die	**Schwimmweste, -n**	life jacket
die	**Sonnenbräune**	suntan
die	**Strömung, -en**	current
die	**Welle, -n**	wave

das **Bad**, ⁻er ◇	bathe (*in sea*), swim
das **Badetuch**, ⁻er	(bath) towel
das **Boot**, -e	boat
das **Fischerboot**, -e	fishing boat
das **Meer**, -e	sea, ocean
das **Picknick**, -s	picnic
das **Reisebüro**, -s	travel agent's
das **Ruder**, –	oar; rudder
das **Schiff**, -e	ship, vessel
das **Schwimmen**	swimming
das **Segel**, –	sail
das **Segeln**	sailing
das **Teleskop**, -e	telescope
das **Ufer** ◇ ▭	shore
das **Wasser**	water

das **Deck**, -s	deck (*of ship*)
das **Fahrgeld**, -er	fare
das **Floß**, ⁻e	raft
das **Steuer**, – ◇	helm, tiller
das **Tretboot**, -e	pedal boat, pedalo

das **Gummiboot**, -e	inflatable (boat)
das **Rennboot**, -e	speedboat
das **Ruderboot**, -e	rowing boat
das **Seebad**, ⁻er	seaside resort
das **Segelboot**, -e	sailing boat
das **Strandgut**	flotsam and jetsam

stürmisch *stormy*
bewegt *choppy*
ans Meer or **an die See fahren** *to go to the seaside*
es ist Flut/Ebbe *the tide is in/out*
sich sonnen *to sunbathe*

ESSENTIAL WORDS (m)

der **Apotheker, –**	(dispensing) chemist, pharmacist
der **Artikel, –**	article
der **Aufzug, ¨e** 📖	lift
der **Ausverkauf, ¨e**	(clearance) sale
der **Bäcker, –**	baker
der **Buchhändler, –**	bookseller
der **Drogist, -en**	retail chemist
der **Einkauf, ¨e**	shopping; purchase
der **Einkaufskorb, ¨e**	shopping basket
der **Einkaufswagen, –**	shopping trolley
der **Fahrstuhl, ¨e**	lift
der **Fischhändler, –**	fishmonger
der **Fleischer, –**	butcher
der **Friseur, -e**	hairdresser
der **Geschäftsmann, (-leute)**	businessman
der **Groschen, –**	10-pfennig piece
der **Händler, –**	dealer
der **Herrenfriseur, -e**	barber, men's hairdresser
der **Juwelier, -e**	jeweller
der **Kassenzettel, –**	receipt
der **Kaufmann, (-leute)** ⇨ 📖	merchant
der **Kiosk, -e**	kiosk
der **Kunde, -n** 📖	customer, client
der **Laden, ¨**	shop
der **Lift, -e**	lift
der **Markt, ¨e**	market
der **Metzger, –**	butcher
der **Obsthändler, –**	fruiterer
der **Obst- und Gemüsehändler, –**	greengrocer
der **Pfennig, -e**	pfennig
der **Preis, -e** ⇨	price
der **Ruhetag, -e**	(early) closing day
der **Schallplattenhändler, –**	record dealer
der **Schalter, –** ⇨	counter (*post office, bank etc*)
der **Scheck, -s**	cheque
der **Schein, -e** ⇨	(bank)note
der **Schilling, –**	schilling
der **Schlußverkauf, ¨e**	(end-of-season) sale

ESSENTIAL WORDS (m) (cont)

der **Schuhmacher**, –	shoemaker; shoe repairer
der **Sommerschlußverkauf** ▭	summer sale
der **Sonderpreis**, -e ▭	special price
der **Stock**, – ◇	floor
der **Supermarkt**, ⁻e	supermarket
der **Tabakladen**, ⁻	tobacconist's (shop)
der **Umtausch**	exchange (*of goods*)
der **Verkauf**, ⁻e	sale
der **Verkäufer**, –	salesman, shop assistant
der **Winterschlußverkauf**	winter sale
der **Zeitungshändler**, –	newsagent

IMPORTANT WORDS (m)

der **Buchmacher**, –	bookmaker, 'bookie'
der **Eisenwarenhändler**, –	ironmonger
der **Gelegenheitskauf**, ⁻e	bargain
der **Grundstücksmakler**, –	estate agent
der **Gutschein**, -e	voucher
der **Handel** ◇ ▭	trade, business
der **Ladentisch**, -e	counter (*in shop*)
der **Lebensmittelhändler**, –	grocer
der **Optiker**, –	optician
der **Schuster**, –	cobbler, shoe repairer
der **Uhrmacher**, –	watchmaker
der **Waschsalon**, -s	launderette

einen Schaufensterbummel machen to go window-shopping
einen Scheck ausstellen to write out a cheque
bar bezahlen to pay cash
ich habe 15 Mark dafür bezahlt I paid 15 marks for it
Geld für Pralinen ausgeben to spend money on chocolates
zu teuer too dear
wählen to choose
wiegen to weigh
was macht das? what does that come to?
was kostet es? what does it cost?
das gefällt mir I like that

USEFUL WORDS (m)

der	**Automat, -en**	vending machine
der	**Bioladen, -̈**	health food shop
der	**Dienstleistungsabend, -e**	late-closing night
der	**Duty-free-Shop, -s**	duty-free shop
der	**Einkaufsbummel, –**	shopping spree
der	**Einzelhändler, –**	retailer
der	**Fischladen, -̈**	fishmonger's
der	**Flohmarkt, -̈e**	flea market
der	**Gebrauchtwarenhändler, –**	second-hand dealer
der	**Goldschmied, -e**	goldsmith
der	**Großhändler, –**	wholesaler
der	**Großmarkt, -̈e**	hypermarket
der	**Kauf, -̈e**	purchase
der	**Käufer, –**	purchaser
der	**Kettenladen, -̈**	chain store
der	**Kundendienst**	after-sales service
der	**Kürschner, –**	furrier
der	**Ladendieb, -e**	shoplifter
der	**Lagerraum, -̈e**	storeroom
der	**Preisnachlaß, -̈sse**	discount
der	**Rabatt, -e**	reduction, discount
der	**Räumungsverkauf, -̈e**	clearance sale
der	**Schnellimbiß, -sse**	fast-food outlet; snack bar
der	**Stand, -̈e**	stall
der	**Straßenhändler, –**	street trader
der	**Verbrauchermarkt, -̈e**	hypermarket, superstore
der	**Wochenmarkt, -̈e**	weekly market

das ist aber günstig! *what a bargain!*
das habe ich günstig bekommen *I got it at a good price*
ganz billig *quite cheap*
kostenlos *free, free of charge*
umsonst *for nothing*
ein preiswertes Angebot *a bargain*
preiswert *good value*
jdn bedienen *to serve sb*

ESSENTIAL WORDS (f)

die	**Abteilung, -en**	department
die	**Anprobe** ▱	trying on
die	**Apotheke, -n**	chemist's, pharmacy
die	**Auswahl (an** +dat**)** ◇	choice (of)
die	**Bäckerei, -en**	bakery, baker's (shop)
die	**Bank, -en** ◇	bank
die	**Betriebsferien** (pl)	holidays (of a business)
die	**Bibliothek, -en**	library
die	**Brieftasche, -n**	wallet
die	**Buchhandlung, -en**	bookshop, bookseller's
die	**Drogerie, -n**	(retail) chemist's
die	**Etage, -n**	floor
die	**Farbe, -n** ◇	colour
die	**Firma, (-men)**	firm, company
die	**Fleischerei, -en**	butcher's (shop)
die	**Friseuse, -n**	hairdresser
die	**Gaststätte, -n**	restaurant; pub
die	**Geschäftszeit, -en**	business hours
die	**Gesellschaft, -en** ◇	company; society
die	**Größe, -n** ◇	size
die	**Handlung, -en** ◇	shop
die	**Kasse, -n** ◇	till; cash desk; checkout
die	**Kneipe, -n**	pub
die	**Konditorei, -en**	cake shop
die	**Kundin** ▱	customer, client
die	**Liste, -n**	list
die	**Mark, –**	mark (money)
die	**Metzgerei, -en**	butcher's (shop)
die	**Öffnungszeiten** (pl)	opening hours
die	**Packung, -en**	packet, box
die	**Parfümerie, -n**	perfume counter; perfume shop
die	**Post, -en** ◇	post office
die	**Quittung, -en**	receipt
die	**Rechnung, -en** ◇	bill
die	**Schachtel, -n**	box; packet (of cigarettes)
die	**Schaufensterpuppe, -n**	dummy, model
die	**Schlange, -n** ◇ ▱	queue
die	**Schreibwarenhandlung, -en**	stationer's
die	**Schuhgröße, -n**	shoe size

ESSENTIAL WORDS (f) (cont)

die	**Selbstbedienung** ⌑	self-service
die	**Sparkasse, -n**	savings bank
die	**Theke, -n**	counter (*in café, bar etc*)
die	**Tierhandlung, -en**	pet shop
die	**Tüte, -n**	bag
die	**Verkäuferin**	salesgirl, shop assistant
die	**Waren** (*pl*)	goods, wares

IMPORTANT WORDS (f)

die	**Bausparkasse, -n**	building society
die	**Besorgung, -en**	errand; purchase
die	**Bücherei, -en**	library
die	**Bude, -n**	stall
die	**Eisenwarenhandlung, -en**	ironmonger's, hardware shop
die	**Filiale, -n**	branch
die	**Garantie, -n**	guarantee; warranty
die	**Kragenweite, -n**	collar size
die	**Reinigung, -en**	cleaner's
die	**Rolltreppe, -n**	escalator
die	**Versicherungs- gesellschaft, -en**	insurance company
die	**Videothek, -en**	video shop
die	**Wäscherei, -en**	laundry

kann ich Ihnen behilflich sein? can I help you?
verkaufen to sell
was darf es sein, bitte? what would you like?
ich möchte ... I'd like ...
einkaufen gehen to go shopping
Einkäufe machen to do the shopping
kaufen to buy
Schlange stehen to queue up
etw probieren to try sth (taste, sample)
etw anprobieren to try sth on
beim Bäcker/Metzger at the baker's/butcher's (shop)
anbieten to offer
ausverkauft sold out
"vom Umtausch ausgeschlossen" "goods cannot be exchanged"

die	**Antiquitäten** (*pl*)	antiques
die	**Anzahlung, -en**	down-payment, deposit
die	**Auslage, -n**	display
die	**Boutique, -n**	boutique
die	**chemische Reinigung**	dry-cleaner's
die	**Gebrauchtwaren** (*pl*)	second-hand goods
die	**Gemischtwaren-** **handlung, -en**	general store
die	**Geschenkpackung, -en**	gift box
die	**Haushaltswaren** (*pl*)	household goods
die	**Käuferin**	purchaser
die	**Konfektionsware, -n**	ready-to-wear clothing
die	**Kreditkarte, -n**	credit card
die	**Kundschaft**	customers, clientèle
die	**Kurzwarenhandlung, -en**	haberdashery
die	**Ladendiebin**	shoplifter
die	**Ladenkette, -n**	chain of shops
die	**Ladenstraße, -n**	(pedestrianized) shopping street
die	**Lederwaren** (*pl*)	leather goods
die	**Markthalle, -n**	covered market
die	**Plastiktüte, -n**	plastic bag
die	**Rate, -n**	instalment
die	**Spielwarenhandlung, -en**	toy shop
die	**Umkleidekabine, -n**	fitting room
die	**Verpackung, -en**	packaging; wrapping

das	**Antiquariat, -e**	second-hand/antiquarian bookshop
das	**Etikett, -e**	label
das	**Feinkostgeschäft, -e**	delicatessen
das	**Reformhaus, ̈-er**	health food shop
das	**Schallplattengeschäft, -e**	record shop
das	**Scheckheft, -e**	chequebook

ich brauche ... I need ...
etw bezahlen to pay for sth
ich möchte mich nur mal umsehen I'm just looking

ESSENTIAL WORDS (nt)

das	**Büro**, -s	office
das	**Café**, -s	café
das	**Einkaufen**	shopping
das	**Einkaufszentrum**, (-ren)	shopping centre
das	**Erdgeschoß**, -sse	ground floor, ground level
das	**Geld**	money
das	**Geschäft**, -e ◇	shop; trade, business; deal
das	**Geschenk**, -e	present, gift
das	**Juweliergeschäft**, -e	jeweller's (shop)
das	**Kaufhaus**, ⁻er	department store
das	**Kleingeld**	small change
das	**Milchgeschäft**, -e	dairy
das	**Obergeschoß**, -sse	upper floor
das	**Portemonnaie**, -s	purse
das	**Postamt**, ⁻er	post office
das	**Produkt**, -e	product; (*pl*) produce
das	**Reisebüro**, -s	travel agent's
das	**Restaurant**, -s	restaurant
das	**Schaufenster**, –	shop window
das	**Schuhgeschäft**, -e	shoe shop
das	**Sonderangebot**, -e ▭	special offer
das	**Souvenir**, -s	souvenir
das	**Untergeschoß**, -sse	basement
das	**Warenhaus**, ⁻er	department store
das	**Wirtshaus**, ⁻er	pub

IMPORTANT WORDS (nt)

das	**Erzeugnis**, -se	product; produce
das	**Lebensmittelgeschäft**, -e	grocer's, general food store
das	**Parterre**, -s	ground floor
das	**Wechselgeld**	change

auf Kredit kaufen *to buy on credit*
in Raten bezahlen *to pay in instalments*
eine Anzahlung leisten *to pay a deposit*
"besonders günstig" *"at bargain price(s)"*
etw als Geschenk einpacken *to giftwrap sth*
etw umtauschen *to exchange sth*

SOUNDS

das	Ächzen	groaning
der	Applaus	applause
der	Beifall ⌒	applause
der	Beifallssturm, ⸚e	burst of applause
das	Brüllen	bellowing; roaring
das	Brummen	growling; droning
der	Donner ⌒	thunder; rumble
das	Echo, -s	echo
die	Explosion, -en	explosion
das	Flüstern	whisper(ing)
das	Gekicher	giggling, tittering
das	Gelächter	laughter
das	Gemurmel	murmur(ing), mumbling
das	Gepolter	banging; din
das	Geräusch, -e	sound, noise
das	Geschrei	shouts, shouting
das	Gezwitscher	chirruping, twitter(ing)
das	Glockengeläut	(peal of) bells
das	Gluckern	glugging
das	Grölen	bawling
das	Grollen	rumbling; pealing (*of thunder*)
das	Gurgeln	gurgling
das	Hämmern	hammering
das	Heulen	howling; howl
das	Hupen	hooting
das	Jaulen	yelping; howling
das	Kichern	chuckle; giggling
das	Klicken	clicking
das	Klimpern	jingling, clinking
das	Klingeln	ringing
das	Klirren	clinking; tingling
das	Klopfen	knock, knocking
das	Knacken	crackling
der	Knall, -e	bang
das	Knallen	banging, slamming
das	Knarren	creaking
das	Knattern	roar; rattle
das	Knirschen	crunching; grinding
das	Knistern	crackling; rustling
das	Knurren	growling; snarling

der	**Krach** ◇	racket, noise
das	**Kratzen**	scratching; scraping
das	**Kreischen**	screeching
das	**Lachen**	laugh(ing)
die	**Lachsalve, -n**	burst of laughter
der	**Lärm**	noise; din, racket
das	**Läuten**	ringing
das	**Miauen**	miaowing
das	**Pfeifen**	whistling
der	**Pfiff, -e**	whistle
das	**Plärren**	blaring; howling, bawling
das	**Plätschern**	lap(ping)
das	**Prasseln**	crackling (*of fire*)
das	**Quietschen**	squeaking; squealing
das	**Rascheln**	rustle; rustling
das	**Rattern**	rattling, clattering
das	**Rauschen**	rustling; hissing
der	**Ruf, -e** ◇	call; shout; cry
das	**Rumpeln**	rumbling
das	**Scharren**	scraping
das	**Schluchzen**	sobbing
das	**Schnurren**	purr(ing)
der	**Schrei, -e**	cry; shout; scream
das	**Schreien**	yelling, crying
der	**Seufzer, –**	sigh
das	**Stöhnen**	groaning, moaning
das	**Summen**	buzzing; buzz
das	**Ticken**	ticking
der	**Ton, ¨e** ◇	sound
der	**Tumult**	din, uproar
das	**Zirpen**	chirping (*of crickets*)
das	**Zischen**	hissing; sizzling

hören *to hear*
bemerken *to notice*
(wider)hallen *to reverberate, resound*
ertönen, erklingen *to ring out*
laut *loud*
leise *quiet*

SPORT AND KEEPING FIT

der	**Ball, ⸚e**	ball
der	**Basketball**	basketball
der	**Fußball, ⸚e**	football
der	**Fußballfan, -s**	football supporter
der	**Fußballplatz, ⸚e**	football pitch
der	**Fußballspieler, –**	footballer
der	**Golfplatz, ⸚e**	golf course
der	**Golfschläger, –**	golf club (*stick*)
der	**Läufer, –** ◇	runner
der	**Netzball**	netball
der	**Paß, ⸚sse** ◇	pass (*football etc*)
der	**Platz, ⸚e** ◇	ground, playing field
der	**Pokal, -e** ◇	cup
der	**Profi, -s**	pro
der	**Radsport**	cycling
der	**Rollschuh, -e**	roller skate
der	**Schläger, –**	racket/bat/club *etc*
der	**Schlittschuh, -e**	ice skate
der	**Ski, -er**	ski
der	**Spieler, –**	player
der	**Sport**	sport
der	**Sportplatz, ⸚e**	sports ground, playing field
der	**Teilnehmer, –** ▭	competitor
der	**Tennisplatz, ⸚e**	tennis court
der	**Volleyball**	volleyball
der	**Wasserball**	water polo
der	**Wintersport**	winter sport(s)
der	**Zuschauer, –** ◇	spectator

joggen *to go jogging*
laufen *to run*
trainieren *to train*
verlieren *to lose*
gewinnen *to win*
den Ausgleich erzielen *to score the equalizer*
unentschieden enden *to end in a draw*
springen *to jump*
spielen *to play*
werfen *to throw*

IMPORTANT WORDS (m)

der **Bergsteiger,** –	mountaineer
der **Federball,** ⸚e	badminton; shuttlecock
der **Gegner,** –	opponent
der **Hochsprung**	high jump
der **Kampf,** ⸚e ▭	fight; contest
der **Meister,** –	champion
der **Rekord,** -e	record
der **Rodel,** –	toboggan
der **Satz,** ⸚e ◇	set (*tennis*)
der **Schiedsrichter,** – ▭	referee; umpire
der **Schlitten,** –	sledge
der **Sieger,** –	winner
der **Stoß,** ⸚e	kick; push, thrust
der **Titelverteidiger,** –	titleholder
der **Torwart,** -e	goalkeeper
der **Trainer,** –	trainer, coach; manager
die **Turnschuhe** (*pl*)	tennis *or* gym shoes
der **Unparteiische*,** -n	umpire; referee
der **Weitsprung**	long jump
der **Weltrekord,** -e	world record
der **Wettbewerb,** -e	competition
der **Wettkampf,** ⸚e	match, contest

USEFUL WORDS (m)

der **Abfahrtslauf**	downhill skiing
der **Ausscheidungskampf,** ⸚e	heat
der **Boxer,** –	boxer
der **Butterfly**	butterfly (stroke)
der **Dreisprung**	triple jump
der **Eiskunstlauf**	figure skating
der **Eislauf**	ice skating
der **Eisschnellauf**	speed skating
der **Elfmeter,** –	penalty (kick)
der **Endspurt**	final spurt
der **Handball**	handball
der **Kajak,** -s	kayak
der **Langlauf**	cross-country skiing
der **Langstreckenläufer,** –	long-distance runner
der **Linksaußen,** –	outside left

SPORT AND KEEPING FIT — 3

der	Marathonlauf, ¨e	marathon
der	Marathonläufer, –	marathon runner
der	Mittelstürmer, –	centre-forward
der	Radrennfahrer, –	racing cyclist
der	Rechtsaußen, –	outside right
der	Rennfahrer, –	racing driver
der	Salto, -s	somersault
der	Schlepplift, -e	ski tow
der	Sieg, -e	victory
der	Skilift, -e	ski lift
der	Skistock, ¨e	ski stick
der	Spagat	splits
der	Sportverein, -e	sports club
der	Stabhochsprung	pole vault
der	Strafstoß, ¨e	penalty (kick)
der	Tennisschläger, –	tennis racket
der	Verteidiger, –	defender
der	Wassersport	water sports

die	Aschenbahn, -en	cinder track
die	Ausdauer	endurance
die	Dopingkontrolle, -n	drugs test
die	Eisbahn, -en	ice rink, skating rink
die	Endrunde, -n	finals
die	Gymnastik	gymnastics
die	Kondition	form; stamina
die	Läuferin	runner
die	Lockerungsübungen (*pl*)	limbering-up exercises
die	Niederlage, -n	defeat
die	Partie, -n	game, match
die	Plazierung, -en	placing
die	Punktzahl, -en	score
die	Regatta, (-ten)	regatta
die	Schwimmflosse, -n	flipper (*for swimming*)
die	Stoppuhr, -en	stopwatch
die	Tabelle, -n	league table
die	Versammlung, -en	meeting
die	Vorrunde, -n	qualifying round

ESSENTIAL WORDS (f)

die	**Angelrute, -n**	fishing rod
die	**Bundesliga** 🕮	national league
die	**Fußballmannschaft, -en**	football team
die	**Halbzeit, -en**	half (*of match*); half-time
die	**Leichtathletik**	athletics
die	**Mannschaft, -en** ⬦	team
die	**Rennbahn, -en**	racecourse; track
die	**Spielerin**	player
die	**Spielhälfte, -n**	half (*of match*)
die	**Teilnehmerin**	competitor
die	**Turnhalle, -n**	gym(nasium)
die	**Weltmeisterschaft, -en**	world championship

IMPORTANT WORDS (f)

die	**Bahn, -en** ⬦	track
die	**Gegnerin**	opponent
die	**Kegelbahn, -en**	bowling lane; bowling alley
die	**Meisterschaft, -en**	championship
die	**Runde, -n** ⬦	lap, round
die	**Siegerin**	winner
die	**Tabellenspitze, -n**	top of the league
die	**Tribüne, -n** ⬦	stand
die	**Unparteiische*, -n**	umpire; referee

USEFUL WORDS (m&f)

der/die	**Eisläufer(in), –**	(ice) skater
der/die	**Junior(in), -en**	junior
der/die	**Leichtathlet(in), -en**	athlete
der/die	**Mannschafts-**	
	kamerad(in), -en	team-mate
der/die	**Ringer(in), –**	wrestler
der/die	**Schwimmer(in), –**	swimmer
der/die	**Skifahrer(in), –**	skier
der/die	**Taucher(in), –**	diver
der/die	**Tennisspieler(in), –**	tennis player
der/die	**Turner(in), –**	gymnast
der/die	**Verlierer(in), –**	loser
der/die	**Volleyballspieler(in), –**	volleyball player

ESSENTIAL WORDS (nt)

das	**Angeln**	fishing, angling
das	**Billard**	billiards
das	**Boxen**	boxing
das	**Eishockey**	ice hockey
das	**Endspiel, -e**	final(s)
das	**Ergebnis, -se** ▢	result
das	**Fitneßzentrum, (-ren)**	health club
das	**Freibad, ⸚er**	open-air swimming pool
das	**Golf(spiel)** ◇	golf
das	**Hallenbad, ⸚er**	indoor swimming pool
das	**Hockey**	hockey
das	**Jogging**	jogging
das	**Kricket**	cricket
das	**Laufen**	running
das	**Netz, -e** ◇	net
die	**Olympischen Spiele** (*pl*)	Olympic Games
das	**Pferderennen, –**	horse racing; horse-race
das	**Radfahren**	cycling
das	**Reiten**	horse-riding
das	**Rennen, –**	race
das	**Rudern**	rowing
das	**Rugby**	rugby
das	**Schießen**	shooting
das	**Schlittschuhlaufen**	(ice) skating
das	**Schwimmbad, ⸚er**	swimming baths
das	**Schwimmen**	swimming
das	**Segeln**	sailing
das	**Skifahren**	skiing
das	**Skilaufen**	skiing
das	**Spiel, -e** ◇	play; game, match
das	**Squash**	squash
das	**Stadion, (-ien)**	stadium
das	**Tauchen**	(underwater) diving
das	**Tennis**	tennis
das	**Tischtennis**	table tennis
das	**Tor, -e** ◇	goal
das	**Training**	training
das	**Turnen** ◇	gymnastics
das	**Ziel, -e** ◇	finish, finishing post

das	**Bergsteigen**	mountaineering
das	**Bogenschießen**	archery
das	**Bowls-Spiel**	bowls
das	**Drachenfliegen**	hang-gliding
das	**Fechten**	fencing
das	**gemischte Doppel**	mixed doubles
das	**Jagen**	hunting; shooting
das	**Klettern**	climbing, mountaineering
das	**Ringen**	wrestling
das	**Surfbrett, -er**	surfboard
das	**Tauziehen**	tug-of-war
das	**Turnier, -e**	tournament
das	**Wasserski**	water-skiing

das	**Aerobic**	aerobics
das	**Aufputschmittel, –**	dope
das	**Bodybuilding**	body-building
das	**Brustschwimmen**	breaststroke
das	**Doping**	doping
das	**Finale, –** ◇	final
das	**Freistilschwimmen**	freestyle swimming
das	**Gewichtheben**	weightlifting
das	**Halbfinale, –**	semifinal
das	**Joga**	yoga
das	**Judo**	judo
das	**Karate**	karate
das	**Kraulen**	crawl
das	**Kugelstoßen**	shot put
das	**Rückenschwimmen**	backstroke
das	**Speerwerfen**	javelin throwing
das	**Sprungbrett, -er**	diving board
das	**Surfen**	surfing
das	**Trikot, -s**	shirt, jersey; leotard
das	**Unentschieden, –**	draw
das	**Viertelfinale, –**	quarterfinals
das	**Wandern**	hiking, rambling
das	**Windsurfen**	windsurfing

STAGE AND SCREEN

der Applaus	applause
der Ausgang, ¨-e	exit, way out
der Balkon, -s ◇	(dress) circle
der Beifall ⌑	applause
der Bühneneingang	stage door
der Dramatiker, –	dramatist, playwright
der Eingang, ¨-e	entrance, way in
der erste Rang	dress circle
der Film, -e	film
der Filmstar, -s	film star
der Kinobesucher, –	cinema-goer
der Komiker, –	comedian
der Konzertsaal, (-säle)	concert hall
der Krimi, -s	thriller
der Kritiker, –	critic
der Platz, ¨-e ◇	seat
der Quatsch	rubbish
der Rang	circle (*in theatre*)
der Regisseur, -e	producer; director
der Saal, (Säle)	hall; room
der Schauspieler, –	actor
der Spaß ◇	fun
der Spielfilm, -e	feature film
der Spielplan, ¨-e	programme
der Text, -e ◇	script
der Theaterbesucher, –	theatre-goer
der Titel, –	title
der Untertitel, –	subtitle
der Vorhang, ¨-e ⌑	curtain
der Western, –	western
die Zuhörer (*pl*)	audience (*listeners*)
die Zuschauer (*pl*) ◇	audience (*viewers*)
der zweite Rang	upper circle

die Bühne betreten to step onto the stage
meine Damen und Herren! ladies and gentlemen!
(kaum) sehenswert (hardly) worth seeing
langweilig boring

STAGE

IMPORTANT WORDS (m)

der	Abgang, ¨e	exit (of actor)
der	Auftritt, -e	entrance (of actor); scene (of play)
der	Intendant, -en	stage manager
der	Orchesterraum, ¨e	orchestra pit
der	Produzent, -en ◇	(film) producer
der	Souffleur, -e	prompter
der	Spionagefilm, -e	spy film
der	Thriller, –	thriller
der	Zeichentrickfilm, -e	cartoon

USEFUL WORDS (m)

der	Akt, -e	act
der	Bauchredner, –	ventriloquist
der	Boulevardstück, -e	light comedy
die	Buhrufe (pl)	boos, booing
der	Filmfan, -s	film buff
der	Horrorfilm, -e	horror film
der	Jongleur, -e	juggler
der	Kassenschlager, –	box-office hit
der	Kinohit, -s	blockbuster
der	Klappsitz, -e	jump or foldaway seat
der	Kulissenmaler, –	scene-painter
der	Kultfilm, -e	cult film
der	Kurzfilm, -e	short (film)
der	Nachspann, -e	credits, credit titles
der	Notausgang, ¨e ▭	emergency exit
der	Pantomime, -n ◇	mime (actor)
der	Requisiteur, -e	property manager
der	Sitz, -e	seat
der	Sketch, -e	sketch
die	Spezialeffekte (pl)	special effects
der	Stummfilm, -e	silent movie
der	Stuntman, (-men)	stuntman
die	Toneffekte (pl)	sound effects
der	Trailer, –	trailer
der	Vorfilm, -e	supporting film, short
der	Vorspann, -e	opening credits
der	Zauberer, –	conjurer, magician

ESSENTIAL WORDS (f)

die **Aufführung, -en**	performance
die **Bühne, -n**	stage; platform
die **Ermäßigung, -en**	reduction (*in price*); concession
die **Figur, -en** ⟡	character
die **Freizeit**	free time, spare time
die **Garderobe, -n** ⟡	cloakroom; wardrobe
die **Handlung, -en** ⟡	plot, action
die **Hauptrolle, -n**	main role *or* part
die **Karte, -n** ⟡	ticket
die **Kasse, -n** ⟡	box office, ticket office
die **Kinobesucherin**	cinema-goer
die **Komödie, -n** ▭	comedy
die **Kritikerin**	critic
die **Musik**	music
die **Oper, -n**	opera; opera house
die **Reklame, -n** ▭	advertisements; advertising
die **Reservierung, -en**	booking
die **Rolle, -n**	role, part
die **Saison, -s** ▭	season
die **Schauspielerin**	actress
die **Schlange, -n** ⟡ ▭	queue
die **Show, -s**	show
die **Szene, -n**	scene
die **Theatergruppe, -n**	dramatic society
die **Theaterkarte, -n**	theatre ticket
die **Theaterkasse, -n**	box office
die **Tragödie, -n**	tragedy
die **Vorstellung, -en** ⟡	performance, show

---

ein Stück geben to put on a play
klatschen to clap
an der Vorverkaufskasse at the booking office
"ausverkauft" "sold out"
ich gehe gern ins Kino/ins Theater I like going to the cinema/the theatre
spannend exciting
ein Film mit Untertiteln a film with subtitles
mein Lieblingsfilmstar my favourite film star

IMPORTANT WORDS (f)

die **Farce**, -n	farce
die **Galerie**	gods, gallery
die **Generalprobe**, -n	dress rehearsal
die **Inszenierung**, -en	production
die **Kapelle**, -n ◇	band
die **Kritik**, -en	review
die **Leinwand**, ¨-e ◇ ⊞	screen
die **Loge**, -n	box
die **Pause**, -n ◇	interval
die **Platzanweiserin**	usherette
die **Probe**, -n	rehearsal
die **Schauspielkunst**	acting
die **Souffleuse**, -n	prompter
die **Tribüne**, -n ◇	platform
die **Zugabe**, -n	encore

USEFUL WORDS (f)

die **Bearbeitung**, -en	adaptation
die **Eintrittskarte**, -n	(admission) ticket
die **Filmmusik**	film music; soundtrack
die **Kamera**, -s	camera
die **Komikerin**	comedian
die **Kulissen** (*pl*)	scenery
die **Marionette**, -n	puppet
die **Operette**, -n	operetta
die **Originalfassung**, -en	original version
die **Pantomime**, -n ◇	mime show
die **Premiere**, -n	premiere
die **Reihe**, -n ◇	row
die **Schauspieltruppe**, -n	theatrical company
die **Schießerei**, -en	shooting
die **Statistenrolle**, -n	walk-on part
die **Synchronisation**	dubbing
die **Uraufführung**, -en	premiere, first night/showing
die **Vorpremiere**, -n	preview

mit X und Y in den Hauptrollen *starring X and Y*

der/die **Animator(in)**, -en	animator
der/die **Beleuchter(in)**, –	lighting engineer
der/die **Bühnenarbeiter(in)**, –	scene shifter, stagehand
der/die **Cineast(in)**, -en	film expert; film fan
der/die **Filmemacher(in)**, –	film-maker
der/die **Garderobier(e)**, -s	wardrobe master/mistress
der/die **Imitator(in)**, -en	impersonator
der/die **Kameramann**, ¨er/	
Kamerafrau, -en	cameraman/-woman
der/die **Kinogänger(in)**, –	cinemagoer
der/die **Maskenbildner(in)**, –	make-up artist
der/die **Nebendarsteller(in)**, –	supporting actor
der/die **Seiltänzer(in)**, –	tightrope walker
der/die **Statist(in)**, -en	walk-on; extra
der/die **Trapezkünstler,(in)** –	trapeze artist
der/die **Zauberkünstler(in)**, –	conjurer, magician

das **Double**, -s	stuntman, stunt girl, stand-in
das **Filmarchiv**, -e	film archives
das **Finale**, – ◇	finale
das **Kasper(le)theater**	Punch and Judy show
das **Kinocenter**, –	multi-screen cinema
das **Lampenfieber**	stage fright
das **Meisterwerk**, -e	masterpiece
das **Musical**, -s	musical
das **Programm**, -e ◇	programme
das **Publikum**	audience
das **Requisit**, -en	prop
das **Showgeschäft**	show business
das **Straßentheater**	street theatre
das **Trapez**, -e	trapeze
das **Varieté**	variety entertainment, vaudeville
das **Volksstück**, -e	dialect folk play

ESSENTIAL WORDS (nt)

das	**Ballett**	ballet
das	**Drama, (-men)**	drama
das	**Foyer, -s**	foyer
das	**Kino, -s**	cinema
das	**Konzert, -e** ◇	concert
das	**Kostüm, -e** ◇	costume
das	**Kriminalstück, -e**	thriller
das	**Make-up**	make-up
das	**Opernglas, ‥er**	(pair of) opera glasses
das	**Opernhaus, ‥er**	opera house
das	**Orchester, –**	orchestra; band
das	**Parkett, -e** ◇	stalls
das	**Schauspiel, -e**	play
das	**Schauspielhaus, ‥er**	theatre
das	**Spiel, -e** ◇	acting; play
das	**Stück, -e** ◇	play
das	**Theater, –**	theatre
das	**Theaterstück, -e**	play

IMPORTANT WORDS (nt)

das	**Lustspiel, -e**	comedy
das	**Plakat, -e**	poster, notice
das	**Rampenlicht**	footlights
das	**Scheinwerferlicht, -er**	spotlight
das	**Trauerspiel, -e**	tragedy

etw beiseite sprechen to say sth in an aside
die Hauptattraktion sein to be top of the bill
vor ausverkauftem Haus spielen to play to a full house
der Film ist nicht jugendfrei the film is for adults only
spielen to play
tanzen to dance
singen to sing
einen Film drehen to shoot a film
"Zugabe! Zugabe!" "encore! encore!"
"die Bretter, die die Welt bedeuten" "the stage"

TIME

der	**Abend, -e**	evening
der	**Augenblick, -e**	moment, instant
der	**Beginn**	beginning
der	**Mittag**	midday, noon
der	**Moment, -e**	moment
der	**Monat, -e**	month
der	**Morgen, –**	morning
der	**Nachmittag**	afternoon
der	**Tag, -e**	day
der	**Vormittag**	morning
der	**Wecker, –**	alarm clock

der	**Einbruch der Nacht**	nightfall
der	**Kalender, –**	calendar
der	**Tagesanbruch**	daybreak
der	**Uhrzeiger, –**	hand (*of clock etc*)
der	**Zeitabschnitt, -e**	time, period

der	**Minutenzeiger, –**	minute hand
der	**Sekundenzeiger, –**	second hand
der	**Sonnenaufgang**	sunrise
der	**Sonnenuntergang**	sunset
der	**Stundenzeiger, –**	hour hand
der	**Zeitunterschied, -e**	time difference

fast *almost*
pünktlich *punctual*
später *later*
bald *soon*
vierundzwanzig Stunden am Tag *twenty-four hours a day*
halb 3 *half past 2*
halb 9 *half past 8*
es ist genau or **Punkt 2 Uhr** *it is exactly 2 o'clock*
um 7 Uhr aufstehen *to get up at 7 o'clock*
um 11 Uhr zu Bett gehen *to go to bed at 11 o'clock*

ESSENTIAL WORDS (f)

die	**Armbanduhr, -en**	(wrist)watch
die	**Essenszeit, -en**	mealtime
die	**Gelegenheit, -en**	opportunity; occasion
die	**halbe Stunde**	half-hour, half-an-hour
die	**Jahreszeit, -en**	season
die	**Kuckucksuhr, -en**	cuckoo clock
die	**Minute, -n**	minute
die	**Mitte**	middle
die	**Mitternacht**	midnight
die	**Nacht, ⁻e**	night; night-time
die	**Sekunde, -n**	second
die	**Stunde, -n** ◇	hour
die	**Tageszeit**	daytime
die	**Uhr, -en** ◇	clock; watch
die	**Uhrzeit, -en**	time of day
die	**Viertelstunde, -n**	quarter of an hour
die	**Weile, -n**	while, short time
die	**Woche, -n**	week
die	**Zeit, -en**	time

IMPORTANT WORDS (f)

die	**Epoche, -n**	epoch, period
die	**Gegenwart**	present
die	**Mittagszeit, -en**	lunchtime
die	**Pause, -n** ◇	interval; pause; break
die	**Standuhr, -en**	grandfather clock
die	**Stoppuhr, -en**	stopwatch
die	**Vergangenheit**	past
die	**Verspätung**	delay
die	**Zukunft**	future

wieviel Uhr ist es?, wie spät ist es? *what time is it?*
spät *late*
früh *early*
den wievielten haben wir heute? *what is today's date?*
gegen 8 Uhr *round about 8 o'clock*

USEFUL WORDS (f)

die **Ära**, (-ren)	era
die **Bürostunden** (*pl*)	office hours
die **Digitaluhr**, -en	digital clock/watch
die **Kindheit**	childhood
die **Nachkriegszeit**	post-war years
die **Sanduhr**, -en	hourglass
die **Sonnenwende**, -n	solstice
die **Tagundnachtgleiche**	equinox
die **Zeitzone**, -n	time zone

ein anderes Mal another time
nächstes Mal next time
diesmal this time
das erste/letzte Mal the first/last time
zum ersten/letzten Mal for the first/last time
anderthalb Stunden warten to wait an hour and a half
damals at that time
jemals ever
nie, niemals never
eine Zeitlang bleiben to stay for a while
gestern/heute vor einer Woche a week ago yesterday/today
gestern/heute vor 2 Jahren 2 years ago yesterday/today
vor einer Woche/einem Monat/2 Jahren a week/a month/2 years ago
in einer Woche/einem Monat/2 Jahren in a week/a month/2 years(' time)
am Wochenende at the weekend
über das Wochenende for the weekend
nachts at night, by night
ich habe es eilig I'm in a hurry
ich habe keine Zeit (dazu) I have no time (for it)
es hat keine Eile there's no hurry
ich habe keine Eile I'm in no hurry
morgen/heute in einer Woche a week tomorrow/today
tagsüber, am Tage during the day
stündlich hourly
täglich daily
wöchentlich weekly

ESSENTIAL WORDS (nt)

das **Datum**, (-ten)	date
das **Ende**	end
das **Jahr**, -e	year
das **Jahrhundert**, -e	century
das **Mal**, -e	time, occasion
das **Wochenende**, -n	weekend

IMPORTANT WORDS (nt)

das **Futur**	future tense
das **Jahrzehnt**, -e	decade
das **Präsens**	present tense
das **Schaltjahr**, -e	leap year
das **Zeitalter**, –	age, time
das **Zifferblatt**, ¨er	(clock) face, dial

USEFUL WORDS (nt)

das **Alter** ◇	age; old age
das **Jahrtausend**, -e	millenium
das **Mittelalter**	Middle Ages

es ist Viertel nach/vor 5 *it is a quarter past/to 5*
morgens *in the morning*
abends *in the evening*
nachmittags *in the afternoon*
es ist Zeit zum Essen *it is time for lunch/dinner etc*
im selben Augenblick *at that very moment*
in diesem/dem Augenblick *at this/that moment*
(sich) die Zeit vertreiben *to pass the time*
monatlich *monthly*
jährlich *annually*
einen Augenblick! *just a minute!*
heutzutage *nowadays*
zu einer bestimmten Zeit *at a set time*
im Uhrzeigersinn *clockwise*
gegen den Uhrzeigersinn *anticlockwise*
wochentags *on weekdays*

TOOLS

ESSENTIAL WORDS (m)

der **Bastler**, –	handyman
der **Bohrer**, –	drill
der **Dosenöffner**, –	tin-opener
der **Hammer**, ̈	hammer
der **Holzhammer**, ̈	mallet
der **Klebstoff**, -e	glue
der **Korkenzieher**, –	corkscrew
der **Schlüssel**, –	key

IMPORTANT WORDS (m)

der **Bolzen**, –	bolt
der **Büchsenöffner**, –	tin-opener
der **Draht**, ̈e ▭	wire
der **Flaschenöffner**, –	bottle-opener
der **Hobel**, –	plane
der **Meißel**, –	chisel
der **Nagel**, ̈	nail
der **Pickel**, – ◇	pick, pickaxe
der **Pinsel**, – ▭	paintbrush
der **Preßluftbohrer**, –	pneumatic drill
der **Schraubenschlüssel**, –	spanner
der **Schraubenzieher**, –	screwdriver
der **Schraubstock**, ̈e	vice
der **Stacheldraht**	barbed wire
der **Stift**, -e	peg
der **Tesafilm** ®	Sellotape ®
der **Werkzeugkasten**, ̈	toolbox

USEFUL WORDS (m)

der **Blasebalg**, ̈e	bellows
der **Brieföffner**, –	paper knife
der **Haken**, – ◇	hook
der **Handbohrer**, –	gimlet
der **Kompaß**, -sse	compass
der **Magnet**, -e	magnet
der **Rasenmäher**, –	lawnmower
der **Schweißbrenner**, –	welding torch; blowlamp
der **Spaten**, –	spade

ESSENTIAL WORDS (f)

die	**Batterie**, -n	battery
die	**Baustelle**, -n 🕮	building site
die	**Gabel**, -n	fork
die	**Maschine**, -n ◇ 🕮	machine; engine
die	**Werkstatt**, ⁻en	workshop

IMPORTANT WORDS (f)

die	**Feder**, -n ◇	spring, coil
die	**Feile**, -n	file
die	**Heftzwecke**, -n	drawing pin, thumbtack
die	**Kelle**, -n	trowel
die	**Leiter**, -n ◇	ladder
die	**Nadel**, -n	needle; pin
die	**Planke**, -n	plank
die	**Reißzwecke**, -n	drawing pin, thumbtack
die	**Säge**, -n	saw
die	**Schaufel**, -n	shovel; scoop
die	**Schere**, -n 🕮	(pair of) scissors
die	**Schnur**, ⁻e ◇	string; cord; wire, flex
die	**Schraube**, -n	screw
die	**Wasserwaage**, -n	spirit level
die	**Zange**, -n	(pair of) pliers

USEFUL WORDS (f)

die	**Axt**, ⁻e	axe
die	**Drahtschere**, -n	wire-cutters
die	**Drehbank**, ⁻e	lathe
die	**Harke**, -n	rake
die	**Kettensäge**, -n	chain saw
die	**Kurbel**, -n	crank
die	**Luftpumpe**, -n	air pump
die	**Metallschere**, -n	metal shears
die	**Mutter**, -n ◇	nut
die	**Pinzette**, -n	tweezers
die	**Sichel**, -n	sickle
die	**Sicherheitsnadel**, -n	safety pin
die	**Taschenlampe**, -n	torch
die	**Werkbank**, ⁻e	(work)bench

ESSENTIAL WORDS (nt)

das	Ding, -e	thing, object
das	Do-it-yourself	do-it-yourself, D.I.Y.
das	Gummi	rubber; gum
das	Gummiband, ⁻er	rubber band
das	Kabel, –	wire; cable
das	Schloß, ⁻sser ◊	lock

IMPORTANT WORDS (nt)

das	Brett, -er ◊	plank, board; shelf
das	Gerüst, -e	scaffolding
das	Seil, -e	rope; cable
das	Tau, -e ◊	rope
das	Werkzeug, -e ▭	tool

USEFUL WORDS (nt)

das	Beil, -e	axe; hatchet
das	Brecheisen, –	crowbar
das	Taschenmesser, –	penknife, pocketknife

etw reparieren lassen *to have sth repaired*
reparieren *to repair*
nageln *to nail*
sägen *to saw*
er kann gut basteln *he is good with his hands*
wozu benutzt man ...? *what do you use ... for?*
einen Nagel in die Wand schlagen *to hammer a nail into the wall*
"frisch gestrichen" *"wet paint"*
streichen *to paint*
tapezieren *to wallpaper*

ESSENTIAL WORDS (m)

der	**Bahnhof, ⸚e**	(railway) station
der	**Betrieb, -e** ◇	bustle
der	**Bezirk, -e** ⌑	district
der	**Biergarten, ⸚**	beer garden
der	**Bürgermeister, –**	mayor
der	**Bürgersteig, -e** ⌑	pavement
der	**Busbahnhof, ⸚e**	bus *or* coach station
der	**Dom, -e**	cathedral
der	**Einwohner, –**	inhabitant
der	**Friedhof, ⸚e** ⌑	cemetery, graveyard
der	**Fußgänger, –** ⌑	pedestrian
der	**Laden, ⸚**	shop
der	**Markt, ⸚e**	market
der	**Markttag, -e**	market day
der	**Park, -s**	(public) park
der	**Parkplatz, ⸚e**	parking space; car park
der	**Platz, ⸚e** ◇	square
der	**Polizist, -en**	policeman
der	**Turm, ⸚e**	tower; (church) steeple
der	**Verkehr**	traffic
der	**Weg, -e** ◇	way

IMPORTANT WORDS (m)

der	**Abwasserkanal, ⸚e**	sewer
der	**Bürger, –**	citizen
der	**Fußgängerüberweg, -e**	pedestrian crossing
der	**Kinderwagen, –**	pram
der	**Ort, -e**	place, spot
der	**Passant, -en**	passer-by
der	**Pflasterstein, -e**	paving stone
der	**Rad(fahr)weg, -e**	cycle path *or* track
der	**Stadtbewohner, –**	town *or* city dweller
der	**Städter, –**	town *or* city dweller
der	**Stadtrand**	outskirts
der	**Taxistand, ⸚e**	taxi rank
der	**Vorort, -e**	suburb
der	**Wegweiser, –**	road sign
der	**Wohnblock, -s**	block of flats
der	**Wolkenkratzer, –**	skyscraper

TOWN

289

USEFUL WORDS (m)

der **Bettler,** –	beggar
der **Briefkasten,** ̈ ◇	postbox, pillar box
der **Brunnen,** – ◇	fountain
der **Durchgang,** ̈e	alleyway
der **Einheimische*,** -n	local (resident)
der **Geldautomat,** -en	cash dispenser
der **Kirchturm,** ̈e	church tower, steeple
der **Kreisverkehr,** -e	roundabout
der **Marktplatz,** ̈e	marketplace
der **Parkscheinautomat,** -en	parking ticket machine
der **Pendelverkehr**	commuter traffic
der **Pfad,** -e	path
der **Stadtplan,** ̈e	street map
der **Stadtstreicher,** –	tramp
der **Stadtteil,** -e	part of town
der **Straßenhändler,** –	street trader
der **Straßenkehrer,** –	roadsweeper
der **Tourist,** -en	tourist
der **Weihnachtsmarkt,** ̈e	Christmas fair
der **Zeitungsverkäufer,** –	newspaper seller

"Vorfahrt achten!" *"give way"*
"Parken verboten" *"no parking"*
"bitte freihalten" *"please keep clear"*
"Betreten der Baustelle verboten" *"building site: keep out"*
"Anlieger frei" *"residents only"*
schmutzig *dirty*
modern *modern*
sauber *clean*
alt *old*
typisch *typical*
an der Ecke *at* or *on the corner*
ins Theater/ins Kino gehen *to go to the theatre/the cinema*
zum Markt gehen, auf den Markt gehen *to go to the market*
eine Stadtrundfahrt machen *to go on a tour of the city*
zu Fuß gehen *to walk*
mit dem Bus/mit dem Zug fahren *to go by bus/by train*

ESSENTIAL WORDS (f)

die **Aussicht, -en** 📖	view
die **Brücke, -n** ◇	bridge
die **Burg, -en**	castle
die **Bürgermeisterin**	mayoress
die **Bushaltestelle, -n**	bus stop
die **Ecke, -n**	corner
die **Einbahnstraße, -n** 📖	one-way street
die **Einwohnerin**	inhabitant
die **Fabrik, -en** 📖	factory
die **Fahrt, -en** ◇	journey
die **Feuerwache, -n**	fire station
die **Haltestelle, -n**	(bus or tram) stop
die **Hauptstraße, -n**	main road; main street
die **Kirche, -n**	church
die **Klinik, -en**	hospital, clinic
die **Menge, -n** ◇	crowd
die **Nebenstraße, -n**	side street; minor road
die **Polizei**	police
die **Polizeiwache, -n**	police station
die **Polizistin**	policewoman
die **Post** ◇	post office
die **Rundfahrt, -en**	tour
die **Schlange, -n** ◇ 📖	queue
die **Sehenswürdigkeiten** (pl)	sights, places of interest
die **Stadt, ⁻e**	town; city
die **Straße, -n** ◇	street, road
die **Straßenecke, -n**	street corner
die **Tankstelle, -n**	petrol station, garage
die **U-Bahn**	underground
die **Umgebung**	surroundings
die **Verkehrsstauung, -en** 📖	traffic jam

in die Stadt gehen or **fahren** to go into town
in der Stadtmitte in the centre of town
ein Taxi rufen to call a taxi
in der Stadt/am Stadtrand wohnen to live in the town/in the suburbs
auf dem Platz in or on the square
die Straße hinübergehen to cross the road

IMPORTANT WORDS (f)

die **Bevölkerung**, -en ⌑	population
die **Gasse**, -n	lane, alley
die **Großstadt**, ¨e	city
die **Kreuzung**, -en	crossroads
die **Kunstgalerie**, -n	art gallery
die **Leuchtreklame**, -n	neon sign
die **Meinungsumfrage**, -n	opinion poll
die **Prozession**, -en	procession
die **Sackgasse**, -n	dead end, cul-de-sac
die **Siedlung**, -en	housing estate
die **Sozialwohnung**, -en	council flat *or* house
die **Spitze**, -n ◇	spire
die **Stadtmitte**	town centre; city centre
die **Statue**, -n	statue
die **Straßenlaterne**, -n	street lamp
die **Tour**, -en	tour
die **Umgehungsstraße**, -n	bypass; ring road
die **Vorstadt**, ¨e	suburbs

USEFUL WORDS (f)

die **Altstadt**	old (part of) town
die **Baustelle**, -n	building site
die **Bettlerin**	beggar
die **Bücherei**, -en	library
die **Bürgerin**	citizen
die **City**	city centre
die **Einheimische***, -n	local (resident)
die **Fahrbahn**, -en	roadway
die **Fußgängerzone**, -n	pedestrian precinct
die **Gosse**, -n	gutter
die **Innenstadt**, ¨e	city centre
die **Ladenstraße**, -n	shopping street
die **Parkuhr**, -en	parking meter
die **Stadtstreicherin**	tramp
die **Straßenbahn**, -en	tram
die **Straßenkehrmaschine**, -n	roadsweeper machine
die **Touristin**	tourist
die **Unterführung**, -en	subway; underpass
die **Zeitungsverkäuferin**	newspaper seller

---

das	Büro, -s	office
das	Denkmal, ¨er ▱	monument
das	Fahrscheinheft, -e	book of tickets
das	Fahrzeug, -e ▱	vehicle
das	Gebäude, – ▱	building; edifice
das	Geschäft, -e ◇	shop
das	Hotel, -s	hotel
das	Kaufhaus, ¨er	department store
das	Kino, -s	cinema
das	Krankenhaus, ¨er	hospital
das	Museum, (Museen)	museum
das	Parken	parking
das	Parkhaus, ¨er	multi-storey car park
das	Postamt, ¨er	post office
das	Rathaus, ¨er	town hall
das	Restaurant, -s	restaurant
das	Schloß, ¨sser ◇	castle
das	Stadtzentrum, (-tren)	city centre, town centre
das	Straßenschild, -er	road sign
das	Taxi, -s	taxi
das	Theater, –	theatre
das	Tor, -e ◇	gate(way), arch
das	Verkehrsamt, ¨er	tourist information office

das	Gedränge	crowd
das	Kopfsteinpflaster	cobblestones
das	Plakat, -e	poster, notice
das	Viertel, - ◇ ▱	district
das	Werk, -e ◇	factory, works
das	Wohngebiet, -e	built-up area

das	Elendsviertel, –	shanty town; slums
das	Industriegebiet, -e	industrial estate
das	Marktstädtchen, –	market town
das	Schild, -er ◇	notice, sign
das	Spielkasino, -s	casino

TRAINS

der	**Anschluß,** ¨sse ◇	connection
der	**Ausgang,** ¨e	exit, way out
der	**Ausstieg,** -e ▢	exit (*from train*)
der	**Bahnhof,** ¨e	station
der	**Bahnsteig,** -e	platform
der	**Dienstwagen,** –	guard's van
der	**D-Zug,** ¨e ▢	through train
der	**Eilzug,** ¨e ▢	limited-stop train
der	**Eingang,** ¨e	entrance
der	**Eisenbahner,** –	railwayman
der	**Entwerter,** – ▢	ticket punching machine
der	**Fahrausweis,** -e ▢	ticket
der	**Fahrgast,** ¨e ▢	passenger
der	**Fahrkartenschalter,** –	ticket *or* booking office
der	**Fahrplan,** ¨e	timetable
der	**Fahrschein,** -e ▢	ticket
der	**Gepäckwagen,** –	luggage van
der	**Hauptbahnhof,** ¨e	main *or* central station
der	**Inter-City-Zug,** ¨e ▢	inter-city train
der	**Koffer,** –	case, suitcase
der	**Liegewagen,** –	couchette coach
der	**Lokomotivführer,** –	train driver
der	**Nahverkehrszug,** ¨e ▢	local train
der	**Paß,** ¨sse ◇	passport
der	**Passagier,** -e	passenger
der	**Platz,** ¨e ◇	seat
der	**Reisende*,** -n	traveller
der	**Reisepaß,** ¨sse	passport
der	**Rucksack,** ¨e	rucksack, backpack
der	**Schaffner,** –	guard; ticket collector
der	**Schlafwagen,** –	sleeping car, sleeper
der	**Schnellimbiß,** -sse	snack bar
der	**Schnellzug,** ¨e	fast train, express train
der	**Speisewagen,** –	dining car
der	**U-Bahnhof,** ¨e	underground station
der	**Wagen,** – ◇	carriage, coach
der	**Zollbeamte*,** -n	customs officer
der	**Zug,** ¨e ◇	train
der	**Zuschlag,** ¨e	extra charge

IMPORTANT WORDS (m)

der	**Anhänger,** – ◇	label, tag
der	**Bahnhofsvorsteher,** –	stationmaster
der	**Bahnübergang,** ¨-e	level crossing
der	**Bestimmungsort,** -e	destination (*of goods*)
der	**Dienst,** -e	service
der	**Fahrpreis,** -e	fare
der	**Gepäckträger,** – ◇	porter
der	**Güterzug,** ¨-e	goods train
der	**Heizer,** –	fireman, stoker
der	**Imbiß,** -sse	snack
der	**Kofferkuli,** -s	luggage trolley
der	**Personenzug,** ¨-e	slow *or* stopping train; passenger train
der	**Pfiff,** -e	whistle
der	**Schrankkoffer,** –	trunk
der	**Taxistand,** ¨-e	taxi rank
der	**Vorortzug,** ¨-e	commuter train
der	**Wartesaal,** (-säle)	waiting room

USEFUL WORDS (m)

der	**Bahndamm,** ¨-e	embankment
der	**Fahrkartenautomat,** -en	ticket machine
der	**Triebwagen,** –	railcar
der	**Tunnel,** –	tunnel
der	**Waggon,** -s	waggon

hier ist besetzt this seat is taken
verspätet delayed
auf dem Bahnhof at the station
sich erkundigen to make inquiries
ist dieser Platz frei? is this seat free?
"nicht hinauslehnen" "do not lean out of the window"
den Zug erreichen/verpassen to catch/miss one's train

ESSENTIAL WORDS (f)

die	**Abfahrt, -en** ⌐	departure
die	**Ankunft, ⁻e** ⌐	arrival
die	**Auskunft, ⁻e** ◇	information; information desk
die	**Bahn** ◇	railway
die	**Bahnhofsgaststätte, -n**	station buffet
die	**Bahnlinie, -n**	railway line
die	**Bremse, -n** ◇	brake
die	**Brücke, -n** ◇	bridge
die	**Deutsche Bundesbahn (DB)** ⌐	German Railways
die	**einfache Fahrkarte, -n -n**	single ticket
die	**Einfahrt, -en**	entrance
die	**Eisenbahn, -en**	railway
die	**Fahrkarte, -n**	ticket
die	**Fahrt, -en** ◇	journey
die	**Gepäckaufbewahrung** ⌐	left-luggage office
die	**Grenze, -n**	border, frontier
die	**Haltestelle, -n**	stop, station
die	**Klasse, -n** ◇	class
die	**Linie, -n**	line
die	**Mehrfahrtenkarte, -n** ⌐	season ticket
die	**Notbremse, -n** ⌐	alarm, communication cord
die	**Reise, -n**	journey
die	**Reisende*, -n**	traveller
die	**Richtung, -en**	direction
die	**Rückfahrkarte, -n**	return (ticket)
die	**S-Bahn** ⌐	high-speed railway; suburban railway
die	**Station, -en** ◇	station
die	**Tasche, -n** ◇	bag
die	**U-Bahn**	underground
die	**U-Bahn-Station, -en**	underground station
die	**Uhr, -en** ◇	clock
die	**Verbindung, -en**	connection
die	**Verspätung, -en**	delay
die	**Zollbeamtin**	customs officer
die	**Zollkontrolle**	customs control *or* check

die	**Entgleisung, -en**	derailment
die	**Lokomotive, -n**	locomotive, engine
die	**Monatskarte, -n**	monthly season ticket
die	**Nummer, -n**	number
die	**Rolltreppe, -n**	escalator
die	**Schienen** (*pl*)	rails
die	**Schranke, -n** ☐	level crossing gate
die	**Sperre, -n**	barrier
die	**Strecke, -n** ◇	(section of) railway line *or* track
die	**Wochenkarte, -n**	weekly ticket

das	**Abteil, -e**	compartment
das	**Fahrgeld, -er**	fare
das	**Fundbüro, -s**	lost property office
das	**Gepäck**	luggage
das	**Gepäcknetz, -e**	luggage rack
das	**Gleis, -e**	platform; track, rails
das	**Nichtraucherabteil, -e**	non-smoking compartment
das	**Rad, ̈er** ◇	bike
das	**Raucherabteil, -e**	smoking compartment, smoker
das	**Reiseziel, -e**	destination
das	**Schließfach, ̈er**	left-luggage locker
das	**Taxi, -s**	taxi

mit der Bahn by rail
muß ich umsteigen? do I have to change (trains)?
"bitte einsteigen!" ''all aboard''
"alles aussteigen!" ''all change''
für diese Züge muß man Zuschlag bezahlen there is an extra charge for these trains
einen Platz reservieren to book a seat
nach Bonn und zurück a return to Bonn
zweimal nach Bonn und zurück two returns to Bonn
nach Bonn einfach a single to Bonn

TREES AND FORESTS

der **Baum**, ¨-e	tree
der **Christbaum**, ¨-e	Christmas tree
der **Forst**, -e 📖	forest
der **Obstbaum**, ¨-e	fruit tree
der **Obstgarten**, ¨-	orchard
der **Schatten**	shade; shadow
der **Wald**, ¨-er 📖	wood(s), forest
der **Weihnachtsbaum**, ¨-e	Christmas tree

der **Ahorn**, -e	maple
der **Ast**, ¨-e 📖	branch
der **Buchsbaum**, ¨-e	box tree
der **Busch**, ¨-e	bush, shrub
der **Kastanienbaum**, ¨-e	chestnut tree
der **Kiefernzapfen**, –	pine cone
der **Lindenbaum**, ¨-e	lime tree
der **Mistelzweig**, -e	(sprig of) mistletoe
der **Rotdorn**, -e	hawthorn
der **Stamm**, ¨-e ⋄ 📖	trunk
der **Strauch**, ¨-er	bush, shrub
der **Tannenbaum**, ¨-e	fir tree
der **Tannenzapfen**, –	fir cone
der **Weidenbaum**, ¨-e	willow
der **Weinberg**, -e	vineyard
der **Wipfel**, –	treetop
der **Zweig**, -e 📖	branch

auf einen Baum klettern to climb a tree
im Schatten eines Baumes in the shade of a tree
im Herbst werden die Blätter gelb the leaves turn yellow in autumn
entwurzeln to uproot

der **Apfelbaum, ¨e**	apple tree
der **Baumstamm, ¨e**	tree trunk
der **Baumstumpf, ¨e**	tree stump
der **Birnbaum, ¨e**	pear tree
der **Farn, -e**	fern
der **Holunder, –**	elder
der **Holzfäller, –**	woodcutter, lumberjack
der **Kiefernwald, ¨er**	pinewood, pine forest
der **Kiefernzapfen, –**	pine cone
der **Kirschbaum, ¨e**	cherry tree
der **Laubbaum, ¨e**	deciduous tree
der **Laubwald, ¨er**	deciduous forest
der **Mischwald, ¨er**	mixed woodland
der **Nadelbaum, ¨e**	conifer
der **Nadelwald, ¨er**	coniferous forest
der **Olivenbaum, ¨e**	olive tree
der **Pilz, -e**	fungus; mushroom; toadstool

die **Beere, -n**	berry
die **Birke, -n**	birch
die **Blutbuche, -n**	copper beech
die **Buche, -n**	beech tree
die **Eibe, -n**	yew
die **Eiche, -n**	oak (tree)
die **Esche, -n**	ash
die **Fichte, -n**	spruce, pine
die **Föhre, -n**	Scots pine
die **Kastanie, -n**	chestnut; chestnut tree
die **Kiefer, -n** ◇	pine
die **Knospe, -n**	bud
die **Linde, -n**	lime tree
die **Mistel, -n**	mistletoe
die **Pappel, -n**	poplar
die **Pinie, -n**	pine
die **Platane, -n**	plane tree
die **Rinde, -n**	bark
die **Roßkastanie, -n**	horse chestnut
die **Stechpalme, -n**	holly

die	**Tanne**, -n	fir tree
die	**Trauerweide**, -n	weeping willow
die	**Ulme**, -n	elm
die	**Weide**, -n ⬦	willow
die	**Wurzel**, -n	root

die	**Baumkrone**, -n	treetop
die	**Baumschule**, -n	nursery
die	**Eichel**, -n	acorn
die	**Entwaldung**	deforestation
die	**Eßkastanie**, -n	sweet chestnut
die	**Lichtung**, -en	clearing
die	**Schonung**, -en	plantation
die	**Wiederaufforstung**	reafforestation
die	**Zeder**, -n	cedar (tree)
die	**Zypresse**, -n	cypress

das	**Blatt**, ¨-er ⬦	leaf
das	**Gebüsch**, -e	bushes; undergrowth
das	**Holz**	wood (*material*)

das	**Dickicht**, -e	thicket
das	**Geäst**	branches
das	**Unterholz**	undergrowth

der	**Blumenkohl**	cauliflower
der	**Champignon, -s**	(button) mushroom
der	**Knoblauch** ▭	garlic
der	**Kohl**	cabbage
der	**Kopfsalat, -e**	lettuce
der	**Pilz, -e**	mushroom
der	**Rosenkohl**	Brussels sprouts
der	**Salat, -e** ◇	lettuce; salad
der	**Vegetarier, –**	vegetarian

der	**Gartenkürbis, -se**	marrow
der	**Kürbis, -se**	pumpkin
der	**Lauch, -e**	leek
der	**Mais** ◇	sweetcorn
der	**Maiskolben, –**	corncob
der	**Paprika, -s**	pepper (*red/green*)
der	**Porree, -s**	leek
der	**Rettich, -e**	(*large*) radish
der	**Sellerie**	celeriac; celery
der	**Spargel**	asparagus
der	**Spinat**	spinach
der	**Stangensellerie**	celery

der	**Chicorée**	chicory
der	**Chinakohl**	Chinese cabbage
der	**Dill**	dill
der	**Fenchel**	fennel
der	**Grünkohl**	curly kale
der	**Kohlrabi**	kohlrabi
der	**Rhabarber**	rhubarb
der	**Rotkohl**	red cabbage
der	**Salbei**	sage
der	**Schnittlauch**	chives
der	**Thymian**	thyme
der	**Weißkohl**	white cabbage
der	**Wirsing**	savoy cabbage

ESSENTIAL WORDS (f)

die	**Aubergine,** -n	aubergine
die	**Avocado,** -s	avocado (pear)
die	**Bohne,** -n	bean
die	**Brokkoli** (*pl*)	broccoli
die	**Erbse,** -n	pea
die	**grüne Bohne,** -n -n	French bean
die	**Gurke,** -n	cucumber
die	**Karotte,** -n	carrot
die	**Kartoffel,** -n	potato
die	**Tomate,** -n	tomato
die	**Vegetarierin**	vegetarian
die	**Zwiebel,** -n	onion

IMPORTANT WORDS (f)

die	**Artischocke,** -n	artichoke
die	**Brunnenkresse**	watercress
die	**Endivie,** -n	endive
die	**Erdartischocke,** -n	Jerusalem artichoke
die	**Essiggurke,** -n	gherkin
die	**Kresse**	cress
die	**Möhre,** -n	carrot
die	**Mohrrübe,** -n	carrot
die	**Paprikaschote,** -n	pepper, capsicum
die	**Pastinake,** -n	parsnip
die	**Petersilie**	parsley
die	**rote Rübe,** -n -n	beetroot
die	**Rübe,** -n	turnip
die	**Zucchini,** –	courgette

USEFUL WORDS (f)

die	**dicken Bohnen** (*pl*)	broad beans
die	**Kichererbsen** (*pl*)	chickpeas
die	**Linsen** (*pl*)	lentils
die	**Schalotten** (*pl*)	shallots
die	**Schwarzwurzeln** (*pl*)	salsifies
die	**Stangenbohnen** (*pl*)	runner beans
die	**Steckrübe,** -n	swede

ESSENTIAL WORDS (nt)

das	**Gemüse, –**	vegetable(s)
das	**Gewürz, -e**	spice
das	**Kraut, ¨er**	herb

USEFUL WORDS (nt)

das	**Bohnenkraut**	savory
das	**Radieschen, –**	radish
das	**Sauerkraut**	sauerkraut, pickled cabbage

organisch organic
Pommes frites chips, French fries
Knoblauchwurst garlic sausage
rot wie eine Tomate as red as a beetroot
vegetarisch vegetarian
geraspelte Möhren grated carrots
Gemüse anbauen to grow vegetables
Salzkartoffeln boiled potatoes
Pellkartoffeln potatoes boiled in their jackets

VEHICLES

ESSENTIAL WORDS (m)

der	Bulldozer, –	bulldozer
der	Bus, -se	bus
der	Dampfer, –	steamer
der	Fahrpreis, -e	fare
der	Feuerwehrwagen, –	fire engine
der	Flugzeugträger, –	aircraft carrier
der	Hubschrauber, –	helicopter
der	Jeep, -s	jeep
der	Krankenwagen, –	ambulance
der	Lastkraftwagen (LKW), – ⌑	lorry, truck
der	Lieferwagen, –	van; delivery van
der	Möbelwagen, –	furniture van, removal van
der	Motorroller, –	motor scooter
der	Personenkraftwagen (PKW), – ⌑	private car
der	Polizeiwagen, –	police car
der	Reisebus, -se	coach
der	Rücksitz, -e	back seat
der	Straßenbahnwagen, –	tramcar
der	Tanker, –	tanker
der	Transporter, –	van; transporter
der	Vordersitz, -e	front seat
der	Wagen, – ◇	car; cart; carriage
der	Wohnwagen, –	caravan
der	Zug, ¨e ◇	train

eine Höchstgeschwindigkeit von 50 Kilometern pro Stunde a maximum
  speed of 50 kilometres per hour
seine Fahrkarte entwerten to cancel one's ticket (in machine)
trampen, per Anhalter fahren to hitch-hike
zu Fuß gehen to walk, go on foot
ein Mietauto (nt) a hired car
gebrauchte Autos, Gebrauchtwagen second-hand cars
mieten to hire
öffentliche Verkehrsmittel public transport
gute Reise! have a good trip!
mit der Bahn or *mit dem Zug fahren* to go by rail or by train
mit dem Auto fahren to drive, go by car

IMPORTANT WORDS (m)

der **Anhänger**, – ◇	trailer
der **Ballon**, -s	balloon
der **Karren**, –	cart
der **Kinderwagen**, –	pram
der **Kombiwagen**, –	estate car, station wagon
der **Lastkahn**, ˙-e	barge
der **Omnibus**, -se	bus
der **Panzer**, - ◇ ▢	tank; armoured car
der **Sattelschlepper**, –	articulated lorry
der **Schlepper**, –	tug, tugboat
der **Sessellift**, -e	chairlift
der **Streifenwagen**, –	(police) patrol car
der **Vergnügungsdampfer**, –	pleasure steamer

USEFUL WORDS (m)

der **Bagger**, –	excavator
der **Einbaum**, ˙-e	dugout (*canoe*)
der **Einsitzer**, –	single-seater (*car, plane*)
der **Firmenwagen**, –	company car
der **Fischdampfer**, –	trawler
der **Go-Kart**, -s	kart, go-cart
der **Kleinbus**, -se	minibus
der **Kleintransporter**, –	small van
der **Kran**, ˙-e	crane
der **Kutter**, –	cutter
der **Laster**, –	lorry
der **Leichenwagen**, –	hearse
der **Pferdetransporter**, –	horsebox
der **Schlitten**, –	sleigh; sledge
der **Schoner**, –	schooner
der **Sportwagen**, – ◇	pushchair; sports car
der **Straßenkreuzer**, –	limousine
der **Tankwagen**, –	tanker
der **Viehwagen**, –	cattle truck

die **Autofähre, -n** ⌼	car ferry
die **Fähre, -n** ⌼	ferry (boat)
die **fliegende Untertasse, -n -n**	flying saucer
die **Gefahr, -en** ⌼	danger, risk
die **Lokomotive, -n**	locomotive, engine
die **Straßenbahn, -en**	tram
die **U-Bahn**	underground

die **Dampfwalze, -n**	steamroller
die **Drahtseilbahn, -en**	cable railway, funicular
die **Düse, -n**	jet (plane)
die **Jacht, -en**	yacht
die **Planierraupe, -n**	bulldozer
die **Rakete, -n**	rocket
die **Schwebebahn, -en**	cable railway; overhead railway

die **Karosserie, -n**	body, coachwork
die **Kutsche, -n**	(*horse-drawn*) coach
die **Limousine, -n**	saloon (*car*)
die **Raumfähre, -n**	space shuttle

das **Coupé, -s**	coupé
das **Dreirad, ¨er**	tricycle
das **Floß, ¨e**	raft
das **Flugboot, -e**	hydroplane
das **Kabriolett, -s**	convertible
das **Rennauto, -s**	racing car
das **Schulschiff, -e**	training ship
das **Wohnmobil, -e**	camper, Dormobile ®
das **Zweirad, ¨er**	two-wheeled vehicle

nach Frankfurt fliegen *to fly to Frankfurt*

ESSENTIAL WORDS (nt)

das	**Auto**, -s	car
das	**Boot**, -e	boat
das	**Fährboot**, -e	ferry (boat)
das	**Fahrgeld**, -er	fare
das	**Fahrrad**, ̈-er	bicycle
das	**Fahrzeug**, -e ▢	vehicle
das	**Feuerwehrauto**, -s	fire engine
das	**Flugzeug**, -e	plane, aeroplane
das	**Kanu**, -s	canoe
das	**Mofa**, -s	small moped
das	**Moped**, -s	moped
das	**Motorboot**, -e	motorboat
das	**Motorrad**, ̈-er	motorbike, motorcycle
das	**Rad**, ̈-er ◇	bike
das	**Raumschiff**, -e	spaceship
das	**Rettungsboot**, -e	lifeboat
das	**Ruderboot**, -e	rowing boat
das	**Schiff**, -e	ship, vessel
das	**Schnellboot**, -e	speedboat
das	**Segelboot**, -e	sailing boat
das	**Taxi**, -s	taxi
das	**UFO**, -s	UFO (unidentified flying object)

IMPORTANT WORDS (nt)

das	**Düsenflugzeug**, -e	jet plane
das	**Luftkissenboot**, -e	hovercraft
das	**Paddelboot**, -e	canoe
das	**Schlauchboot**, -e	inflatable (dinghy)
das	**Segelflugzeug**, -e	glider
das	**Tankschiff**, -e	tanker
das	**Transportmittel**, –	means of transport (*goods*)
das	**U-Boot**, -e	submarine
das	**Verkehrsmittel**, –	means of transport

fahren *to go*
eine Reise machen *to go on a journey*
reisen *to travel*

WEATHER

ESSENTIAL WORDS (m)

der	**Abend**, -e	evening
der	**Berg**, -e	mountain; hill
der	**Blitz**, -e	(flash of) lightning
der	**Donner** ▭	thunder
der	**Donnerschlag**, ̈-e	thunderclap
der	**Frost**, ̈-e	frost
der	**Frühling**	spring
der	**Grad**, -e	degree
der	**Hagel**	hail
der	**Herbst**	autumn
der	**Himmel** ◇	sky
der	**Monat**, -e	month
der	**Mond**	moon
der	**Morgen**, –	morning
der	**Nachmittag**	afternoon
der	**Nebel**	fog, mist
der	**Niederschlag**, ̈-e ▭	rainfall, precipitation
der	**Norden**	north
der	**Osten**	east
der	**Regen**	rain
der	**Regenschauer**, –	shower (*of rain*)
der	**Regenschirm**, -e	umbrella
der	**Regentropfen**, –	raindrop
der	**Schatten**	shadow; shade
der	**Schauer**, –	shower
der	**Schirm**, -e	umbrella
der	**Schnee**	snow
der	**Schneefall**, ̈-e	snowfall
der	**Schneeregen**	sleet
der	**Schneesturm**, ̈-e	snowstorm
der	**Smog**	smog
der	**Sommer**	summer
der	**Sonnenschein**	sunshine
der	**Stern**, -e	star
der	**Sturm**, ̈-e	storm, gale; tempest
der	**Süden**	south
der	**Westen**	west
der	**Wetterbericht**, -e ▭	weather report
der	**Wind**, -e	wind
der	**Winter**	winter

IMPORTANT WORDS (m)

der **Blitzableiter**, –	lightning conductor
der **Dunst** ◇	haze
der **Eiszapfen**, –	icicle
der **Gefrierpunkt**	freezing point
der **Mondschein**	moonlight
der **Orkan**, -e	hurricane
der **Ort**, -e	place
der **Planet**, -en	planet
der **Platzregen**	downpour
der **Regenbogen**, ¨	rainbow
der **Schaden**, ¨	damage
der **Sonnenaufgang**, ¨e	sunrise
der **Sonnenschirm**, -e	parasol, sunshade
der **Sonnenstrahl**, -en	ray of sunshine
der **Sonnenuntergang**, ¨e	sunset
der **Tagesanbruch**	dawn, break of day
der **Tau** ◇	dew
der **Windstoß**, ¨e	gust of wind

USEFUL WORDS (m)

der **Hagelschauer**, –	hailstorm
der **Luftdruck**	atmospheric pressure
der **Meteorologe**, -n	meteorologist
der **Monsun**	monsoon
der **Nieselregen**	drizzle
der **Sprühregen**	drizzle
der **Taifun**, -e	typhoon
der **Tornado**, -s	tornado
der **Wetterhahn**, ¨e	weather cock
der **Wettersturz**	sudden fall in temperature
der **Wetterumschwung**, ¨e	sudden change in the weather
der **Wirbelwind**	whirlwind
der **Wolkenbruch**, ¨e	cloudburst
der **Zenit**	zenith

*so ein **Sauwetter**!* *what awful weather!*
plus *plus*
minus *minus*

ESSENTIAL WORDS (f)

die **Front, -en** 📖	front
die **Hitze**	heat
die **Insel, -n**	island
die **Jahreszeit, -en**	season
die **Kälte**	cold
die **Luft**	air
die **Nacht, ¨e**	night
die **Natur**	nature
die **Sonne**	sun
die **Temperatur, -en**	temperature
die **Verbesserung, -en**	improvement
die **Welt**	world
die **Wetterlage** 📖	weather situation
die **Wettervorhersage, -n** 📖	weather forecast
die **Wolke, -n**	cloud

es fängt an zu schneien it's beginning to snow
wie ist das Wetter heute? what's the weather like today?
wie ist das Wetter bei euch? what's the weather like with you?
scheinen (die Sonne scheint) to shine
schneien (es schneit) to snow
regnen (es regnet) to rain
blitzen (es blitzt) to flash
donnern (es donnert) to thunder
nieseln (es nieselt) to drizzle
gießen (es gießt) to pour
frieren (es friert) to freeze
bedeckt overcast
bewölkt cloudy
feucht damp
heiß hot
heiter bright
herrlich marvellous
kalt cold
kühl cool

IMPORTANT WORDS (f)

die	**Atmosphäre**	atmosphere
die	**Aufheiterungen** (*pl*)	bright periods
die	**Bö, -en**	squall, gust of wind
die	**Brise, -n**	breeze
die	**Dürre, -n**	(period of) drought
die	**Flut, -en** ◇	flood
die	**Hitzewelle, -n**	heat wave
die	**Kältewelle, -n**	cold spell
die	**Morgendämmerung**	dawn
die	**Pfütze, -n**	puddle
die	**Schneeflocke, -n**	snowflake
die	**Schneewehe, -n**	snowdrift
die	**Überschwemmung, -en**	flood, deluge

USEFUL WORDS (f)

die	**Akklimatisierung**	acclimatization
die	**Klimazone, -n**	(climatic) zone
die	**Luftfeuchtigkeit**	(atmospheric) humidity
die	**Meteorologie**	meteorology
die	**Meteorologin**	meteorologist
die	**Nässe**	wetness
die	**Trockenheit**	dryness
die	**Wetterwarte, -n**	weather station
die	**Windstille, -n**	lull in the wind

mild *mild*
naß *wet*
neblig *misty*
regnerisch *rainy*
schön *lovely*
schwül *sultry, close*
sonnig *sunny*
stürmisch *stormy*
trocken *dry*
trüb *dull*
warm *warm*
windig *windy*

das	**Eis** ◇	ice
das	**Gewitter, –**	thunderstorm
das	**Glatteis** ▭	black ice
das	**Halbdunkel**	semi-darkness
das	**Jahr, -e**	year
das	**Klima, -s**	climate
das	**Land, ¨er** ◇	country
das	**Licht**	light
das	**Mondlicht**	moonlight
das	**Sauwetter**	awful weather
das	**Wetter**	weather

das	**Barometer, –**	barometer
das	**Schneegestöber, –**	snowstorm
das	**Tauwetter**	thaw
das	**Unwetter, –**	thunderstorm

das	**Hagelkorn, ¨er**	hailstone
das	**Regenwetter**	raininess; rainy weather
das	**Tageslicht**	daylight
das	**Thermometer, –**	thermometer
das	**Wetterleuchten**	sheet lightning
das	**Zwielicht**	twilight

vereinzelt bewölkt *with (occasional) cloudy patches*
herrschen *to prevail*
zeitweise *for a time*
wie ist die Wettervorhersage? *what's the weather forecast?*
die Hitze war nicht auszuhalten *the heat was unbearable*
es regnet in Strömen *it's pouring*
sich unterstellen *to shelter (from the rain etc)*
atmosphärische Störungen *atmospherics*
bei guter/schlechter Witterung *when the weather is good/bad*

ESSENTIAL WORDS (m)

der	**Aufenthalt, -e**	stay
der	**Empfang** ☐	reception
der	**Feuerlöscher, –** ☐	fire extinguisher
der	**Herbergsvater, ¨**	warden
der	**Junge, -n** ◇	boy
der	**Mülleimer, –**	dustbin
der	**Prospekt, -e**	leaflet, brochure
der	**Rucksack, ¨e**	rucksack, backpack
der	**Schlafsaal, (-säle)**	dormitory
der	**Schlafsack, ¨e**	sleeping bag
der	**Spaziergang, ¨e**	walk
der	**Speisesaal, (-säle)**	dining room
der	**Stadtplan, ¨e**	street map
der	**Urlaub, -e**	holiday(s)
der	**Waschsalon, -s**	launderette
der	**Zimmernachweis** ☐	accommodation service

USEFUL WORDS (m)

der	**Erwachsene*, -n**	adult
der	**Jugendliche*, -n**	young person, youth
der	**Laden, ¨**	shop
der	**Reiseführer, –** ◇	guidebook
der	**Waschraum, ¨e**	washroom

USEFUL WORDS (f)

die	**Decke, -n** ◇	blanket; cover
die	**Erwachsene*, -n**	adult
die	**Hausordnung**	house regulations
die	**Jugendliche*, -n**	young person
die	**Thermosflasche, -n**	Thermos ® flask
die	**Wanderung, -en**	walk, hike

"Hausordnung für Jugendherbergen" *"youth hostel rules"*
mieten *to hire*
bleiben *to stay*
übernachten *to spend the night*

ESSENTIAL WORDS (f)

die	**Anmeldung** ◇ ⌑	registration
die	**Bettwäsche**	bed linen
die	**Dusche, -n**	shower
die	**Herbergsmutter, ⸚**	(female) warden
die	**Jugendherberge, -n**	youth hostel
die	**Küche, -n** ◇	kitchen
die	**Landkarte, -n**	map
die	**Mahlzeit, -en**	meal
die	**Mitgliedskarte, -n**	membership card
die	**Nachtruhe** ⌑	lights out
die	**Ruhe** ◇	peace; rest
die	**Toilette, -n**	toilet
die	**Übernachtung, -en**	overnight stay
die	**Unterkunft, ⸚e**	accommodation
die	**Veranstaltung, -en** ⌑	organization
die	**Wäsche**	washing (*things*)

ESSENTIAL WORDS (nt)

das	**Abendessen**	evening meal, supper
das	**Badezimmer, –**	bathroom
das	**Bett, -en**	bed
das	**Büro, -s**	office
das	**Essen** ◇	food; meal
das	**Frühstück**	breakfast
das	**Mädchen, –**	girl
das	**Schwarze Brett** ⌑	notice board

USEFUL WORDS (nt)

das	**Etagenbett, -en**	bunk bed
das	**Kind, -er**	child
das	**Trampen**	hitch-hiking

sich anmelden *to register*

SUPPLEMENTARY VOCABULARY

The vocabulary items on pages 315 to 336 have been grouped under parts of speech rather than topics because they can apply in a wide range of circumstances. You should learn to use them just as freely as the vocabulary already given.

ADJECTIVES

ADJECTIVES

abgenutzt worn out (*object*)
abscheulich hideous
ähnlich (*+dat*) similar (to), like
aktuell topical
albern silly, foolish
allerlei all kinds of
allgemein general
alltäglich ordinary; daily
alt old
altmodisch old-fashioned
amüsant amusing
andere(r,s) other
anders different
angenehm pleasant
angrenzend neighbouring
arm poor
artig well-behaved, good
aufgeregt excited
aufgeweckt bright, sharp
aufregend exciting
aufrichtig sincere
außergewöhnlich extraordinary
außerordentlich extraordinary
ausführlich detailed
ausgestreckt stretched (out)
ausgezeichnet excellent
ausschließlich sole, exclusive
befriedigend satisfactory
begeistert keen, enthusiastic
bekannt (well-)known; famous
belebt busy (*street*)
beleuchtet illuminated, floodlit
beliebt popular

bemerkenswert remarkable
benachbart neighbouring
bereit ready
berühmt famous
beschäftigt (mit) busy (with) (*of person*)
besetzt engaged; taken
besondere(r,s) special
besorgt worried, anxious
besser better
beste(r,s) best
betrunken drunk
beunruhigt worried, disturbed
billig cheap
blöd silly, stupid
breit wide, broad
bunt colourful
dankbar grateful
dauernd perpetual, constant
defekt faulty
delikat delicate; delicious
deutlich clear; distinct
dicht thick; dense
dick thick; fat
doof daft, stupid
dreckig dirty, filthy
dringend urgent
dumm silly, stupid; annoying
dunkel dark
dünn thin
durstig thirsty
dynamisch dynamic
echt real; genuine

ADJECTIVES — 2

ehemalig former, old
ehrlich sincere; honest
eifrig keen, enthusiastic
eigen own
einfach simple; single
einzeln single, individual
einzig only
elegant elegant
elektrisch, Elektro- electric
elend poor, wretched
End- final
endgültig final, definite
endlos endless
eng narrow; tight
entschlossen determined
entsetzlich dreadful
entzückend delightful
erfahren experienced
ernst serious; solemn
ernsthaft serious, earnest
erreichbar reachable, within reach
erschöpft exhausted, worn out
erstaunlich amazing, extraordinary
erstaunt astonished
erste(r,s) first
erstklassig first-rate
erträglich bearable
fähig (zu or +gen) capable (of)
falsch false; wrong
faul rotten; lazy
feierlich solemn
fein fine
fern far-off, distant
fertig prepared, ready
fest firm; hard
fett fat; greasy
finster dark
flach flat
fortgeschritten advanced
fortwährend continual, incessant
frech cheeky
frei free; vacant
frisch fresh

früh early
furchtbar frightful
fürchterlich terrible, awful
ganz whole; complete
geduldig patient
geeignet suitable
gefährlich dangerous
gefroren frozen
geheim secret
geheimnisvoll mysterious
gemischt mixed
gemütlich comfortable
genau exact, precise
gerade straight; even
geringste(r,s) slightest, least
gesamt whole, entire
geschichtlich historical
gewaltig tremendous, huge
gewalttätig violent
gewiß certain
gewöhnlich usual; ordinary;
  common
glatt smooth
gleich same; equal
glücklich happy; fortunate
gnädig gracious
gnädige Frau Madam
graziös graceful
grob coarse; rude
groß big, large; tall; great
großartig magnificent
günstig favourable; convenient
gut good
hart hard
häßlich ugly
Haupt- main
heftig fierce, violent
heiß hot
heiter cheerful; bright; fair
hell pale; bright; light
herrlich marvellous
historisch historical
hoch high

höflich polite, civil
hübsch pretty
hungrig hungry
intelligent intelligent
interessant interesting
jede(r,s) each; every
jung young
kalt cold
kein no, not any
klar clear
klatschnaß wet through, soaking
wet
klein small, little
klug wise; clever
komisch funny
kompliziert complicated
körperlich physical
kostbar expensive; precious
kostenlos free (of charge)
köstlich delicious
kräftig strong
kühl cool
kurz short
lächelnd smiling
lächerlich ridiculous
lahm lame
Landes- national
lang long; tall (*of person*)
langsam slow
langweilig boring
laut loud; noisy
lauwarm lukewarm, tepid
lebendig alive; lively
lebhaft lively (*of person*)
lecker delicious, tasty
leer empty
leicht easy; light (*weight*)
leidenschaftlich passionate
leise quiet; soft
letzte(r,s) last, latest; final
lieb dear
Lieblings- favourite
linke(r,s) left

lustig amusing; cheerful
sich lustig machen über (*+acc*) to
make fun of
luxuriös luxurious
Luxus- luxury, luxurious
mächtig powerful, mighty
mager thin
mehrere several
merkwürdig strange, odd
Militär-, militärisch military
mindeste least
mitleidig sympathetic
modern modern
möglich possible
müde tired
munter lively
mutig courageous
mysteriös mysterious
nachlässig careless, negligent
nächste(r,s) next; nearest
nah(e) near; close
natürlich natural
nett nice; kind
neu new
neugierig curious
niedrig low
nötig necessary
notwendig necessary
nützlich useful
nutzlos useless
obligatorisch compulsory,
obligatory
offen open; frank
offenbar, offensichtlich obvious
öffentlich public
offiziell official
ordentlich (neat and) tidy
Orts- local
pädagogisch educational
passend suitable
persönlich personal
populär popular
prächtig magnificent

ADJECTIVES — 4

privat private; personal
privilegiert privileged
pünktlich punctual
Quadrat-, quadratisch square
rauh rough; harsh
rechte(r,s) right
reich rich
reif ripe
rein clean
reizend charming
religiös religious
reserviert reserved
richtig right, correct
riesig huge, gigantic
romantisch romantic
ruhig quiet, peaceful
rund round
sanft gentle; soft
satt full (*person*)
ich habe es satt I'm fed up (with it)
sauber clean
sauer sour
scharf sharp; spicy
schattig shady
scheu shy
schick smart, chic
schläfrig sleepy
schlank slender, slim
schlau cunning, sly
schlecht bad
schlimm bad
schmal narrow; slender
schmutzig dirty
schnell fast, quick, rapid
schön beautiful
schrecklich terrible; frightful
schroff steep; jagged; brusque
schüchtern shy
schwach weak
schweigsam silent
schwer heavy; serious
schwierig difficult
seltsam strange, odd, curious

sicher sure; safe
sichtbar visible
solche(r,s) such
Sonder- special
sonderbar strange, odd
sorgenfrei carefree
sorgfältig careful
spannend exciting
spät late
Stadt-, städtisch municipal; urban
ständig perpetual
stark strong; heavy
steif stiff
steil steep
still quiet; still
stolz (auf +*acc*) proud (of)
streng severe, harsh; strict
süß sweet
sympathisch likeable
tapfer brave
technisch technical
tief deep
toll mad; terrific
tot dead
tragbar portable
traurig sad
treu true (*friend etc*)
trocken dry
typisch typical
übel wicked, bad
übrig left-over, remaining
unangenehm unpleasant
unartig naughty
unbekannt unknown
uneben uneven
unentschieden undecided
unerreichbar unattainable
unerträglich unbearable
ungeduldig impatient
ungeheuer huge
ungewöhnlich unusual
ungezogen rude
unglaublich incredible

unglücklich unhappy; unfortunate
unheimlich weird
unmöglich impossible
unsicher unsure; unsafe
unvergleichbar incomparable; unique
unwahrscheinlich unlikely
unwesentlich irrelevant
unwichtig unimportant
unzufrieden dissatisfied
ursprünglich original
verantwortlich responsible
verboten prohibited, forbidden
vergleichbar comparable
verlegen embarrassed
verletzt injured
vernünftig sensible, reasonable
verrückt mad, crazy
verschieden various; different
verständlich understandable
viereckig square
volkstümlich popular (*of the people*)
voll (+*gen*) full (of)
vollkommen perfect; complete

vollständig complete
vorderste(r,s) front (*row etc*)
vorletzte(r,s) last but one
wach awake
wahr true
wahrscheinlich likely
warm warm
weich soft
weise wise
weit wide
wert worth
wertlos worthless
wesentlich essential
wichtig important
wild fierce; wild
wohlhabend well-off
wunderbar wonderful, marvellous
zäh tough
zahlreich numerous
zart gentle, tender
zig umpteen
zufrieden satisfied, content(ed)
zusätzlich extra

ADVERBS

absichtlich deliberately, on purpose
allein alone, on one's own
allerdings certainly; of course, to be sure
anders otherwise; differently
äußerst extremely, most
bald soon; almost
beinahe nearly, almost
besonders especially, particularly
am besten best, best of all
bestimmt definitely, for sure
bloß only, merely
da there; here; then
daher from there; from that
dahin (to) there; then
damals at that time
danach after that; afterwards
dann then
darin in it; in there
deshalb therefore, for that reason
doch after all
dort there
dorthin (to) there
draußen out of doors; outside
drinnen inside; indoors
drüben over there; on the other side
durchaus thoroughly; absolutely
eben exactly; just
eher sooner; rather
eigentlich really, actually
einmal once; one day, some day
auf einmal all at once
endlich at last; finally
erst first; only (*time*)
erstens first(ly), in the first place
etwa about; perhaps
fast almost, nearly
ganz quite; completely
gar nicht not at all
gegenwärtig at present, at the
moment
genau exactly, precisely
genug enough
gerade just; exactly
geradeaus straight ahead
gern(e) willingly; gladly
gewöhnlich usually
glücklicherweise fortunately
gut well
häufig frequently
heutzutage nowadays
hier here
hierher this way, here
hin und her to and fro
hinten at the back, behind
höchst highly, extremely
hoffentlich I hope, hopefully
immer always
immer noch still
inzwischen meanwhile, in the meantime
irgendwo(hin) (to) somewhere
je ever
jedenfalls in any case
jedesmal each time, every time
jedesmal wenn whenever
jemals ever; at any time
jetzt now
kaum hardly, scarcely
keineswegs in no way; by no means
komischerweise funnily (enough); in a funny way
künftig in future
lange for a long time
langsam slowly
lauter (*with pl*) nothing but, only
leider unfortunately
lieber rather, preferably
am liebsten most (of all), best (of all)

links left; on *or* to the left
manchmal sometimes
mehr more
meinetwegen for my sake; on my account
am meisten (the) most
meistens mostly; for the most part
mitten (in) in the middle *or* midst (of)
möglicherweise possibly
möglichst as ... as possible
nachher afterwards
natürlich naturally
neu newly; afresh, anew
nicht not
nichtsdestoweniger nevertheless
nie, niemals never
noch still; yet
noch einmal (once) again
normalerweise normally
nun now
nur just, only
oben above; upstairs
oft often
plötzlich suddenly
rechts right; on *or* to the right
richtig correctly; really
rundherum round about, all (a) round
schlecht badly
schließlich finally
schnell quickly
schon already
sehr very, a lot, very much
selbst even
selten seldom, rarely
so so; thus, like this

sofort at once, immediately
sogar even
sogleich at once, straight away
sonst otherwise; or else
überall(hin) everywhere
übrigens besides; by the way
umher about, around
ungefähr about, approximately
unten below; downstairs; at the bottom
unterwegs on the way
versehentlich accidentally
viel much, a lot
vielleicht perhaps, maybe
völlig completely
vorbei by, past
vorher before, previously; beforehand
vorn(e) at the front
wahrscheinlich probably
wann(?) when(?)
warum(?) why(?)
weit far
wie(?) how(?)
wieder again
wirklich really
wo(?) where(?)
woher/wohin(?) from where/(to) where(?)
ziemlich fairly; rather
zu too
zuerst first; at first
zufällig by chance
zurück back
zweitens second(ly), in the second place

CONJUNCTIONS

aber but; however
als when; as; than
als ob, als wenn as if, as though
also therefore; so
bevor before (*time*)
bis until, till; (up) to, as far as
da as, since, seeing (that)
damit so that, in order that
denn for
ehe before
entweder ... oder either ... or
gerade als just as
indem as; while
inwiefern to what extent
je ... desto the more ... the more
nachdem after
nicht nur ... sondern auch not only ... but also
nun (da) now (that)
ob if, whether
obwohl although
oder or

ohne daß without
seit since
seitdem since
sobald as soon as
so daß so that
solange as long as
sondern (*after neg*) but
soweit as far as
sowohl ... als auch both ... and
teils ... teils partly ... partly
und and
während while
wann when
weder ... noch neither ... nor
weil because
wenn when; if
wie as, like
wo where
wohin to where
worauf whereupon; on which
worin in which

SOME EXTRA NOUNS

die **Abhängigkeit** dependence
die **Abkürzung**, -en ◊ abbreviation; shortcut
der **Abschnitt**, -e section
die **Abwesenheit** absence
die **Ahnung**, -en idea, suspicion
der **Alptraum**, ¨e nightmare
die **Änderung**, -en ◊ change
die **Andeutung**, -en innuendo, insinuation
der **Anfall**, ¨e attack, fit
der **Anfang**, ¨e beginning
zu **Anfang** at the beginning
die **Angelegenheit**, -en matter
das **Anliegen**, – request
die **Anmeldung**, -en ◊ announcement
die **Anonymität** anonymity
die **Anstalten** (*fpl*) preparations
die **Anstrengung**, -en effort
der **Antrag**, ¨e application
die **Anweisungen** (*fpl*) orders, instructions
die **Anwesenheit** presence
das **Anzeichen**, – sign, indication
der **Apparat**, -e machine
das **Ärgernis**, -se annoyance
die **Art**, -en way, method; kind, sort
aller **Art** of all kinds
auf meine **Art** in my own way
das **Asyl** asylum
das **Attest**, -e certificate
die **Aufmerksamkeit** attention; attentiveness
die **Aufsicht** supervision
der **Aufstieg** ascent
der **Ausbruch**, ¨e outbreak; break-out; eruption
die **Ausgabe**, -n ◊ edition

der **Ausgangspunkt**, -e starting point
das **Ausmaß**, -e scale, extent
die **Ausnahme**, -n exception
der **Ausschnitt**, -e ◊ cutting; excerpt
die **Äußerung**, -en remark; statement
die **Ausstattung**, -en fittings
die **Auswahl (an** +*dat*) ◊ selection (of)
die **Auswirkung**, -en repercussion
die **Autorität** authority
der **Bau** ◊ construction
die **Beaufsichtigung** supervision
die **Bedeutung**, -en meaning; importance
die **Bedingung**, -en condition, stipulation
das **Bedürfnis**, -se need
der **Befehl**, -e order, command
die **Begabung**, -en talent
der **Begriff: im Begriff sein, etw zu tun** to be about to do sth
das **Beispiel**, -e example
zum **Beispiel** for example
die **Bemerkung**, -en remark
die **Bemühung**, -en trouble, effort
die **Berechnung**, -en calculation
der **Bescheid**, -e ◊ message
jdm **Bescheid sagen** to let sb know
die **Besorgnis**, -se worry
der **Betrag**, ¨e sum, amount (*of money*)
der **blinde Passagier**, -n -e stowaway
der **Blödsinn** nonsense
der **Bogen**, ¨ ◊ bend
die **Botschaft**, -en ◊ message, news

die **Breite, -n** width
der **Bursche, -n** fellow
die **Chance, -n** chance, opportunity
der **Dank** thanks
die **Darstellung, -en** portrayal,
  representation
das **Denken** thinking, thought
das **Diagramm, -e** diagram; chart
die **Dicke, -n** thickness; fatness
der **Dienstwagen, –** company car
die **Dimension, -en** dimension
der **Dreck** dirt, filth
der **Druck** ⟡ pressure
der **Duft, ⁻e** smell; fragrance
die **Dummheit, -en** stupidity;
  stupid mistake
der **Dummkopf, ⁻e** idiot
die **Dunkelheit** dark(ness)
der **Dunst, ⁻e** ⟡ vapour
der **Durchschlag, ⁻e** (carbon) copy
der **Durchschnitt** average
die **Effektivität** efficiency;
  effectiveness
die **Ehre, -n** honour
die **Ehrlichkeit** honesty
die **Eifersucht** jealousy
der/die **Eigentümer(in), –** owner
die **Einbildung, -en** imagination
der **Eindruck, ⁻e** impression
der **Einfall, ⁻e** thought, idea
das **Eintreffen** arrival
die **Einzelheit, -en** detail
die **Eleganz** elegance
die **Empfindung, -en** feeling,
  emotion
die **Entdeckung, -en** discovery
die **Entschlossenheit** resolution,
  determination
die **Erfahrung, -en** experience
die **Erinnerung, -en** memory;
  remembrance
die **Erklärung, -en** explanation
die **Erkundigung, -en** inquiry

die **Erlaubnis, -se** permission;
  permit
das **Erlebnis, -se** experience
der **Ernst** earnestness, seriousness
im **Ernst** in earnest
die **Erwiderung, -en** retort
das **Exil, -e** exile (state)
der **Fall** ⟡ fall; downfall
die **Faulheit** laziness
die **Festigkeit** firmness
der **Fleckentferner** stain remover
der **Fluch, ⁻e** curse
die **Folge, -n** order; series; result
das **Format, -e** size; format
der/die **Freiwillige*, -n** volunteer
der/die **Fremde*, -n** stranger;
  foreigner
die **Freundlichkeit, -en** kindness
die **Frische** freshness
der/die **Führer(in), –** guide; leader
der **Funke, -n** spark
das **Gähnen** yawn(ing)
die **Gebühr, -en** ⟡ fee, charge
das **Gedächtnis, -se** memory
der **Gedanke, -n** thought, idea
die **Geduld** patience
der **Gegenstand, ⁻e** object
das **Gegenteil, -e** opposite
im **Gegenteil** on the contrary
das **Geheimnis, -se** mystery;
  secret
das **Gemisch, -e** mixture
das **Gerät, -e** ⟡ device, tool
der **Geruch, ⁻e** smell
das **Geschick, -e** fate; skill
der **Gesichtspunkt, -e** point of
  view
die **Gewandtheit** skill
der **Gewinn, -e** profit, gain; prize
das **Gleichgewicht** balance
das **Glück** ⟡ (good) luck;
  prosperity; happiness
das **Grab, ⁻er** grave

die **Grausamkeit, -en** cruelty
der **Grund, ⁻e** ✧ reason
die **Grüße** (*mpl*) wishes
die **Güte, -n** ✧ quality
der **Haken, –** ✧ snag
der **Halbschlaf** half-sleep
die **Hauptsache, -n** the main thing
die **Helligkeit** brightness
die **Herausforderung, -en** challenge
die **Herstellung, -en** manufacture
die **Hilfestellung, -en** aid, assistance
das **Hin und Her** coming(s) and going(s)
der **Hintergrund, ⁻e** background
die **Hoffnung, -en** hope
die **Höflichkeit, -en** politeness
die **Höhe, -n** ✧ height; level
die **Hypothese, -n** hypothesis
die **Idee, -n** idea
die **Kalkulation, -en** calculation
das **Kapitel, –** chapter
die **Kenntnis, -se** knowledge
die **Kette, -n** ✧ necklace
der **Klang, ⁻e** sound
das **Klischee, -s** cliché, stereotype
der **Knoten, –** ✧ knot
die **Kohle, -n** ✧ (*fam*) cash
das **Komplott, -s** plot, conspiracy
die **Konstruktion, -en** construction
die **Kontrolle, -n** control, supervision
die **Kopie, -n** copy
die **Kosten** (*pl*) cost(s); expenses
der **Kreis, -e** ✧ circle; district
der **Kreisel, –** spinning top
das **Kriterium, (-ien)** criterion
die **Krone, -n** crown
die **Kugel, -n** ✧ ball, sphere
das **Lächeln** smile
die **Lage, -n** ✧ layer
der **Landstreicher, –** tramp

die **Länge, -n** length
die **Lang(e)weile** boredom
der **Laut, -e** sound
der **Lebenslauf, ⁻e** curriculum vitae, CV
der **Leichtsinn** foolishness, thoughtlessness
das **Leid** sorrow, grief
der **Leiter, –** ✧ chief, leader
der/die **Leser(in)** reader
die **Literatur** literature
die **Lücke, -n** opening, gap
die **Lüge, -n** lie
die **Lust: ich habe Lust, es zu tun** I feel like doing it
die **Macht, ⁻e** power
der **Mangel, ⁻⁺** ✧ (**an** +*dat*) lack (of), shortage (of)
die **Marke, -n** ✧ brand
das **Maß, -e** ✧ measure
die **Meinung, -en** opinion, view
meiner Meinung nach in my opinion
das **meiste; die meisten** most
die **Meldung, -en** announcement
die **Menge, -n** ✧ crowd; quantity, lot
die **Mischung, -en** mixture
das **Mißgeschick, -e** misfortune
die **Mitteilung, -en** communication
das **Mittel, –** means; method
das **Modell, -e** ✧ model, version
die **Möglichkeit, -en** means; possibility
die **Mühe** pains, trouble
das **Muster, –** ✧ specimen
die **Nachrichten** (*fpl*) news; information
der **Nachteil, -e** disadvantage
die **Nähe: in der Nähe** close by
das **Netz, -e** ✧ network

der **Neuling**, -e newcomer
die **Not** need, distress
die **Notiz**, -en note; item
das **Notsignal**, -e distress signal
das **Objekt**, -e object
die **Öffentlichkeit** the general
  public
die **Öffnung**, -en opening
die **Ohrfeige**, -n slap (in the face)
die **Ordnung**, -en order
in **Ordnung** all right
in **Ordnung bringen** to arrange,
  tidy (up)
das **Pech**, -e misfortune, bad luck
der **Pfeil**, -e arrow
der **Plan**, ¨e plan; map
der **Platz**, ¨e ⋄ place; seat; room,
  space; square
die **Plauderei**, -en chat,
  conversation; talk
der **Pokal**, -e ⋄ cup (Sport); goblet
die **Politik** ⋄ politics; policy
die **Politur** polish
das **Pseudonym**, -e fictitious
  name; pen name
die **Publicity** publicity
der **Punkt**, -e point; dot; full stop
die **Puppe**, -n doll
die **Qualität**, -en quality
der **Radau** hullaballoo
der **Rand**, ¨er ⋄ edge; rim
die **Rasse**, -n ⋄ race (of person)
der **Rat**, ¨e (piece of) advice
das **Rätsel** puzzle, riddle
der **Raum**, ¨e ⋄ space; room
die **Regulierung**, -en adjustment
die **Rehabilitation** rehabilitation
die **Reihe**, -n ⋄ series; line
ich bin an der **Reihe** it's my turn
  now
der **Reim**, -e rhyme
der **Reiz**, -e attraction, charm
der **Rest**, -e remainder, rest

der **Revolutionär**, -e revolutionary
der **Rhythmus**, -men rhythm
das **Risiko**, (-ken) risk
der **Rückschlag**, ¨e setback
die **Rückseite**, -n back (of page etc)
der **Ruf**, -e ⋄ call, cry; reputation
die **Ruhe** ⋄ rest; peace; calm; silence
die **Sache**, -n ⋄ thing; matter
der **Sauerstoff** oxygen
der **Schatz**, ¨e treasure
die **Schätzung**, -en estimation
der **Schein**, -e ⋄ appearance
der **Scherz**, -e joke
das **Schicksal** fate
das **Schild**, -er ⋄ sign; label
der **Schlag**, ¨e blow, knock
der **Schluß**, ¨sse end(ing);
  conclusion
der **Schnuller**, – dummy (of baby)
der **Schritt**, -e footstep; step, pace
die **Schuhcreme** shoe polish
die **Schwerelosigkeit**
  weightlessness
die **Schwierigkeit**, -en difficulty
die **Sensation**, -en stir, sensation
die **Sicherheit** security; safety;
  certainty
die **Sicht** sight; view
der **Sinn**, -e mind; sense; meaning
die **Situation**, -en situation
der **Slang** slang
die **Sorte**, -n sort, kind
der **Spalt**, -e crack, opening; split
der **Spartarif** discount rate
der **Spaß**, ¨e ⋄ joke
das **Spielzeug**, -e toy
die **Spur**, -en sign, trace
der **Standpunkt**, -e point of view,
  standpoint
der **Star**, -s ⋄ star (film etc)
die **Stärke** ⋄ power, strength
die **Stelle**, -n ⋄ place

die **Steuer**, -n ⟐ tax
der **Stil**, -e style
die **Stille** stillness
die **Stimmung**, -en ⟐ mood;
  atmosphere
die **Strecke**, -n ⟐ stretch; distance
der **Streich**, -e practical joke
die **Streichung**, -en deletion
die **Strophe**, -n verse, stanza
die **Struktur** structure; framework
das **Stück**, -e ⟐ piece, part
die **Summe**, -n sum
das **System**, -e system
die **Tat**, -en act, action, deed
in der Tat in (actual) fact, indeed
die **Tätigkeit**, -en ⟐ activity
das **Teil**, -e ⟐ part, component
der **Teil**, -e ⟐ part, section
der **Text**, -e ⟐ text
die **Tiefe**, -n depth
die **Tonne**, -n barrel; drum; bin; ton
der **Tor**, -en ⟐ fool
die **Torheit**, -en foolishness
der **Traum**, ̈-e dream
der **Trick**, -s trick
die **Trümmer** (*pl*) wreckage; ruins
das **Tuch**, ̈-er ⟐ cloth
der **Typ**, -en ⟐ type
der **Überblick**, -e general survey;
  perspective
der/die **Überlebende***, -n
  survivor
die **Überraschung**, -en surprise
die **Übertreibung**, -en
  exaggeration
das **Unglück**, -e misfortune; bad
  luck; disaster
das **Unheil** evil; disaster,
  misfortune
die **Unhöflichkeit** impoliteness,
  rudeness
das **Unrecht: Unrecht haben** to be
  wrong, be mistaken

das **Unterbewußtsein**
  subconscious
die **Unterbrechung**, -en
  interruption
die **Unterhaltung**, -en ⟐
  conversation, chat
das **Unternehmen**, – undertaking,
  enterprise
der **Unterschied**, -e difference
die **Untertreibung**, -en
  understatement
die **Ursache**, -n reason, cause
die **Verantwortung** responsibility
der **Vergleich**, -e comparison
das **Vergnügen** pleasure
die **Vergrößerung**, -en
  enlargement
die **Verlegenheit** embarrassment
der **Verlust**, -e loss
der **Verrat** treachery
das **Versprechen**, – promise
das **Versteck**, -e hiding place
der **Versuch**, -e ⟐ attempt
das **Vertrauen** confidence
die **Vorbereitung**, -en preparation
der **Vordergrund** foreground
die **Vorderseite** front
der **Vorgeschmack** foretaste
die **Vorrichtung**, -en device
der **Vorschlag**, ̈-e suggestion
die **Vorstellung**, -en ⟐
  introduction; idea, thought
der **Vorteil**, -e advantage
das **Vorwort**, -e foreword
die **Wahl** ⟐ choice, selection;
  election
die **Wahrheit** truth
das **Wappen**, – coat of arms
das **Wattestäbchen**, – cotton bud
die **Weise**, -n way, method,
  manner
die **Weite**, -n width; distance
der **Wert**, -e value

die **Wette**, -n bet
die **Wichtigkeit** importance
der **Wille** will
die **Willenskraft** willpower
die **Windel**, -n nappy
die **Wirklichkeit**, -en fact; reality
die **Wirkung**, -en effect
der **Witz**, -e joke
der **Wohlstand** prosperity
das **Wohlwollen** goodwill
das **Wort**, ⁼er *or* -e word
der **Wunsch**, ⁼e wish
die **Zahl**, -en number; figure

das **Zeichen**, – ◇ sign
die **Zeile**, -n line (*of text*)
der **Zeitgenosse**, -n contemporary
die **Zeitgenossin** contemporary
die **Zensur**, -en ◇ mark (*school*)
der **Zerstäuber**, – atomizer
das **Zeug** stuff; gear
das **Ziel**, -e ◇ aim, goal; destination
das **Zitat**, -e quotation
der **Zufall**, ⁼e chance, coincidence
die **Zuflucht** refuge
der **Zusatz**, ⁼e addition
der **Zweck**, -e purpose

PREPOSITIONS

- **an** (+*dat or acc*) at; to
- **anstatt** (+*gen*) instead of
- **auf** (+*dat or acc*) on
- **aus** (+*dat*) out of
- **außer** (+*dat*) out of; except
- **außerhalb** (+*gen*) outside
- **bei** (+*dat*) near, by; at the house of
- **beiderseits** (+*gen*) on both sides of
- **diesseits** (+*gen*) on this side of
- **durch** (+*acc*) through
- **entlang** (+*acc*) along
- **für** (+*acc*) for
- **gegen** (+*acc*) against
- **gegenüber** (+*dat*) opposite; to(wards)
- **hinsichtlich** (+*gen*) with regard to
- **hinter** (+*dat or acc*) behind
- **in** (+*dat or acc*) in; into
- **infolge** (+*gen*) as a result of
- **innerhalb** (+*gen*) in(side), within
- **jenseits** (+*gen*) on the other side of
- **mit** (+*dat*) with
- **nach** (+*dat*) after
- **neben** (+*dat or acc*) next to; beside
- **ohne** (+*acc*) without
- **seit** (+*dat*) since
- **statt** (+*gen*) instead of
- **trotz** (+*gen*) despite, in spite of
- **über** (+*dat or acc*) over; above
- **um** (+*acc*) (a)round, about
- **unter** (+*dat or acc*) under; among
- **von** (+*dat*) from
- **vor** (+*dat or acc*) in front of; before
- **während** (+*gen*) during
- **wegen** (+*gen*) because of
- **wider** (+*acc*) against, contrary to
- **zu** (+*dat*) to
- **zwischen** (+*dat or acc*) between

* Does not match details given in German Grammar book.

VERBS

VERBS

abhängen von to depend on
abholen to fetch, go and meet (*somebody*)
ablehnen to refuse
absagen to cancel, call off
abschreiben to copy
akzeptieren to accept
anbeten to adore
anbieten to give, offer
anblicken to look at
ändern to change
anfangen to begin
angeben to state
angehören (*+dat*) to belong to (*club etc*)
angreifen to attack; to touch
anhalten to stop; to continue
ankommen to arrive
ankündigen to announce
annehmen to accept; to assume
anrufen to call, phone
anschalten to switch on
antworten to answer, reply
anzeigen to announce
anziehen to attract; to put on (*clothes*)
sich ärgern to get angry
aufbewahren to keep, store
aufhängen to hang (up)
aufheben to raise, lift
aufhören to stop (*intransitive*)
aufkleben to stick on *or* onto
aufmachen to open
aufpassen (auf *+acc*) to watch; to be careful (of), pay attention (to)
aufstehen to get up
auftreten to appear (on the scene)
aufwachen to wake up (*intransitive*)
aufwärmen to warm up

aufwecken to awaken, wake up(*transitive*)
ausdrücken to express
ausführen to carry out, execute
ausgeben to spend (*money*)
ausgehen to go out
ausgleichen to level out; to reconcile
auslöschen to put out, extinguish
ausrufen to exclaim, cry (out)
sich ausruhen to rest
ausschalten to switch off
ausschlafen to have a good sleep
aussprechen to pronounce
ausstrecken to extend, hold out
sich ausstrecken to stretch out
auswählen to select
beabsichtigen to intend
beachten to observe; to obey
bedanken: sich (bei jdm) bedanken to say thank you (to sb)
bedecken to cover
bedeuten to mean
bedienen to serve; to operate
sich beeilen to hurry
beenden to finish
befehlen (*+dat*) to order
sich befinden to be
begegnen (*+dat*) to meet
beginnen to begin
begleiten to accompany
begreifen to realize
behalten to keep, retain
behaupten to maintain
beherrschen to rule (over)
sich beklagen (über *+acc*) to complain (about)
bekommen to obtain, get
bemerken to notice
benachrichtigen to inform

benutzen to use
beobachten to watch
berichten to report
(sich) beruhigen to calm down
sich beschäftigen mit to attend to;
  to be concerned with
beschmutzen to dirty
beschreiben to describe
beschützen to protect
besiegen to conquer
besitzen to own, possess
besprechen to discuss
bestehen (auf +*dat***)** to insist (upon)
bestehen (aus +*dat***)** to consist (of),
  comprise
bestellen to order
besuchen to attend, be present at; to
  go to; to
betreten to enter
beunruhigen to worry, disturb
(sich) bewegen to move
bewundern to admire
biegen to bend
bieten to offer
binden to tie
bitten to request
bitten um to ask for
bleiben to stay, remain
blicken (auf +*acc***)** to glance (at),
  look (at)
borgen to borrow
jdm etw borgen to lend sb sth
brauchen to need
brechen to break
brennen to burn
bringen to bring, take
bummeln to wander; to skive
danken (+*dat***)** to thank
darstellen to represent
dauern to last
decken to cover
denken to think, believe

denken an (+*acc***)** to think of; to
  remember
deuten (auf +*acc***)** to point (to *or* at)
dienen to serve
diskutieren to discuss
drehen to turn; to shoot (*film*)
drucken to print
drücken to press; to squeeze
durchführen to accomplish, carry
  out
durchqueren to cross; to pass
  through
durchsuchen to search (all over)
dürfen to be allowed to
eilen to rush, dash
einfallen (+*dat***)** to occur to
  (*someone*)
einladen to invite
einnicken to doze off
einrichten to establish, set up
einschalten to switch on
einschlafen to fall asleep
eintreten to come in
eintreten in (+*acc***)** to come into,
  enter
einwickeln to wrap (up)
empfangen to receive (*person*)
empfehlen to recommend
entdecken to discover
entführen to take away
enthalten to contain
(sich) entscheiden to decide
sich entschließen to make up one's
  mind
entschuldigen to excuse
sich entschuldigen (für) to
  apologize (for)
(sich) entwickeln to develop
sich ereignen to happen
erfahren to learn; to experience
erfahren von to hear about
ergreifen to seize
erhalten to receive, get

sich erheben to rise
erinnern (an +*acc*) to remind (of)
sich erinnern (an +*acc*) to remember
erkennen to recognize
erklären to state; to explain
sich erkundigen (nach *or* **über** +*acc*) to inquire (about)
erlauben to allow, permit, let
erleben to experience
ermutigen to encourage
erobern to capture
erregen to excite
erreichen to reach; to catch (*train etc*)
errichten to erect
erschaffen to create
erscheinen to appear
erschrecken to frighten
erschüttern to shake, rock, stagger
erstaunen to astonish
erwachen to wake up (*intransitive*)
erwähnen to mention
erwarten to expect; to await, wait for
erwidern to retort
erwürgen to strangle
erzählen to tell; to explain
erziehen to bring up; to educate
fallen to fall
fallen lassen to drop
falten to fold
fangen to catch
fassen to grasp; to comprehend
fehlen to be missing
er fehlt mir I miss him
etw fertigmachen to bring sth about; to get sth ready
festbinden to tie, fasten
finden to find
fliehen (vor +*dat*) to flee (from)
fließen (in +*acc*) to flow (into)
flüstern to whisper

folgen (+*dat*) to follow
fordern to demand
fortfahren to depart; to continue
fortgehen to go away
fortsetzen to continue (*transitive*)
fragen to ask
sich fragen to wonder
sich freuen to be glad
führen to lead
füllen to fill
funkeln to sparkle
funktionieren to work (*of machine*)
sich fürchten (vor +*dat*) to be afraid *or* frightened (of)
geben to give
gebrauchen to use
gefallen (+*dat*) to please
das gefällt mir I like that
gehen to go
gehorchen (+*dat*) to obey
gehören (+*dat*) to belong (to)
gelingen (+*dat*) to succeed
gelten to be worth
genießen to enjoy
genügen to be sufficient
gernhaben to like
geschehen to happen
gestatten to permit, allow
glauben (+*dat*) to believe
glauben an (+*acc*) to believe in
glühen to glow
gründen to establish
gucken to look
haben to have
halten to keep; to stop; to hold
halten für to consider (as)
handeln: es handelt sich um it is a question of
hängen to hang (up)
hassen to hate, loathe
hauen to cut, hew
heben to lift, raise
helfen (+*dat*) to help

herantreten an (+*acc*) to approach
herausziehen to pull out
hereinkommen to enter, come in
hereinlassen to admit
herstellen to produce, manufacture
herunterlassen to lower
hineingehen (in +*acc*) to enter, go in (to)
hinlegen to put down
sich hinsetzen to sit down
hinstellen to put down
hinübergehen to go over
hinweisen auf (+*acc*) to point out; to refer to
hinzufügen to add
hoffen (auf +*acc*) to hope (for)
holen to fetch
horchen to listen
hören to hear
hüten to guard, watch over
interessieren to interest
sich für etw interessieren to be interested in sth
sich irren to be mistaken *or* wrong
kämpfen to fight
kennen to know (*person, place*)
kennenlernen to meet, get to know
kitzeln to tickle
klagen to complain
klatschen to gossip
klettern to climb
klingeln to ring
klingen to sound
kochen to cook
kommen to come
können to be able (to)
kriegen to get, obtain
kritisieren to criticize
sich kümmern (um) to worry (about)
küssen to kiss
lassen to allow, let; to leave
laufen to run

leben to live
legen to lay
sich legen to lie down
leiden to suffer
ich kann ihn nicht leiden I can't stand him
leihen to lend
(sich *dat*) **etw leihen** to borrow sth
leiten to guide; to lead
lesen to read
lieben to love
liefern to deliver; to supply
liegen to be (situated)
loben to praise
löschen to put out
losmachen to unfasten, undo, untie
loswerden to get rid of
lügen to lie, tell a lie
machen to do; to make
malen to paint
meinen to think, believe
mieten to hire; to rent
mitbringen to bring
mitnehmen to take
mitteilen: jdm etw mitteilen to inform sb of sth
mögen to like
murmeln to murmur
müssen to have to (*must*), be obliged to
nachdenken (über +*acc*) to think (about)
nachsehen to check
nähen to sew
sich nähern (+*dat*) to approach
necken to tease
nehmen to take
nennen to call, name
sich niederlegen to lie down
notieren to note
öffnen to open
organisieren to organize

passen (+*dat*) to suit; to be suitable (for)
passieren to happen
pflegen to take care of
ich pflegte zu tun I used to do
plaudern to chat
pressen to press; to squeeze
produzieren to produce
protestieren to protest
prüfen to examine; to check
raten (+*dat*) to advise
räumen to clear away
recht haben to be right
reden to talk, speak
reinigen to clean; to tidy up
reisen to go; to travel
retten to save, rescue
riechen (nach) to smell (of)
rufen to call
sich rühren to stir
sagen (+*dat*) to say (to), tell
säubern to clean
saugen to suck
schaden (+*dat*) to harm
schallen to sound
schauen (auf +*acc*) to look (at)
scheinen to seem; to shine
schenken to give (*as a present*)
schieben to push, shove
schießen to shoot
schlafen to sleep
schlafen gehen to go to bed
schlagen to hit, strike, knock; to beat
sich schlagen to fight
(sich) schließen to close, shut
schluchzen to sob
schlummern to doze
schmücken (mit) to adorn (with)
schnarchen to snore
schneiden to cut
schnüren to tie
schreiben to write

schreien to shout, cry
schütteln to shake
schützen (vor +*dat*) to protect (from)
schweigen to be silent
schwimmen to swim
schwören to swear
sehen to see
sein to be
senken to lower
setzen to put (down), place, set
sich setzen to sit (down); to settle
seufzen to sigh
singen to sing
sitzen to sit, be sitting
sollen ought (to)
sich sorgen (um) to worry (about)
sorgen für to take care of, look after
sparen to save
spaßen to joke
spazierengehen to go for a walk
sprechen to speak
springen to jump
stattfinden to take place
stecken to put, stick
stehen to stand
stehenbleiben to stop (still)
steigen to come *or* go up, rise; to climb
stellen to put, place; to ask (*a question*)
sterben to die
stimmen to be right
stinken to stink
stoppen to stop (*transitive*)
stören to disturb
stoßen to push, shove
stottern to stutter
strecken to stretch
streichen to paint; to delete
streiten to argue, fight
sich streiten to quarrel
stürzen to fall

sich stürzen (in or **auf** +*acc*) to rush or dash (into)
suchen to look for, search for
tanzen to dance
teilen to share, divide
teilnehmen an (+*dat*) to attend, be present at, go to; to take
telefonieren to phone
töten to kill
tragen to carry; to wear
träumen to dream
treffen to meet; to strike (*transitive*)
treiben to drive; to go in for
trennen to separate; to divide
trocknen to dry
tun to do
so tun, als ob to pretend (that)
üben to practise
überkochen to boil over
überlegen to consider
überraschen to surprise
überreden to persuade
übersetzen to translate
(sich) umdrehen to turn round
umgeben to surround
umgehen to avoid; to bypass
umkehren to turn back
umleiten to divert
umwerfen to overturn, knock over
unterbrechen to interrupt
unterhalten to support; to entertain
sich unterhalten (über +*acc*) to converse or talk (about)
sich unterscheiden to differ, be different
unterschreiben to sign
untersuchen to examine
sich verabreden to make an appointment
verbergen to conceal
verbessern to improve
verbieten to forbid, prohibit
verbinden to connect; to bandage

verbringen to pass or spend (*time*)
verdecken to hide; to cover up
verderben to spoil, ruin
verdienen to deserve; to earn
vereinigen to unite
vergessen to forget
sich verhalten to act, behave
verhindern to prevent
verlangen to demand
verlassen to leave
verleihen (an +*acc*) to lend (to)
verletzen to harm
verlieren to lose
es vermeiden, etw zu tun to avoid doing sth
vermieten to let, rent
versäumen to miss
verschließen to lock
verschmutzen to soil, make dirty
verschwinden to disappear, vanish
versehen (mit) to provide (with)
versichern (+*dat*) to assure
versprechen to promise
(sich) verstecken (vor +*dat*) to hide (from)
verstehen to understand
was verstehen Sie darunter? what do you understand by that?
versuchen to try, taste, sample; to attempt to
verteidigen to defend
verteilen to distribute
verzeihen to pardon, forgive
vollenden to finish
vorbereiten to prepare
vorgeben to pretend
vorschlagen to suggest
(sich) vorstellen to introduce (oneself)
sich (*dat*) **etw vorstellen** to imagine sth
wachen to be awake
wachsen to grow

wagen to dare
wählen to elect; to choose
warten (auf +*acc*) to wait (for)
(sich) waschen to wash
wechseln to exchange; to change (*money*)
wecken to awaken, wake up (*transitive*)
wegnehmen to take off *or* away
sich weigern to refuse
weinen to cry
sich wenden an (+*acc*) to apply to; to turn to
werden to become, grow, turn (out)
werfen to throw
wetten (auf +*acc*) to bet (on)
wiederholen to repeat
wiedersehen to see again
wischen to wipe
wissen to know
wohnen (in +*dat*) to live (in)
wohnen (bei +*dat*) to lodge (with), live (with)
wollen to want (to), wish (to)
sich wundern (über +*acc*) to wonder (at), be astonished (at *or* by)

es wundert mich I am surprised (at it)
das würde mich wundern! that would surprise me!
wünschen to wish
zahlen to pay
zählen to count
zeichnen to draw
zeigen to show; to point
zelten to go camping
zerbrechen to break
zerreißen to tear up
zerstören to destroy
zerstreuen to scatter
ziehen to draw; to pull; to tug
zittern (vor) to tremble (with)
zögern to hesitate
zugeben to confess, admit
zuhören (+*dat*) to listen (to)
zumachen to close, shut (*transitive*)
zurückkehren to come back, return
zurückkommen to go *or* come back
zurücksetzen, zurückstellen to replace
zustimmen (+*dat*) to assent (to)
zweifeln to doubt
zwingen to force, oblige

The following German words can have more than one translation, depending on context. If you do not already know these translations, check them up on the pages shown.

das Gerät   142, 324
das Gericht   125, 202
das Geschäft   32, 46, 267, 293
die Geschichte   79, 132
das Geschirr   18, 37, 102, 125, 177, 194
die Gesellschaft   31, 41, 264
das Glas   37, 91, 125; 194, 206, 225
das Glück   113, 324
der/das Golf   143, 274
die Größe   69, 106, 264
der Grund   61, 229, 325
die Güte   70, 325
der Hahn   25, 98, 173
der Haken   114, 174, 286, 325
der Handel   29, 39, 262
die Handlung   264, 278
der/die Heide   63, 100, 241
der Hering   36, 114
das Herz   135, 182
der Himmel   25, 241, 308
die Höhe   10, 325
die Höhle   15, 63, 144
der Hörer   184, 208
die Hütte   170, 231
der/das Junge   17, 66, 92, 313
der Kanal   87, 143, 208
die Kapelle   218, 244, 279
die Karte   79, 278
die Kasse   186, 264, 278
der Kaufmann   29, 261
die Kette   23, 227, 325
der/die Kiefer   178, 299
die Klasse   79, 296
der Knoten   67, 325
die Kohle   169, 205, 325
das Konzert   220, 281
der Korb   22, 204
das Kostüm   109, 281
der Krach   110, 269
der Krebs   114, 153, 257
der Kreis   51, 325
das Kreuz   51, 135, 245

die Küche   169, 314
die Kugel   215, 325
der/die Künstler(in)   44, 219
der Kurs   77, 184
die Lage   169, 325
das Lager   33, 216
das Land   65, 91, 102, 240, 312
der Läufer   174, 270
die Leinwand   205, 279
der/die Leiter   44, 100, 175, 231, 287, 325
der Mais   98, 301
die Mandel(n)   137, 158, 181
der Mangel   66, 325
der Mann   66, 92
die Mannschaft   259, 273
die Marke   250, 325
die/das Maß   124, 325
die Maschine   10, 249, 287
die Melone   107, 137
die Menge   225, 291, 325
die Messe   48, 131, 243
das Modell   134, 325
das Muster   109, 325
die Mutter   94, 287
das Netz   274, 325
die Note   80, 218
der/die Otter   13, 16
das Paar   97, 225
der/die Pantomime   277, 279
der Panzer   12, 212, 305
das Parkett   172, 281
der Paß   8, 143, 270, 294
die Pause   80, 279, 283
der Pickel   66, 179, 286
der Platz   270, 276, 289, 294, 326
der Pokal   270, 326
die Politik   236, 326
der/das Pony   17, 66
die Post   186, 264, 291
der Preis   77, 164, 184, 261
der Produzent   39, 277
das Programm   54, 133, 211, 280

die Prothese   159, 181
das Rad   24, 252, 297, 307
der Rand   52, 326
die Rasse   16, 326
der Raum   139, 167, 326
die Rechnung   31, 121, 165, 264
die Regel   81, 181
die Reihe   80, 279, 326
der Reiseführer   163, 313
das Rezept   125, 161, 177
das Rohr   171, 177, 207
der Ruf   269, 326
die Ruhe   37, 155, 314, 326
die Runde   124, 273
die Sache   37, 227, 326
der Salat   116, 301
der Satz   78, 140, 271
die Schale   121, 137
der Schalter   163, 173, 184, 261
der Schein   261, 326
das Schild   293, 326
die Schlange   15, 264, 278, 291
das Schloß   24, 65, 172, 288, 293
die Schnur   205, 287
der Schornstein   167, 258
die Schuld   199
der/die See   61, 87, 89, 143, 144, 259
die Seite   80, 180, 209
der Sekretär   43, 140
der Spaß   276, 326
der Speicher   52, 168
das Spiel   133, 274, 281
der Spion   168, 196
die Spitze   63, 144, 205, 292
der Sportwagen   247, 305
der Stachel   12, 26, 230
der Stamm   229, 298
der Stammbaum   14, 93
der Star   25, 326
die Stärke   124, 326
die Station   156, 296
der Stein   61, 136, 167, 203, 229, 257

die Stelle   41, 326
die/das Steuer   89, 187, 237, 260, 327
der Stich   19, 25, 152
die Stimme   180, 236
die Stimmung   69, 327
der Stock   61, 163, 167, 262
die Strafe   81, 200
die Straße   63, 144, 169, 250, 291
der Strauß   25, 230
die Strecke   297, 327
der Streit   110, 195, 234
der Strom   61, 87, 139, 143
das Stück   128, 225, 281, 327
die Stunde   80, 283
die Tafel   80, 225, 255
die Tasche   10, 106, 165, 186, 198, 296
die Taste   53, 186, 218
die Tätigkeit   42, 327
der/das Tau   230, 288, 309
der/die Taube   27, 71
der/das Teil   327
der/das Terminal   8, 54
die Terrasse   165, 169
der Text   217, 276, 327
der Ton   203, 217, 269
der/das Tor   65, 172, 274, 293, 327
die Tribüne   273, 279
das Tuch   327
das Turnen   84, 274
der Typ   68, 327
das Ufer   65, 260
die Uhr   10, 141, 283, 296
der Umschlag   154, 184, 254
der Umzug   140, 167
die Unterhaltung   131, 327
die Untersuchung   155, 198
der Versuch   77, 327
das Viertel   225, 293
die Vorstellung   278, 327
der Wagen   294, 304
die Wahl   236, 327

The vocabulary lists on the following pages cover all of the English nouns in the first two levels of the book, i.e. ESSENTIAL and IMPORTANT.

The vocabulary lists on the following pages cover all of the German nouns in the first two levels of the book, i.e. ESSENTIAL and IMPORTANT.